Stitched
PICTURES

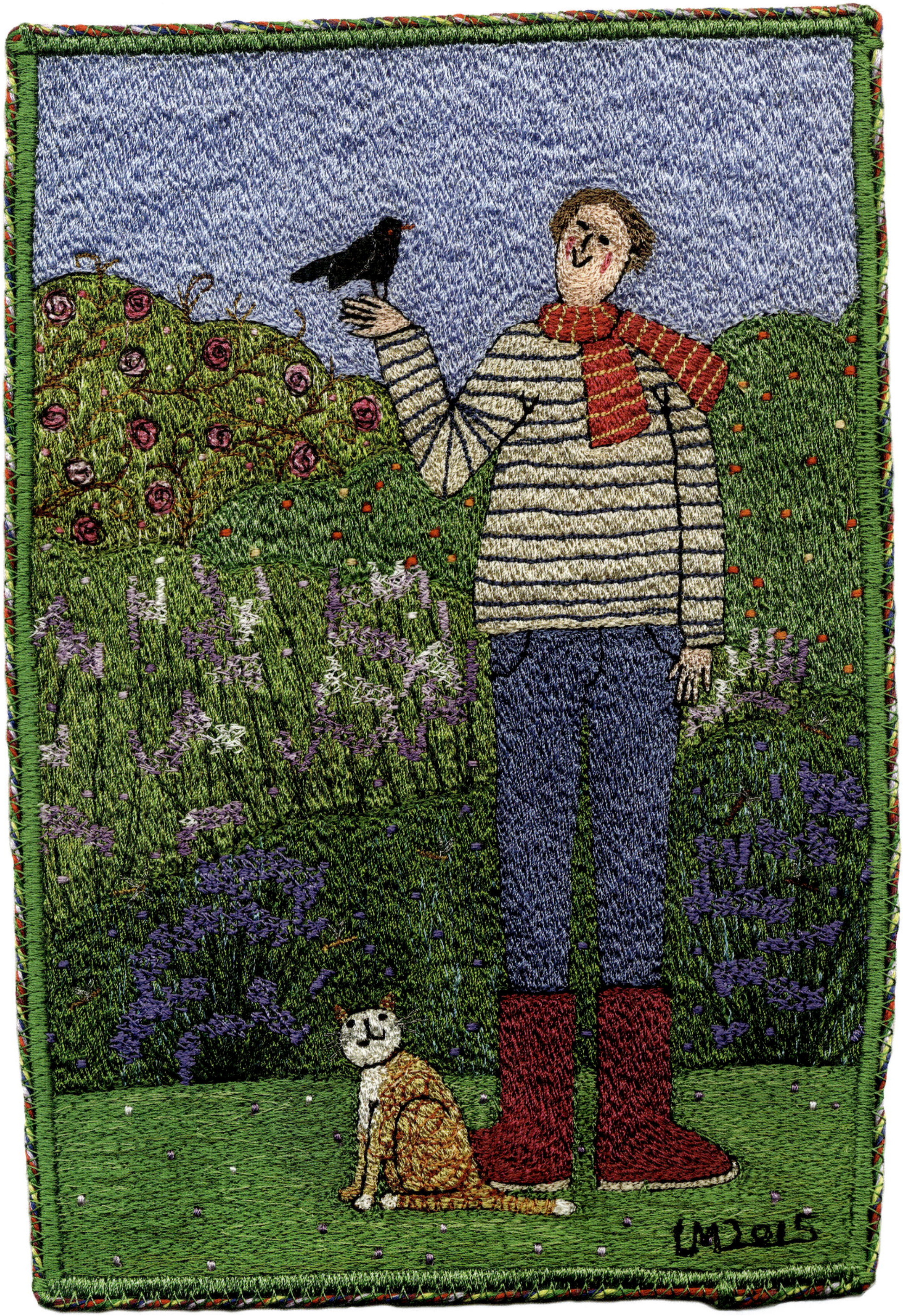
LM 2015

Linda Miller

Stitched
PICTURES

techniques and projects

THE CROWOOD PRESS

First published in 2022 by
The Crowood Press Ltd
Ramsbury, Marlborough
Wiltshire SN8 2HR

enquiries@crowood.com
www.crowood.com

British Library Cataloguing-in-Publication Data
A catalogue record for this book is available from the British Library.

ISBN 978 0 7198 4037 1

Front cover design: Sergey Tsvetkov
Front cover: *The Birds Sing Your Name by Linda Miller*, 25 × 19cm (10 × 7½in), free machine embroidery
Frontispiece: *Blackbird Garden* by Linda Miller, 23 × 17cm (9 × 6¾in), free machine embroidery. (Photo: Michael Jennings)

All designs by Linda Miller.
All photographs are by Oliver Lane, unless specified otherwise.

Graphic design and typeset by Peggy & Co. Design
Printed and bound in India by Parksons Graphics

CONTENTS

	Introduction	7
1	Tools and Equipment	13
2	Working with your Sewing Machine	25
3	Using the Sewing Machine as a Drawing and Painting Tool	33
4	Fabrics Galore!	47
5	Finding Inspiration for your Imagery and Design	59
6	Colour Exploration through Fabric Appliqué	73
7	Drawing and Design	87
8	Style, Inspiration and Placing Imagery	103
9	Presentation and Framing	117
	Acknowledgements	141
	Suppliers	142
	Index	143

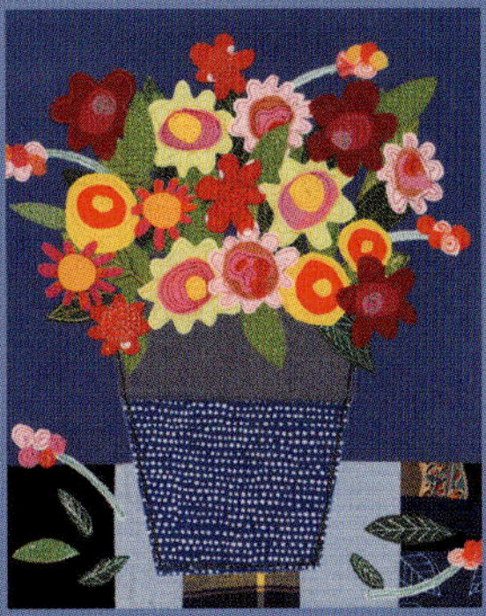

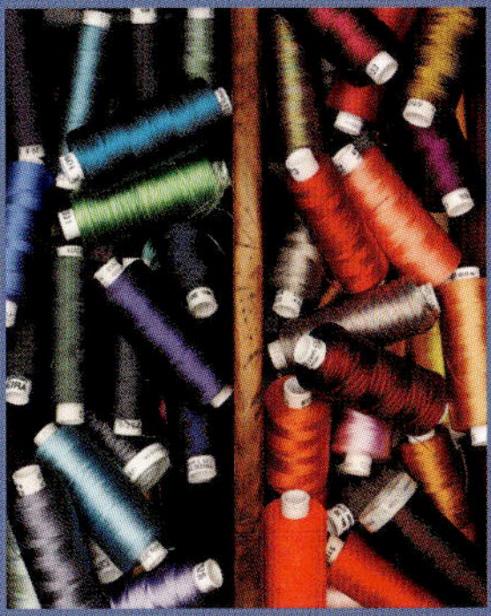

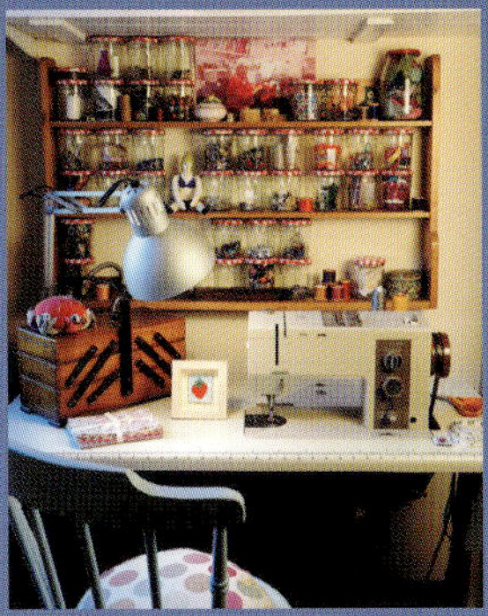

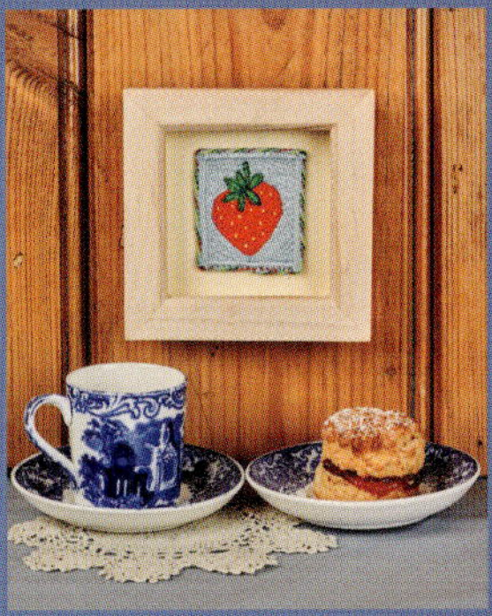

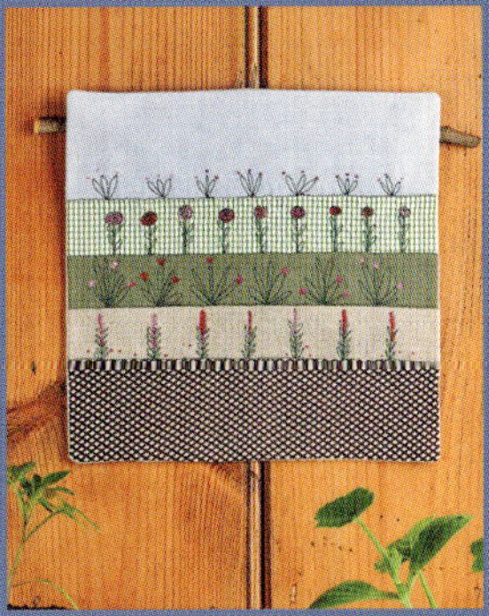

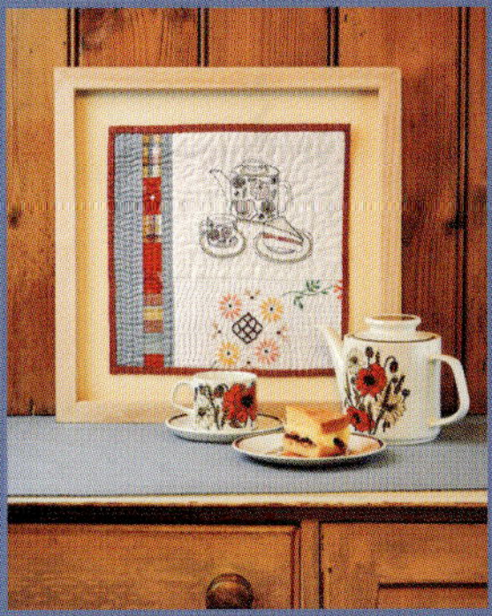

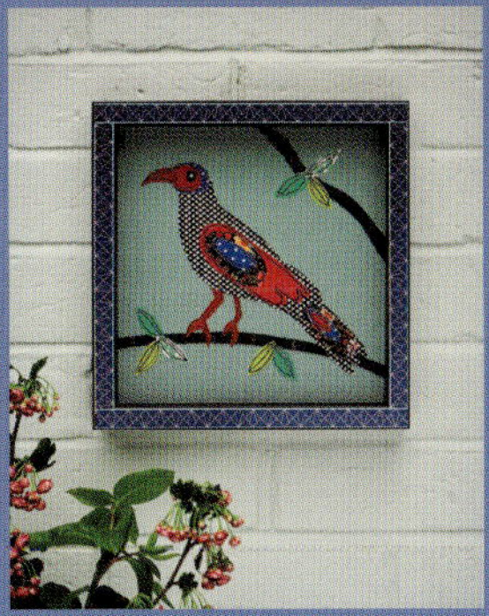

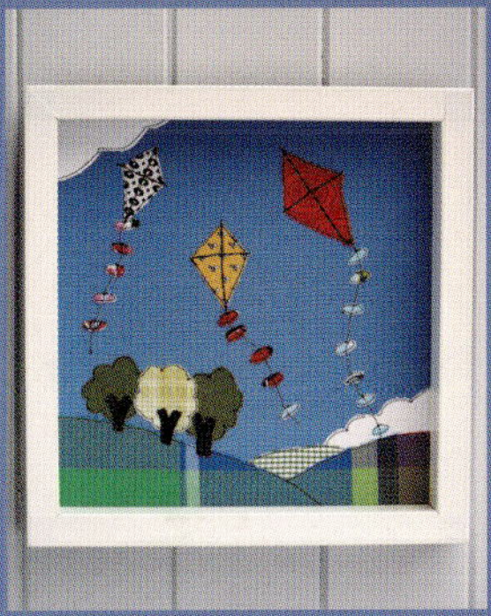

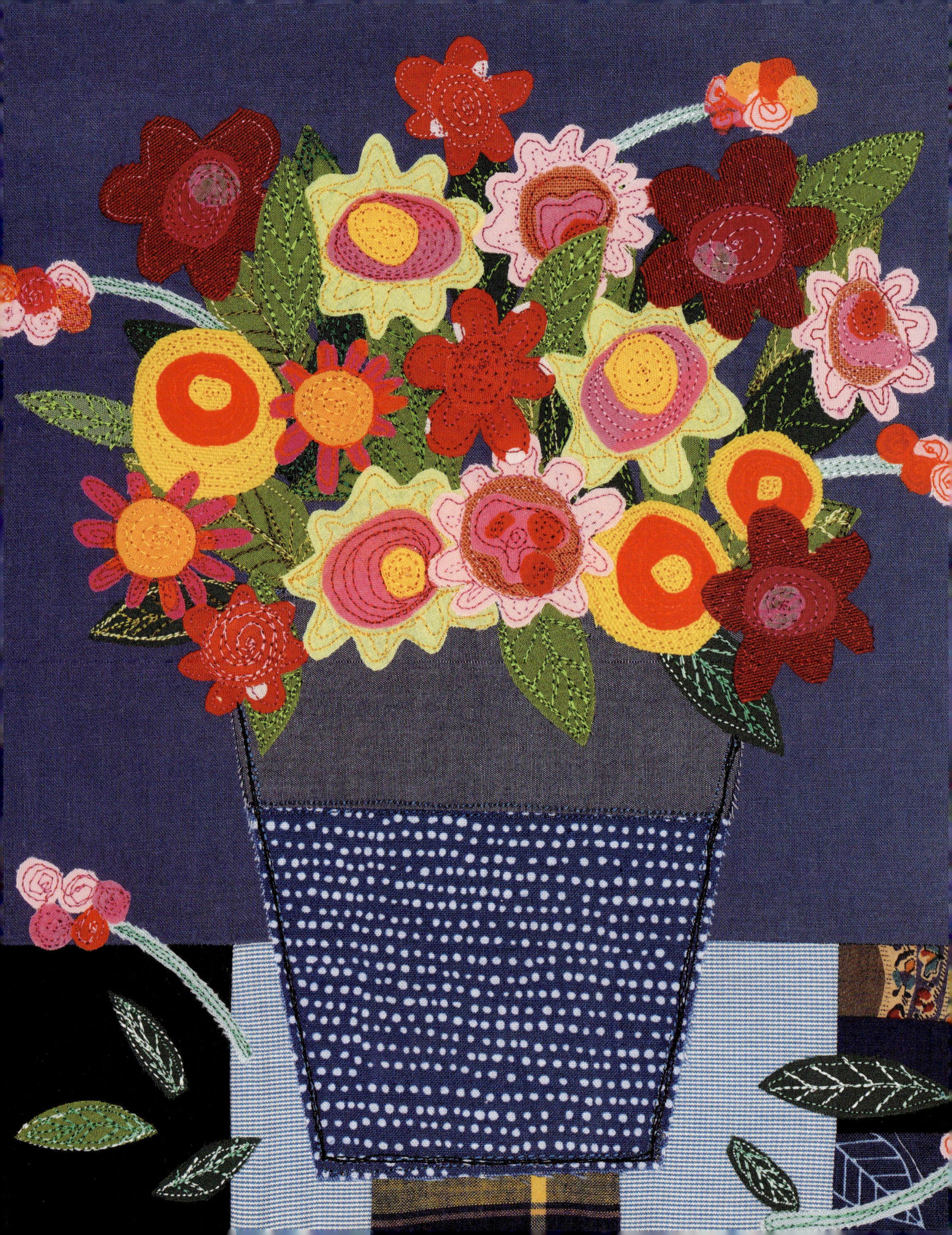

INTRODUCTION

Making textile pictures with a sewing machine is an exciting and innovative way of expressing one's creative ideas. The sewing machine is a wonderful drawing tool, and mark marking with stitch upon pieced and layered fabrics is an ideal medium in which to create exciting and versatile textile pictures. Whatever materials are used in conjunction with stitch, communicating and expressing ourselves through textiles allows us to create a narrative through which we can tell our story.

The Evolution of the Sewing Machine

The simple pleasure of decorative stitching has been experienced since the invention of the sewing machine in the late nineteenth century and is still embraced today. The contemporary domestic sewing machine has changed almost beyond recognition from those early models and the range of precision stitching that can now be achieved is quite phenomenal. Anyone who enjoys machine sewing knows what a beautiful and versatile tool the sewing machine is. It is surely one of the most valued pieces of equipment within the workroom.

The twentieth century saw the mass production of the hand cranked sewing machine, which brought huge domestic change to the lives of women. No longer was home sewing purely achieved by hand. Purchasing a sewing machine for the household enabled women to make garments and create decorative domestic items with greater ease and speed for the whole family and home. This gave many women more time to pursue other activities, both within and away from the household. Later still, the electric domestic sewing machine further transformed machine sewing for women, enabling them to produce a greater variety of textiles at speed.

Social and economic change has altered our lives unrecognizably from that of our forebears and one of the many qualities it has brought to domestic life is more free time in which to enjoy interests and pastimes. Household sewing is no longer a necessity, and for the devotee it is a pleasure. Over the twentieth century the critical profile of textiles as an art form was raised and imbued with a greater value and respect. This, alongside the technical development of the sewing machine, has enabled its change in use from that of a solely domestic object to a drawing and painting tool and this transformation in turn has empowered its user to become a respected and valued creator.

Flower Bouquet by Linda Miller, 29 × 29cm (11½ × 11½in), fabric appliqué and free machine embroidery.

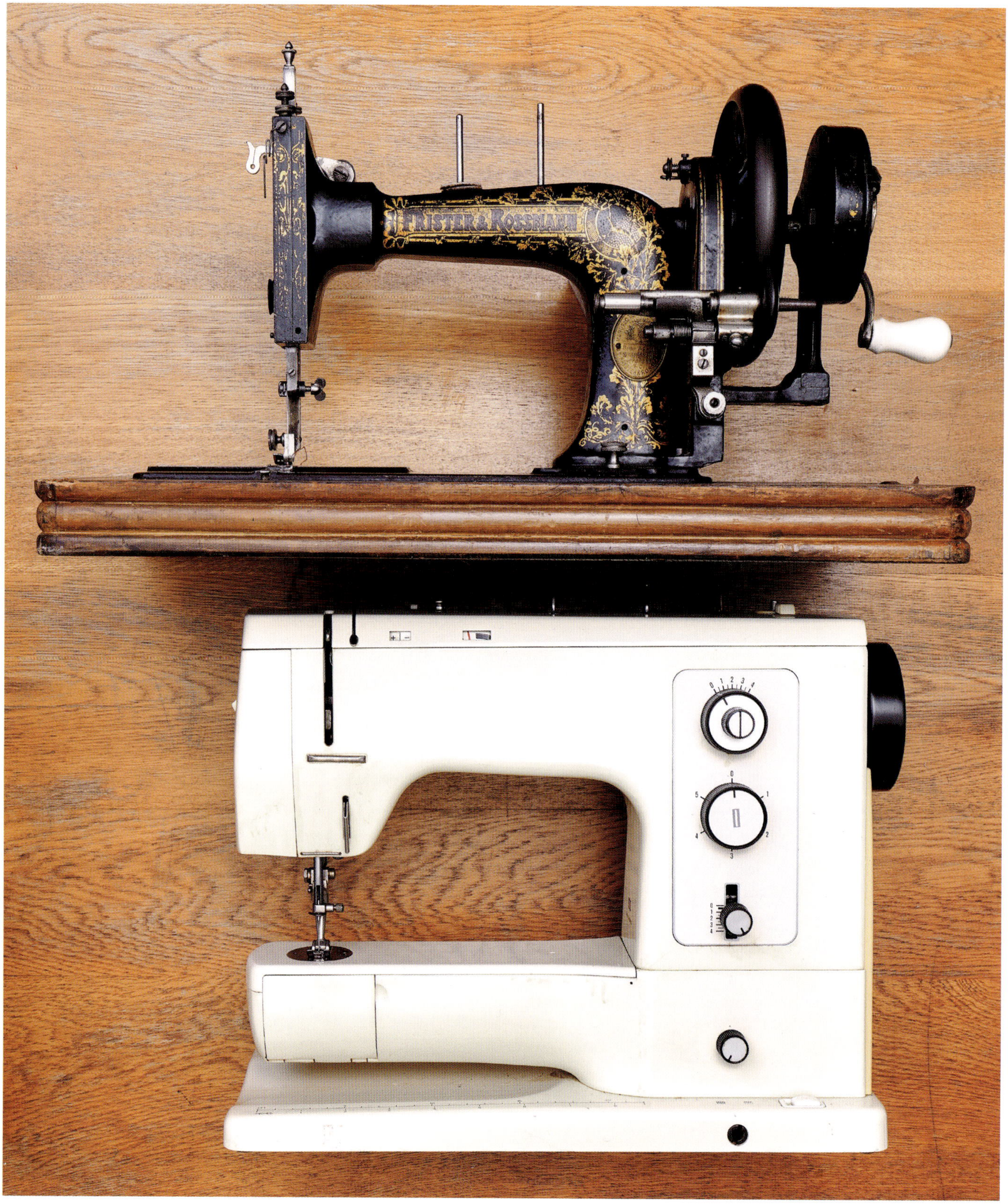

Through the centuries, the changing look of the sewing machine.

Exploring Textiles

Textiles as a medium can be very versatile. Fabric can be cut, manipulated and stitched with the greatest of ease and the simplest of tools. The wide range and availability of both fabric and thread has given the maker an exciting pallet of textile materials to use and explore. We can choose to use new or recycled fabrics, or a combination of both, and these can be used either on their own or mixed with an array of other art materials such as paper, card and found objects.

Museums and galleries hold a wealth of textiles in all forms, from every corner of the world. If you are unable to physically visit a museum or gallery, most can be accessed online. Whichever way you visit installations and exhibitions, the experience is invaluable. Looking and observing allows our creative knowledge and understanding to grow and develop. To see how a piece has been conceived and constructed enables us to further our own thought process and gain technical knowledge to utilize within our own work, and this in turn expands our own creative journey.

There are many things to consider when making and creating textile work, including the colour palette, the use of expressive stitch, fabric texture, subject matter, and the choice and placement of imagery. The process can consist of a series of questions as you try out different visual scenarios to develop before finding a final design you wish to develop into your textile artwork. Whichever fabric we are drawn to and whatever technique we favour, it is important for us to study work in as many disciplines as we can in order to further our knowledge of the many and varied textile media. Each textile artist creates their own unique style in the way in which they use and treat their chosen medium.

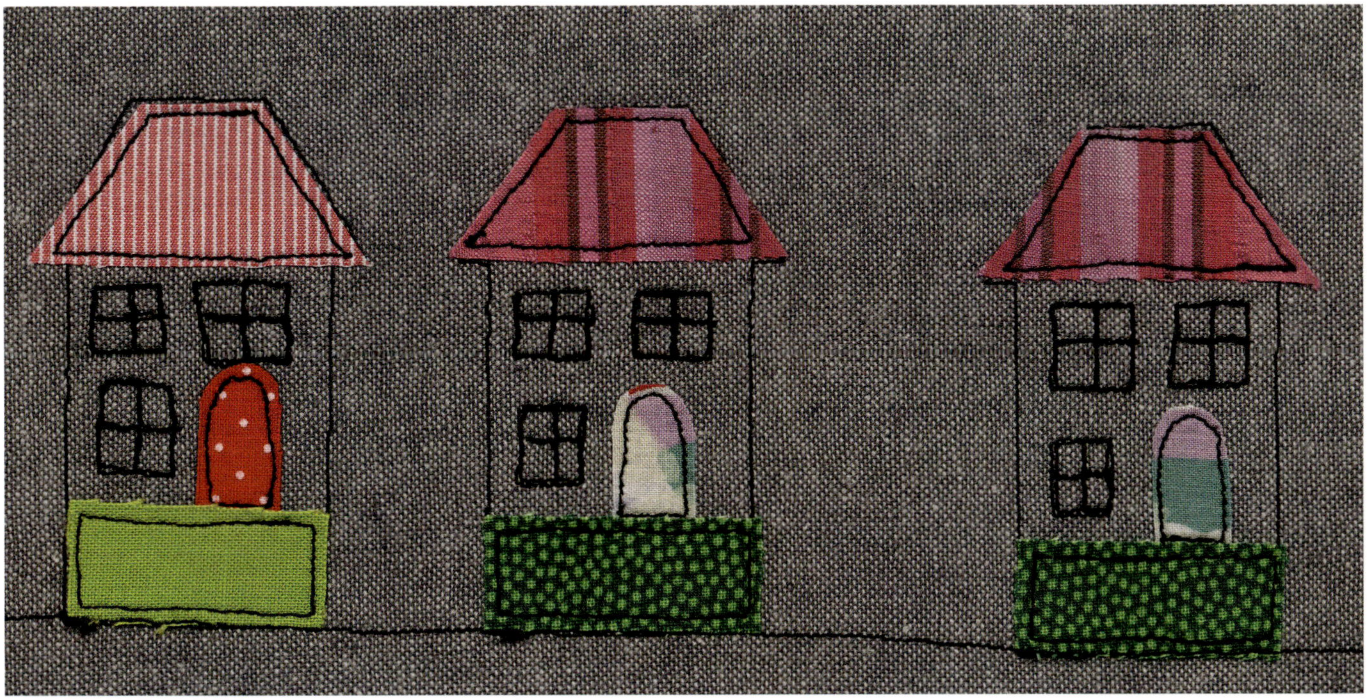

Three Houses by Linda Miller, 10 × 19cm (4 × 7½in), fabric appliqué and free machine embroidery. (Photo: Michael Jennings)

Creating a Mood Board

The starting point for a textile picture can be achieved by creating a mood board. This can be an invaluable way in which to collate a group of visual references that can be then formed into an idea. Any visual and written sources that interest us can be used; items such as pictures, photographs, fabric swatches and overheard snippets of conversation. All at some stage will make it onto our mood board, ready to ignite our imagination. Items can be arranged by colour, theme, style or a mix of collaged pieces. There is no right or wrong way in which to create a mood board – whatever works for the individual is the best way.

Mood boards can either be kept digitally on a phone or tablet or physically presented upon a wall. If buying a board for a workspace, choose a pinboard made of cork as they are easy to pin into. However, they can also be easily made from a piece of cardboard, and the size can reflect on the volume of inspirational material your project demands. After the gathered reference material has served its purpose, remove it carefully from the pinboard and stick the assortment into a sketchbook. This simple action will keep all the information stored neatly away and easy to find for future use. The arrangement can always be rearranged or added to, creating new ideas for any future picture project. This will make the beginning of any textile project a straightforward and pleasurable task.

The Joys of Stitching

It is important for us all to take time away from our busy lives and spend some quality hours for ourselves. In this fast-paced life that we all lead, hobbies and pastimes are a valuable outlet for us to rejuvenate ourselves. The pleasure of sewing and making is full of many benefits; it improves our hand and eye coordination, whilst enhancing our motor skills – using our brain helps to stimulate growth. The art of sewing, making and communicating through our stitching is an outlet for our creativity, it makes us individual and unique. We feel energised while active in mind and body, and it gives us a great sense of achievement.

The activity of sewing is incredibly versatile and does not have to be a solitary endeavour. Getting together with friends to stitch is a wonderful way in which to share projects, swap ideas and exchange technical knowledge, while socializing with like-minded people. Our making is valid and needed; it is what makes us complete and able to contribute to the world around us.

In the chapters ahead, there are six exciting and versatile picture projects to make. Each one is full of clear photographs that accompany the informative text, allowing you to work at your own pace. All you need is an electric sewing machine, together with a small selection of tools and equipment and a collection of fabrics of your choice to begin your exciting adventure in sewing and making stitched pictures.

Happy stitching!

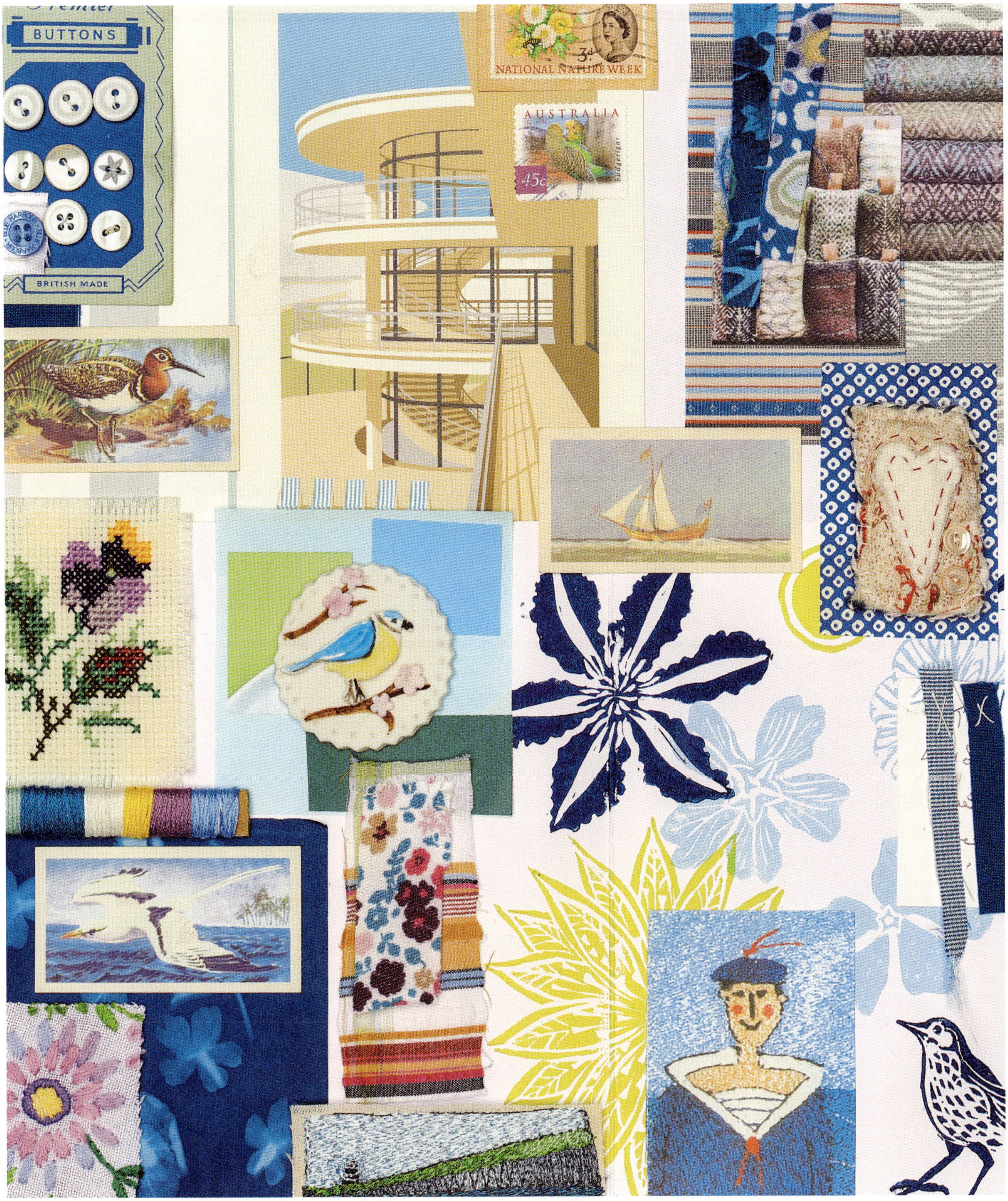

Creating a mood board can offer inspiration time and time again.

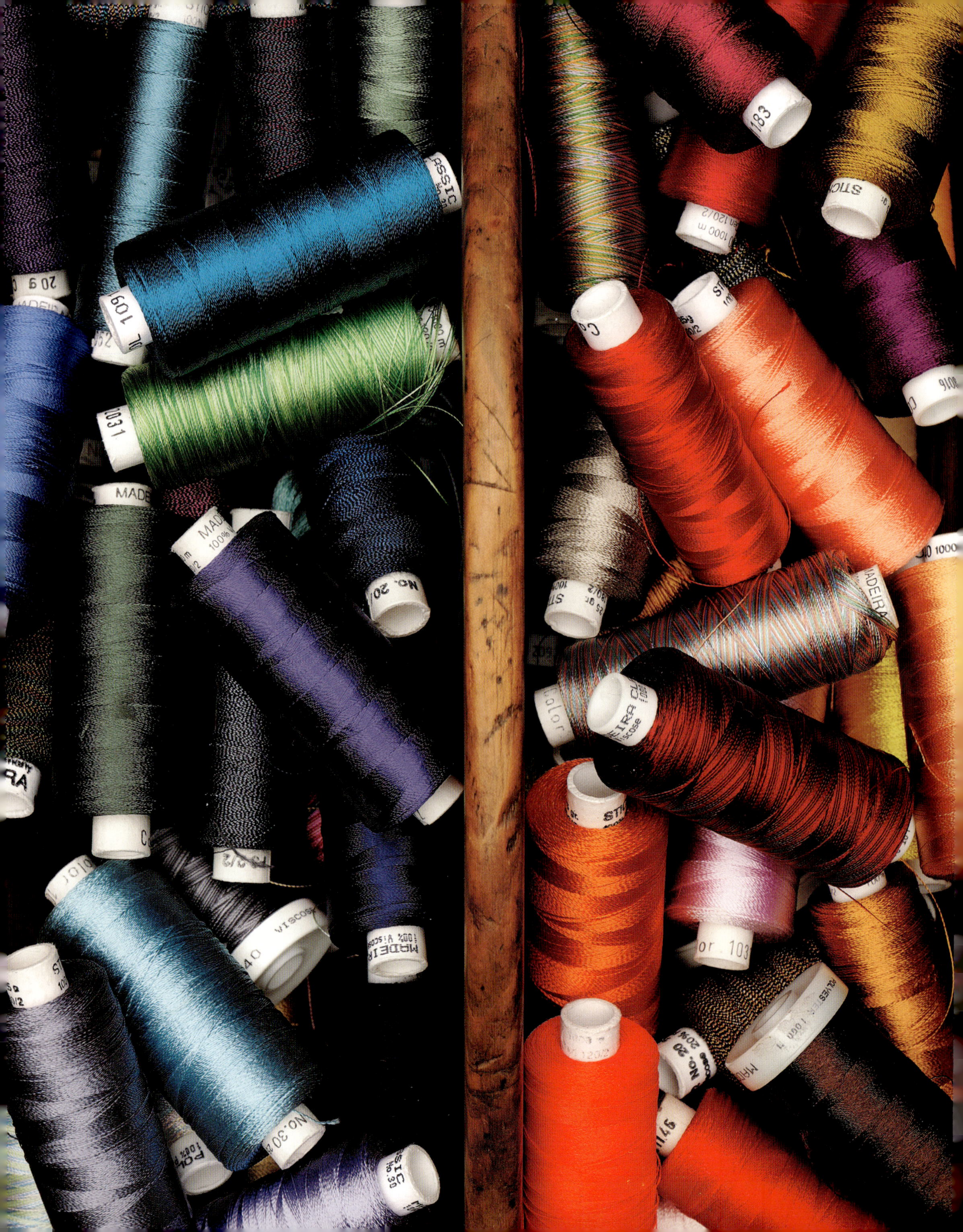

183
MADEIRA

CHAPTER 1

TOOLS AND EQUIPMENT

This chapter lists all the tools and equipment you will need to create the picture projects in *Stitched Pictures*. If you are already an avid sewer or an enthusiastic maker, then no doubt you will have an existing collection of materials and equipment that you can use for these projects, but if you are new to sewing and making then you may need to start to gather together a set of basic materials, which you can add to as you progress.

BASIC TOOL KIT

- An electric sewing machine, in good working order, which can drop the feed dog teeth or which has a plate that fits over the teeth
- The sewing machine's manual and its tool kit, which should include items such as oil, a screwdriver, bobbin spools and a selection of sewing machine feet
- A free motion machine embroidery foot or a darning foot, which must be compatible with your sewing machine and allows you to free machine embroider
- Size 80 universal machine sewing needles
- Hand sewing needles
- Dressmaking pins or sewing clips
- Calico in a selection of weights such as heavy, medium and lightweight
- Decorative 100 per cent cotton fabrics in a selection of patterns, colours and textures
- Fusible fabric for bonding
- Iron-on light interfacing fabric
- Stabilizing fabric
- Machine embroidery threads and general sewing threads
- Hand embroidery threads
- Beeswax
- Dressmaking or fabric scissors/rotary cutter
- Paper scissors
- Small embroidery/sharp scissors
- Corner and edge shaper
- Quick unpick/seam ripper
- 15cm (6in) wooden embroidery hoop
- Notebook and sketchbook
- Ruler and tape measure
- Lightbox
- Good lighting/Anglepoise light/daylight bulbs
- Pen, pencil, paper, eraser, pencil sharpener, masking tape and clear sticky tape
- HB and colouring pencils
- Air-soluble drawing pen and permanent marker pen
- Tailor's chalk
- Cutting mat
- Art and craft utility knife
- Mount board
- Hook and loop fastener tape
- Steam iron, ironing board and linen cloth for pressing (you can use a clean linen tea towel)

A sumptuous array of colourful machine embroidery threads in the weights of 30 and 40.

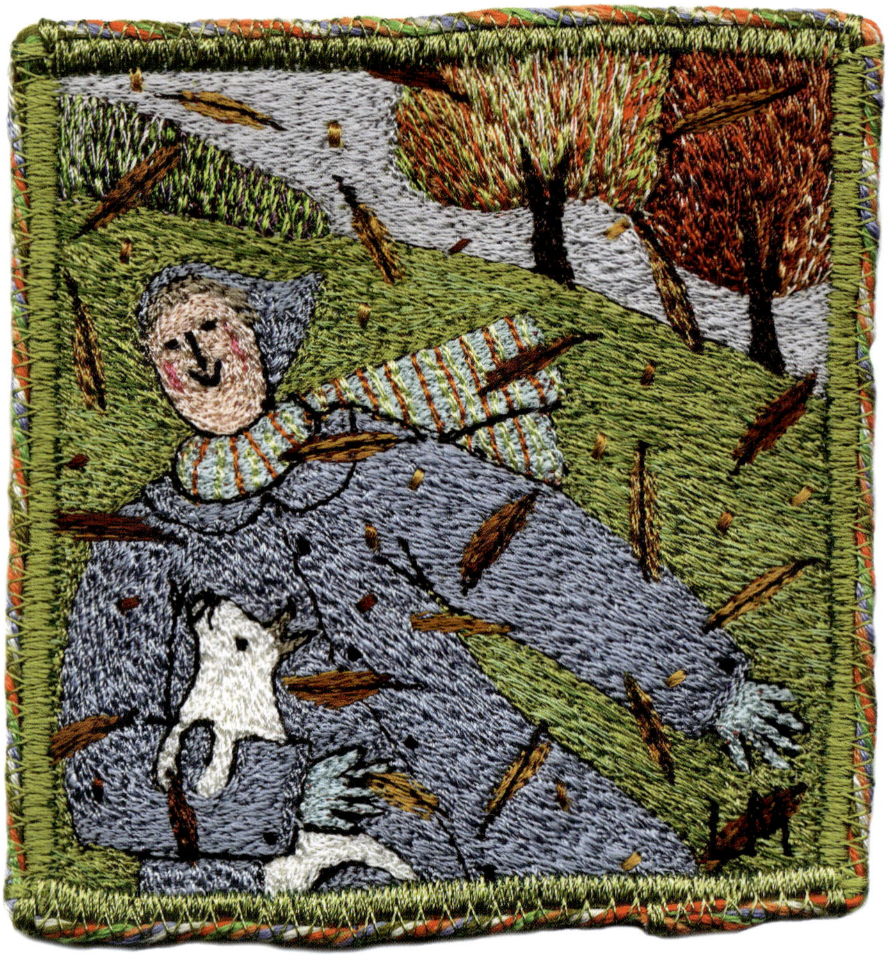

Hurrying Home by Linda Miller, 10 × 10cm (4 × 4in), free machine embroidery. (Photo: Michael Jennings)

TOOLS AND EQUIPMENT

Sewing Machines

The most important piece of equipment that you will need to make these picture projects is an electric sewing machine, which can lower and raise the feed dog teeth. It needs to be in good working condition and should be earthed and wired correctly. Guidance on how to choose a sewing machine can be found in Chapter 2.

Feed Dog Teeth

The feed dog teeth are two rows of small spiky metal teeth situated beneath the presser foot of the sewing machine. More detail about the feed dog teeth can be found in Chapter 3.

Sewing Machine Feet and the Free Machine Embroidery Foot

All modern sewing machines come with a standard set of feet. Generally, this includes a general-purpose sewing foot, a zigzag or satin stitch foot and a zipper foot. Some machines also come with a free machine embroidery or darning foot, depending on the age of the machine. All sewing machine feet can be purchased from a sewing machine retailer.

Sewing Machine Needles

Sewing machine needles come in a range of sizes to suit sewing in different weights and types of fabric. Each needle has two numbers: one is the European size and the other is the American size. The European size ranges from 60 to 110 and the American range is from 8 to 18 (thinnest to thickest size). Sewing machine needles also range in quality – for further guidance on making the correct choice, see Chapter 2.

Bobbin Spools

The brand of machine will determine what type of bobbin spool it uses. Some machines have a drop-in bobbin spool system beneath the stitch plate, while others require the user to place the spool in its bobbin case and then insert that into the machine beneath the stitch plate. Note: not all bobbin spools are the same size and therefore you must ensure you are using the correct size bobbin for your machine; the machine will not work correctly if the wrong size bobbin spools are used.

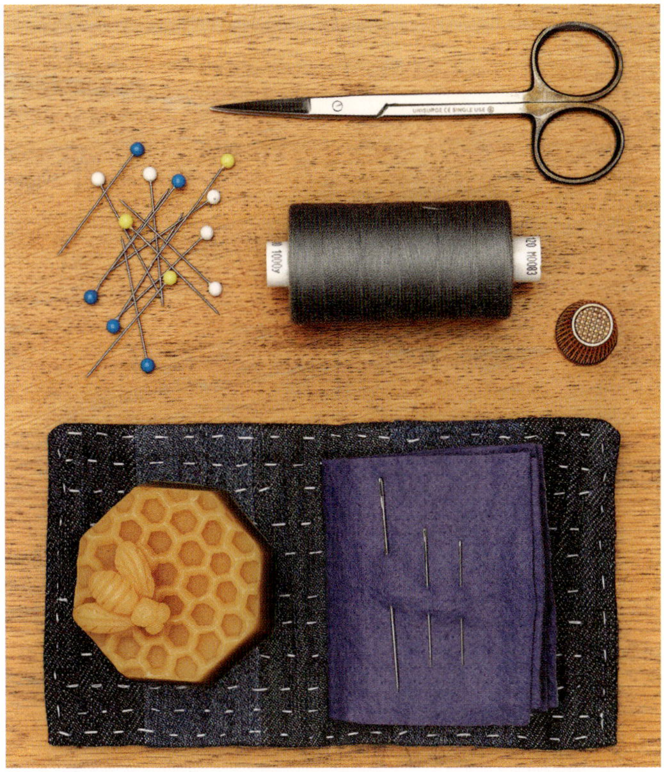

A hand sewing kit. Coating the thread first with beeswax will make hand sewing easy.

Hand Sewing Needles

As with machine needles, hand sewing needles also differ in quality, size and usage. They are relatively cheap, so always choose good-quality branded needles. A selection packet of good-quality needles in various sizes should last you a long time and will increase the quality of your hand sewing.

Pins and Sewing Clips

A box of good-quality dressmaking pins is an essential piece of equipment for any basic sewing kit. An alternative to pins are sewing clips, which are nowadays very popular. Unlike traditional pins, these do not pierce the fabric but clip it together; the flat bottom of the clip is marked with lines of 5mm, 7mm and 1cm (3/8in), and by placing the clip on the fabric edge the precise measured sewing line can be sewn.

FABRICS

Base Fabrics

There are three main types of base fabrics used in these picture projects: lightweight, medium weight and heavyweight cotton calico. All these calico fabrics are unwashed and undyed and maintain their original stiffness to provide a rigid surface to work upon.

The lightweight calico is a soft, manageable cloth suitable to be used as a backing fabric. The medium weight calico is a good all-round material that responds well when it is adhered to other cotton fabrics. Finally, the heavyweight calico will hold layer upon layer of machine embroidery stitch. All of these plain-woven cotton calico fabrics are relatively cheap and easily found in any good fabric or haberdashery shop.

Decorative Fabrics

A selection of dressmaking and patchwork materials will make excellent decorative fabrics to use in these picture projects. These will be used in conjunction with the medium weight calico and appliquéd onto this base fabric with a free machine embroidery stitch. Utilizing household textiles alongside vintage and preloved cotton adds further interest to the palette.

Fusible Fabric for Bonding

Fusible fabric is a double-sided adhesive material that can be used in fabric appliqué to fuse two pieces of fabric together. Once ironed down, the fusible fabric tends not to fray as much as other non-bonded fabrics. See Chapter 6 for further information about using fusible fabric.

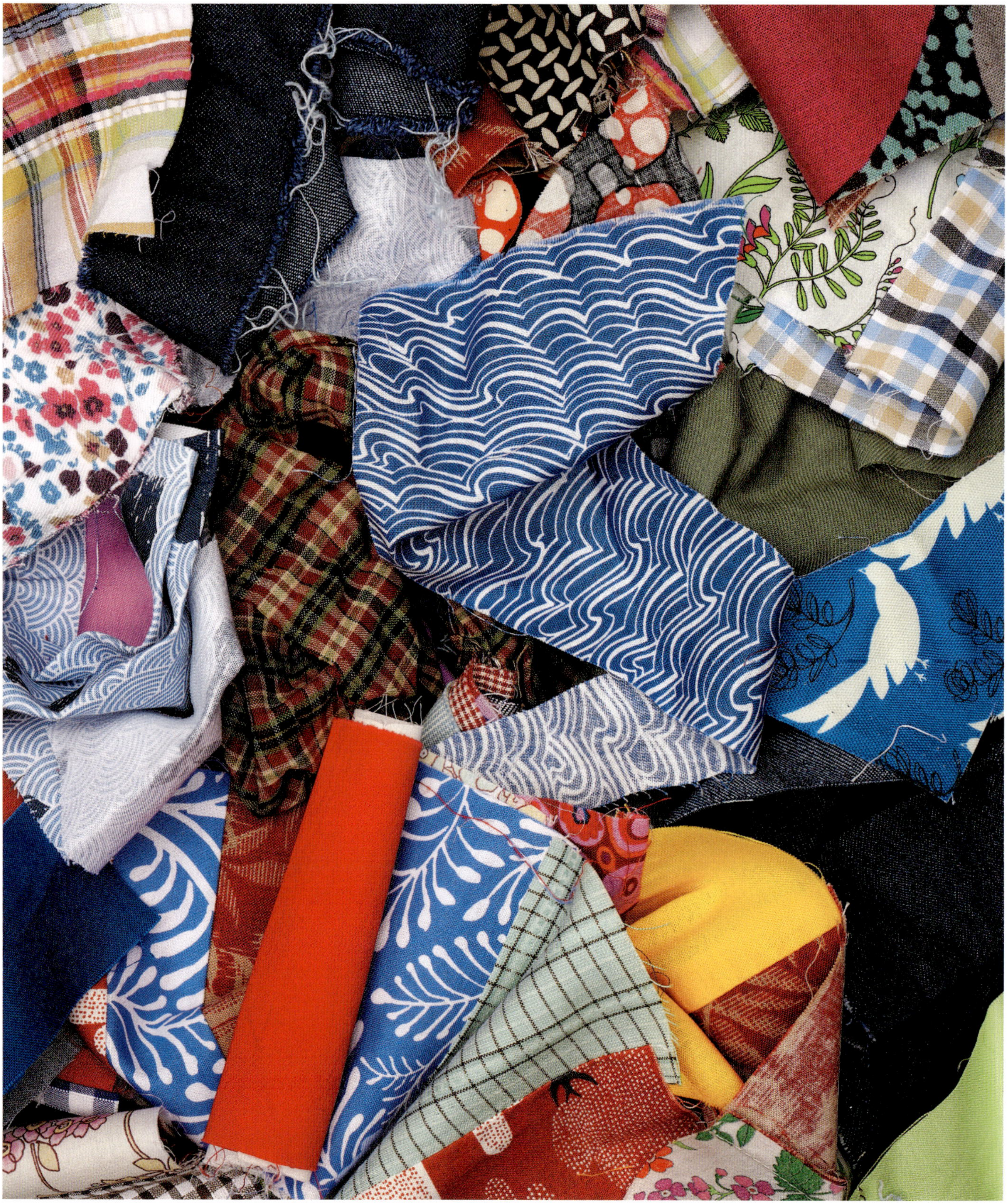

Spoilt for choice! Old, new and preloved cotton fabrics in all colours and patterns.

Iron-on Light Interfacing Fabric

Another type of iron-on fusible fabric used in the projects in this book is interfacing fabric. It is suitable for various fabrics and is mainly used in dressmaking, giving collars and cuffs the required stiffness. Unlike the fusible fabric for bonding, the interface fabric has the adhesive on one side only. It is applied with a hot iron to the back of the base fabric to provide a stabilizing layer. It is especially good for textile art projects as it makes a firm fabric surface and facilitates drawing with stitch.

Stabilizing Fabric

Using a stabilizing fabric when embroidering onto a fine or lightweight fabric prevents the fine fabric from splitting as you sew. When edging fabric with a zigzag satin stitch, the stabilizing fabric will ensure a clean, smooth stitching edge. On completion, any excess can easily be removed.

THREADS

Machine Embroidery Threads and General Sewing Threads

The two main types of thread used in the projects in this book are machine sewing threads and machine embroidery threads. Both types are easily found in any good high-street stockist.

Machine sewing threads are used for general sewing projects, with the most common being polyester thread. This practical polyester thread is strong and has a slight stretch to it, which makes it a good all-rounder that can be used on both stretch and cotton fabrics. When using a polyester thread, a light grey thread suits most coloured fabric and enables one to sew without having to keep changing the sewing thread to suit the fabric colour.

Machine embroidery threads are not suitable for practical sewing and are used purely as a decorative thread. Both types of thread are discussed in more detail in Chapter 2.

Bobbin Threads

These include all threads that are wound onto a bobbin spool and subsequently used in the bobbin and bobbin case.

Top Threads

These are threaded up through the top of the sewing machine and are always in view to the sewer.

Hand Embroidery Threads

For some projects you will need a few hand embroidery threads. These can be made from cotton or viscose. If you have a choice, always opt for cotton hand embroidery threads as they are less slippery than viscose and therefore easier to work with.

The threads consist of six strands wound together, giving you the option of either using one, two or all six of the strands together. Traditionally, hand embroidery thread is used for hand embroidery or cross stitch, and can be found in fabric or haberdashery departments and sometimes in the craft section of an art shop.

Beeswax for Hand Sewing

Beeswax is a natural wax produced by the honeybee. Running hand sewing thread through a piece of beeswax will help it to run smoothly while sewing, without forming knots and tangles.

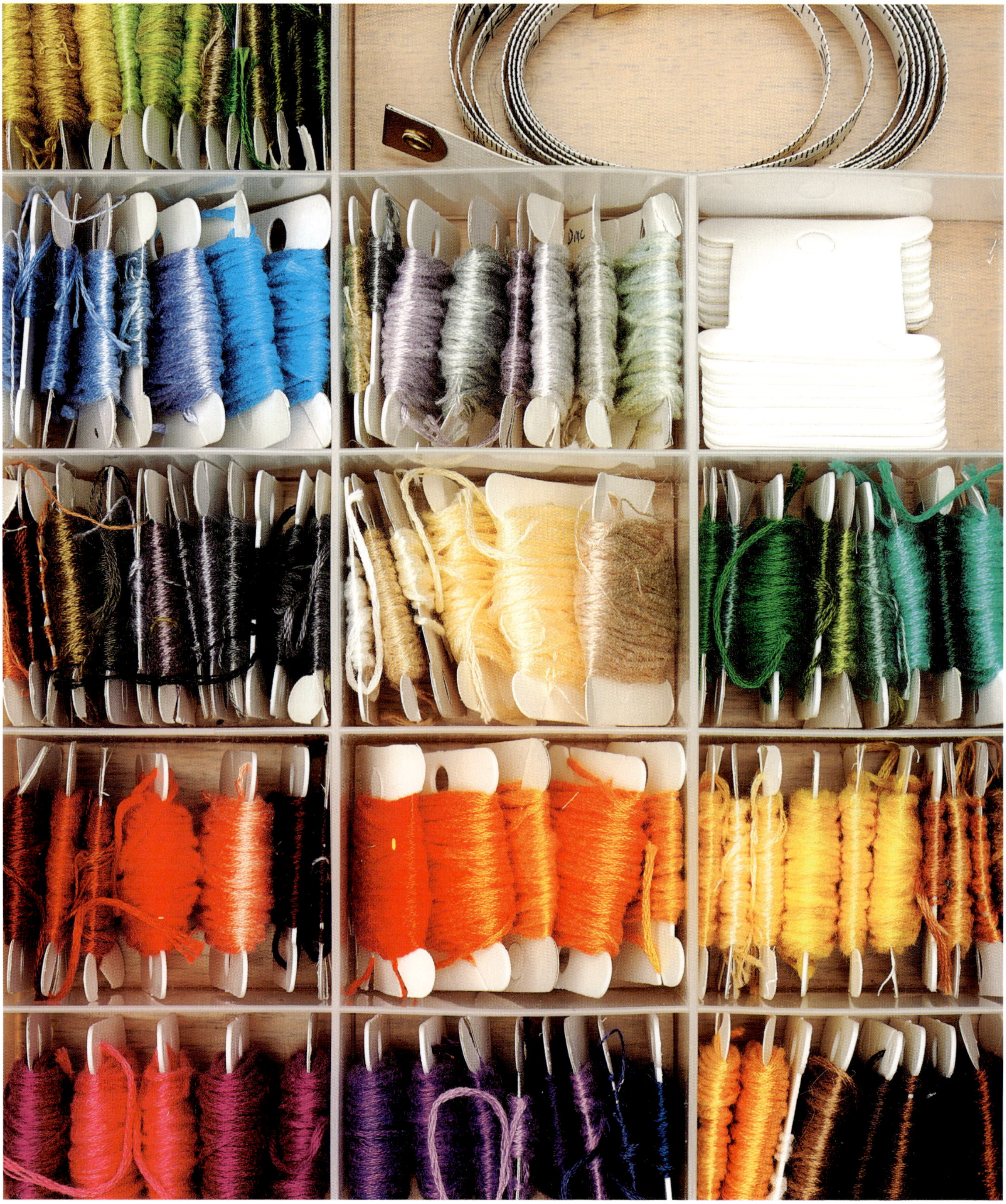

Winding hand embroidery threads onto cards keeps them tangle free and easy to use.

CUTTING TOOLS

Scissors

There are scissors for specific tasks. Generally, you will need a pair of paper scissors, a pair of fabric or dressmaking scissors and a small pair of embroidery scissors.

Good-quality dressmaking scissors are an investment and if well looked after will last you your sewing career. To prolong the life of your scissors, never lend them to anyone else – as we all have our own unique way of cutting – and never use them to cut paper! Fabric or dressmaking scissors need to be sharper to cut material precisely without tearing it. They can be regularly sharpened using a specific scissor-sharpening tool, easily obtained from your local fabric shop.

Specialist embroidery scissors with long, thin pointed tips are ideal to use as you will find it much easier to cut away thread ends in awkward areas. For fabric appliqué works, small appliqué scissors are recommended as they have a paddle-shaped blade that pushes away the bottom layer of fabric, enabling you to make neat and controlled cuts, close to the sewn appliqué edge. However, these are not a necessity and a pair of sharp-pointed embroidery scissors can be just as efficient, although a little more vigilance must be applied when trimming waste material to ensure that the appliqué and the base fabric are not cut away at the same time.

Rotary Cutter

Used in conjunction with a cutting mat and a grid-measured clear ruler, rotary cutters have very sharp blades and come in different sizes. The rotary cutter blade runs against the ruler to ensure a clean straight line. They can easily cut single or multiple layers of fabric.

Cutting Mat

A cut-proof mat with a printed measured grid upon it is perfect for obtaining straight cuts of measured fabric when used with a rotary cutter. The mat is an ideal base for cutting paper and card with an art and craft utility knife.

Art and Craft Utility Knife

A popular retractable craft utility knife that is designed as a multipurpose cutting tool. It often comes with replaceable blades suitable to cut and score a selection of different materials.

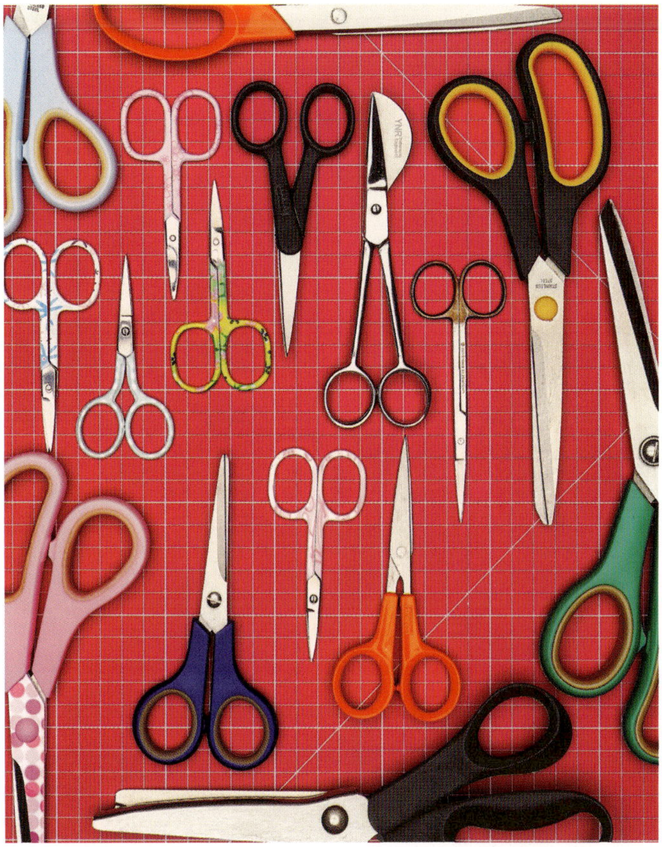

Using set pairs of scissors for dedicated materials will give years of trouble-free cutting.

OTHER USEFUL TOOLS

Wooden Embroidery Hoop

You will need a wooden embroidery hoop for the picture project, *Strawberry Delight* (see Chapter 3), which is a solidly stitched machine embroidery picture. Once the fabric is placed into the hoop and the hoop screw is tightened sufficiently, a wooden embroidery hoop will hold the base fabric tightly, creating the drum-like surface on which to machine embroider. Do not use a plastic spring hoop, which is designed to be used for hand stitch, as this will not hold the fabric tight enough for free machine embroidery.

In terms of size, a 15cm (6in) or 20cm (8in) diameter wooden hoop is ideal to use for machine embroidery. A hoop any larger than this may prove to be unwieldy and will hit the side of the sewing machine as you move it, thereby limiting your working area.

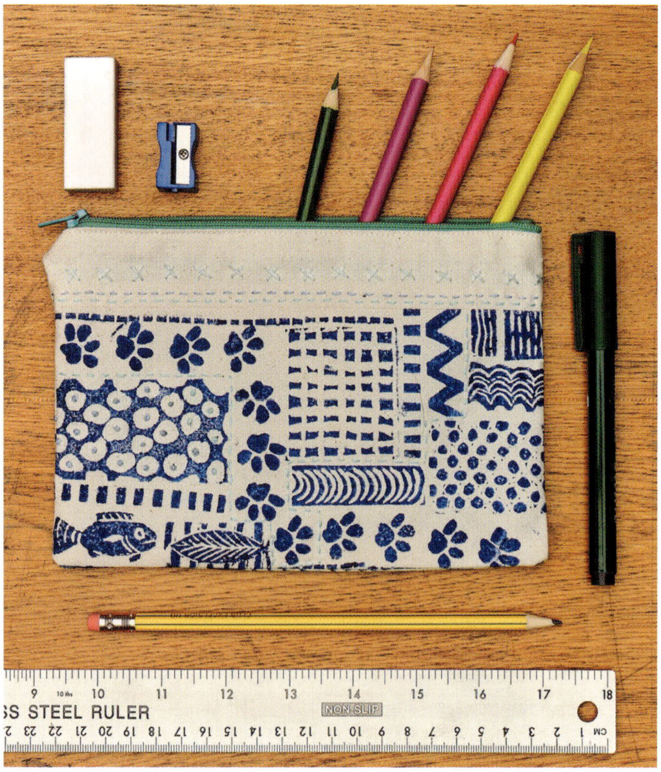

A simple selection of drawing pen, pencils and stationery will assist the starting point of any creative journey.

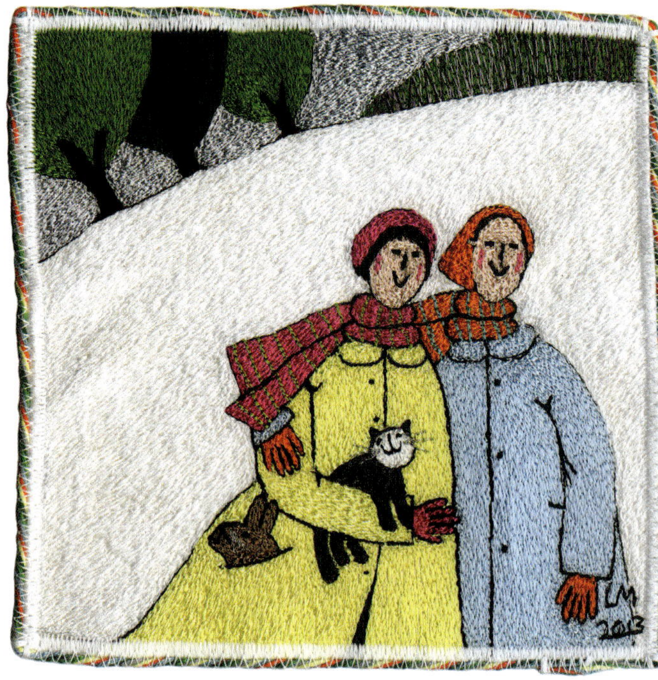

Snow by Linda Miller, 15 × 15cm (6 × 6in), free machine embroidery. (Photo: Michael Jennings)

Corner and Edge Shaper

This handy tool, made from either plastic or bamboo, enables the pushing out of seams and corners without piercing the fabric. It can also be used for taking out basting or tacking stitches.

Quick Unpick/Seam Ripper

This is ideal for unpicking tiny stitches and any stitching mistakes that are difficult to get to with scissors.

Notebook and Sketchbook

Recording notes and ideas in a small bound notebook for future projects is a handy way of keeping track of your creative thoughts. In addition, a small companion sketchbook is ideal for jotting down quick pencil drawings and colour notes, which can be referred to for artistic inspiration.

HB and Colouring Pencils

Simple yet vital tools, and easily sourced. All pencils are marked with their graphite gradient: an H pencil means hard, and a B pencil means black. An HB pencil can be used for drawing on both paper and fabric.

Having a selection of colouring pencils to hand is always useful. They are essential for recording colour ideas in your sketchbook and are easily transported when out and about.

Air-soluble Drawing Pen and Permanent Marker Pen

An air-soluble pen is a great addition to any workbox. Depending on the type of fabric used, the ink on the fabric lasts for about eight hours and then disappears.

Using a permanent marker pen can be useful as the ink will not bleed into your work and the line will remain visible until you cover it either with fabric or stitch. They come in fine, medium and bold nib sizes, which are all useful.

A SIMPLE CHECKLIST FOR GENERAL TROUBLE-FREE SEWING AND EASY MAINTENANCE

If for any reason your sewing machine is not sewing correctly then here are a few handy troubleshooting hints:

- Make sure that your sewing machine is threaded correctly – it does not take any time at all to rethread top and bottom.
- Is the bobbin spool correctly wound – neither too tight nor too loose?
- Check that the bobbin spool is in the bobbin case the right way round, as not all spools and cases are the same. Always refer to your sewing machine manual if you are unsure.
- Make sure that the needle is in the right way round, is pushed up high and clamped tight by the needle clamp screw. Check that it is not blunt or bent. If in doubt, replace it with a brand-new needle.
- Make the most of your needle by fitting a new needle for each project. You may be surprised what a difference this simple rule will make.
- Refer to the sewing machine manual for any oiling that may need to be done – when, where and how – and remember each sewing machine, depending on its manufacturer, will be different.
- Every so often, look beneath the needle plate to check that it is dust and lint free. After a while it will have collected a 'felt carpet', which will need to be brushed away with the small soft sewing machine brush supplied with the machine.
- When not in use, store your sewing machine upright in its case or beneath its cover. Ensure it is stored out of direct sunlight and in a damp-free environment.
- If you treat your machine well, you will get many years' service from it.

Tailor's Chalk

A flat triangle or square-shaped hard chalk used to make a temporary mark on fabric. Use a soft, clean brush to get rid of any unwanted chalk markings.

Hook and Loop Fastener Tape

This is a two-part tape: one tape has hooks, the other loops. It adheres strongly when pressed together. It can be bought in packs of either stick and sew or mixed.

Mount Board

A thin, flat piece of card that comes in a wide range of colours. It can be used either to mount work onto, or for cutting a window into for all framing requirements.

Steam Iron, Ironing Board and Linen Cloth for Pressing

Pressed fabric is much easier to work with than crumpled fabric. Ironing out all the seams allows for precision and tidy sewing.

As with all heavily stitched fabric, the stitching can cause puckering and for the fabric to become uneven in places, especially if the embroidered stitch has been taken in many different directions. To help reduce any wrinkles and to smooth an uneven surface on the front of the work, press the fabric on the reverse with a hot steam iron and a pressing cloth. Always use a dampened linen cloth, such as a clean tea towel, as this helps to protect the fabric from scorching, while at the same time preventing the transference of any dirt from the iron sole plate to the fabric or stitched picture.

Masking Tape

Adhesive tape with a low tack value is great to use for keeping paper and fabric in place when drawing on. It is also ideal for sticking images onto a wall for creative contemplation.

Ruler and Tape Measure

Both are invaluable tools for measuring to ensure precision when cutting. It is always best to have both metric and imperial measurements. A traditional sewer's tape measure can be rolled up for neat storage and is easy to wear around the neck when sewing in the workroom.

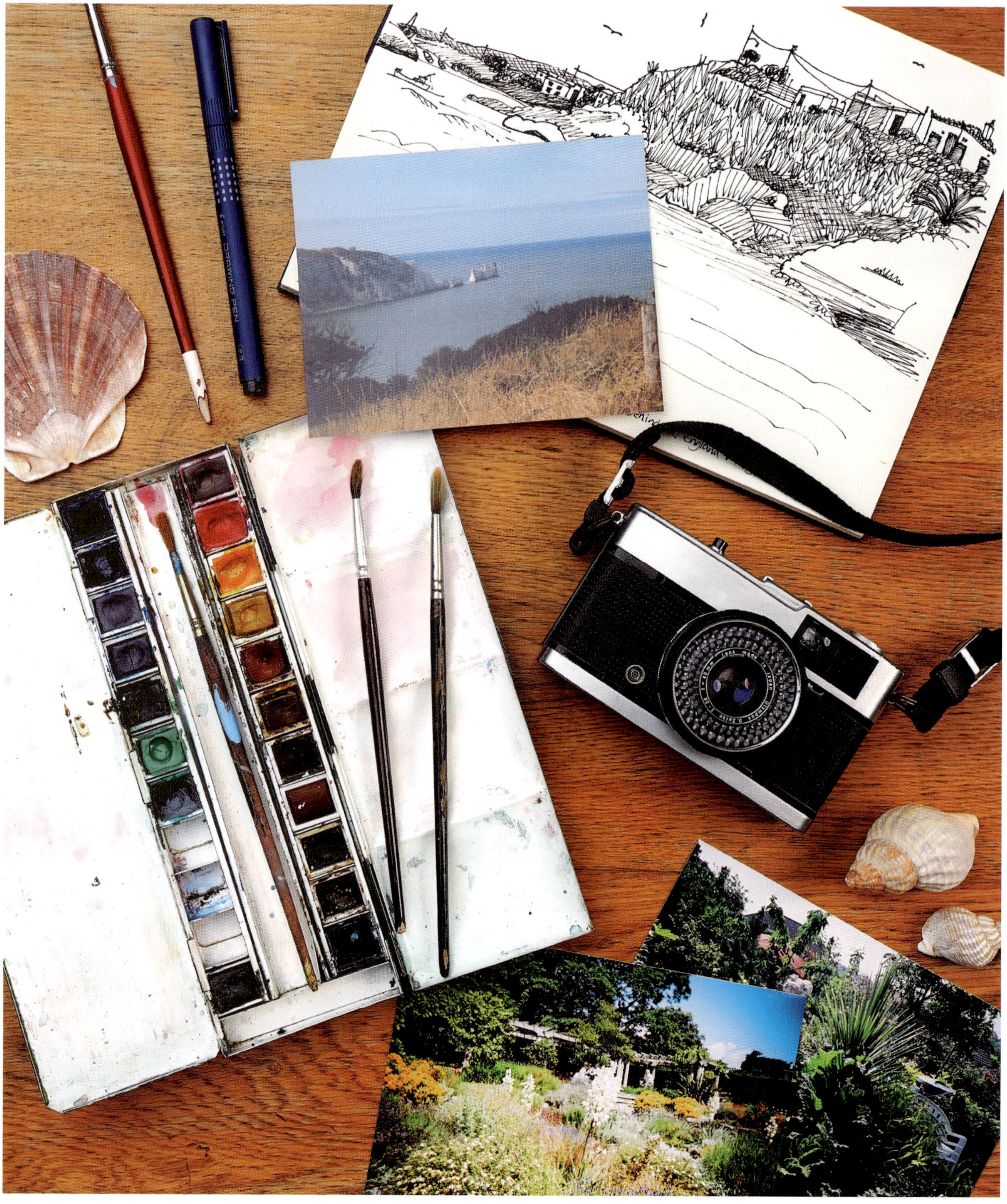

Be prepared for looking and recording; one never knows when inspiration will strike!

Lightbox

A lightbox is a useful tool for tracing images. It has an opaque screen, which is backlit. There are many types to choose from and they can be battery powered or mains operated. The different settings enable you to work with either a very bright or slightly diffused light. You can trace from different sources of inspiration such as photographs, drawings, fabric and text, transferring images directly onto paper, fabric or tracing paper.

If you do not have a lightbox, a bright day and a window pane will act in the same way. Using masking or clear sticky tape, stick the picture that you wish to trace from onto the window, then attach the paper or fabric you wish to trace onto over the top. The sunlight will shine through, illuminating your original picture and enabling you to trace the image.

Good Lighting/Anglepoise Light/Daylight Bulbs

It is essential to see your work properly, so good lighting is a must. If the natural daylight is poor, an Anglepoise light fitted with a daylight bulb is an excellent alternative to natural daylight. A daylight bulb emits a light similar to natural daylight and will not tire your eyes as you work.

All of the projects in this book require a selection of the basic tools and equipment listed in this chapter. In addition, each project requires its own selection of materials, which are listed at the beginning of each of the project chapters.

When you use your sewing machine for the free machine embroidery technique, you must have the compatible free machine embroidery foot fitted and the feed dog teeth lowered, or a plate fitted over the feed dog teeth.

To begin the free machine embroidery technique process in each project, read the section on bringing up the bobbin thread, which is explained in Chapter 3, Step 4.

Unless otherwise stated at the beginning of each project, the sewing machine tension setting is set to ordinary sewing tension. To achieve the recommended sewing tension for your own machine, refer to your sewing machine manual.

A CREATIVE SPACE OF YOUR OWN

It is important as a maker to have a creative workspace; a place that you can go to and work in whenever inspiration strikes, whether it be for a snatched half an hour or a whole day's making. A welcoming and peaceful refuge away from the distractions of everyday life – a bright and cheerful environment which houses all our precious equipment and essential materials – is essential for our creative wellbeing.

When setting out to make your creative space, choose somewhere that has good natural daylight and select a light colour with which to decorate the walls – white walls work very well, as white will maximize the light within the room. Position your sewing machine in an area of the room where the daylight is most constant. Consider what else you require to make your creative space work best for you: a cutting-out table, an ironing board always up and ready, a pinboard for ideas, shelving for reference books and magazines? If your materials and equipment can be left out all the time then even better – perhaps with purpose-built floor-to-ceiling shelves to show off your fabric stash and to provide constant inspiration. There are many shops, both on the high street and on the internet, that sell storage solutions, and there are some inspired storage ideas that can maximize even the smallest of spaces to make a near perfect workspace.

A spare room, a converted garage, a workshop in the garden or even a purpose-built studio on the side of the house – all of these can make a very desirable space in which we can express ourselves creatively. However, sometimes we cannot have exactly what we want, and compromises have to be made. We are not all fortunate enough to have such an ideal self-contained space, so ask yourself: is there a part of your home that could accommodate a sewing machine? A corner of the bedroom, a well-lit cupboard under the stairs, an area on the landing? With a few simple changes and some determination, a desirable making space can be created. For instance, replacing a bed in a spare room with a sofa bed will free up some floor space and enable you to install a worktable or desk for your sewing machine, together with fitting a couple of shelves to store fabric, thread and your essential sewing kit. Even the end of the family dining table can be accommodating if your sewing machine can be left nearby for easy access. With some imagination, any available area has the potential to become a great creative space you can call your own.

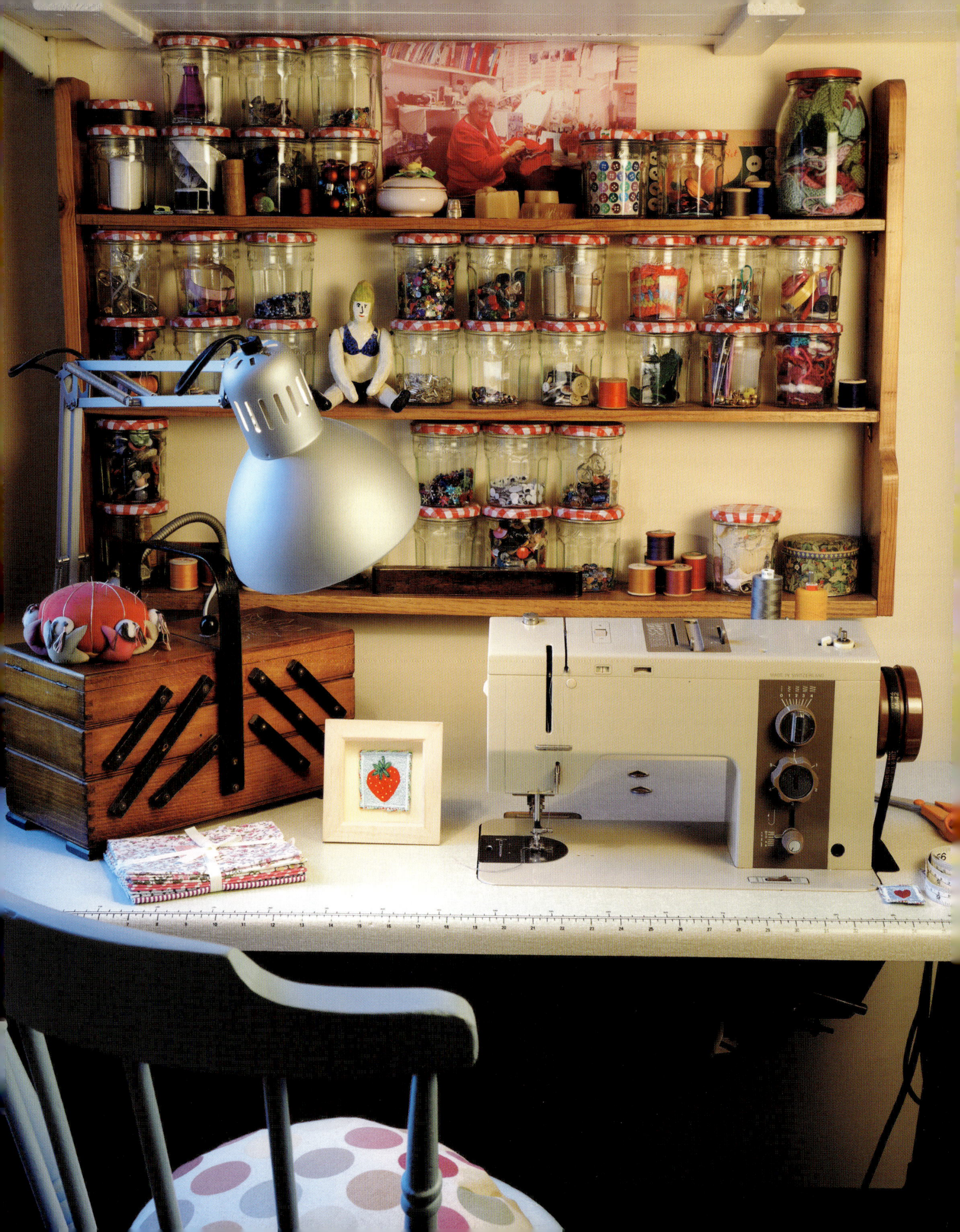

CHAPTER 2

WORKING WITH YOUR SEWING MACHINE

CHOOSING A SEWING MACHINE

Whether you are a beginner or an experienced stitcher there are a vast array of sewing machines to choose from. If you are new to machine sewing and are looking to buy a sewing machine, think carefully about what you will use it for. Occasional hemming and repair? Or as an art and craft tool? Or perhaps you wish to undertake sewing for the home and family? The good news is that the right machine will be able to undertake all these tasks and, if maintained well, should serve you for many years.

Whatever your sewing aspirations, choose a basic good quality sewing machine that can go forwards and backwards, make a zigzag stitch, achieve a few fancy stitches and has an option to do automatic buttonholes. You may already have a well-loved sewing machine that suits all your requirements, and which has more years of service to give in creating a wealth of textile projects. It is worth noting at this point that all the projects in this book require the use of a machine where the feed dog teeth (*see* overleaf) can either be lowered or a plate can be placed over them; check your machine's manual for instructions on how to perform this task.

It is key that the sewing machine you buy is the right one for you, so it is essential to try out a few different models before you make your purchase decision. Bearing in mind the above advice to choose a basic good-quality machine, do not be swayed into buying an overly complicated, fashion-branded, overpriced model, where a simpler machine with fewer features would serve you better. It is always advisable to make your purchase from a reputable retailer where there will be someone on hand to show you how the machine works and what functions it has. Some stockists offer practical workshops where you can learn how to get the best out of your newly acquired sewing machine.

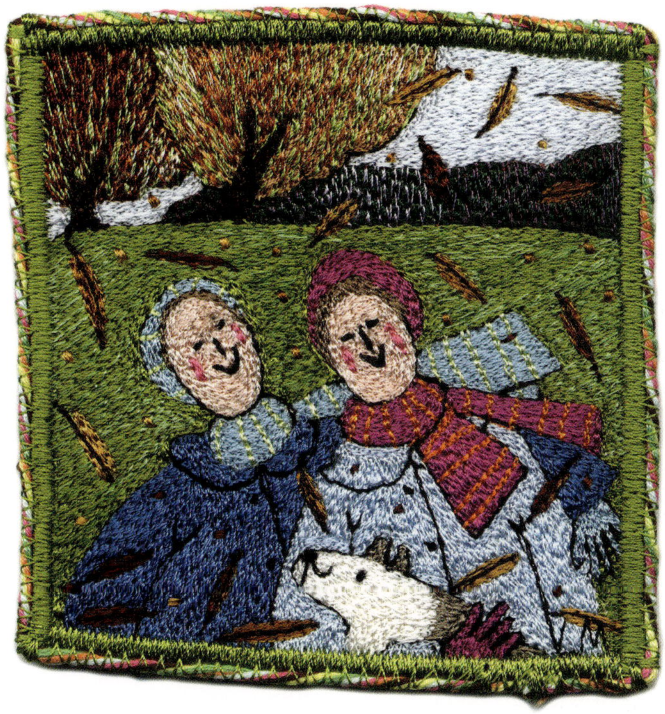

Blowy Hillside by Linda Miller, 10 × 10cm (4 × 4in), free machine embroidery. (Photo: Michael Jennings)

◀ A creative space to call one's own.

An attractive alternative to buying a brand-new machine is to invest in a second-hand model. Often this is a way of securing an extremely good-quality machine at a more affordable price. However, it is crucial to ensure when buying any second-hand machine that it comes with a warranty and has been serviced to a high standard by a specialist sewing machine engineer.

Once you have invested in a new or second-hand machine it is essential to keep it in good running order. Refer to your sewing machine manual for how to clean, oil and generally care for your newly acquired machine. In addition, it is advisable that every so often you have your machine serviced by a qualified sewing machine engineer. A machine that does not work properly is not just frustrating but in some cases can be dangerous too. If you are tackling a challenging sewing project you need to put all your energy and concentration into your assignment and not be distracted by a faulty machine. An unhappy machine makes unhappy work!

SEWING MACHINE PARTS

Feed Dog Teeth

The feed dog teeth are two rows of metal teeth situated beneath the sewing machine foot. When engaged, the teeth's automatic mechanism grips the fabric and pulls it through the machine, which allows the action of the needle to produce the line of stitch.

When using the technique of free machine embroidery, the feed dog teeth must be disengaged and a free machine embroidery foot must be fitted. Using this technique allows the sewer to pull the fabric through the machine manually, enabling the line of stitch to be taken in a multidirectional way, which is ideal for drawing with stitch. This process is only achievable using a compatible free machine embroidery foot, which helps to keep the fabric down as well as protecting the needle and your fingers. Note: machines without a mechanism to lower the feed dog teeth simply have a metal plate to cover the teeth.

Sewing Machine Feet and the Free Machine Embroidery Foot

Depending on the make and model of your machine you will have a selection of sewing machine feet designed solely to fit your machine. The manual will explain in detail what each foot is used for and how to use it correctly. The feet that you will need for the projects in this book are:

- General-purpose sewing foot
- Zigzag/satin stitch foot
- Free machine embroidery/darning foot

For the picture projects in the chapters ahead, the free machine embroidery foot will be the one used to create the machine embroidery technique. Depending on the make, model and age of your machine, it can also be referred to as a free motion quilting foot or a darning foot; it usually comes in the shape of a circle, an oval or a horseshoe. It is designed so that it hops up and down upon the fabric as the needle passes through it, creating the stitch line. The foot helps to keep the fabric down and stops it from puckering, creating a fine, even stitch line. If your sewing machine does not have a free machine embroidery foot you can buy one from a sewing machine retailer; it is sometimes referred to as a free motion foot.

Do not attempt to machine embroider without the correct free machine embroidery foot fitted. An unprotected needle pummelling through the fabric at great speed can be very dangerous as there is a risk of serious injury to one's fingers, the needle breaking and the fabric puckering – all of which you will wish to avoid. It is recommended therefore that you have a well-fitting and compatible foot for your machine to make the process both safer and easier.

Bobbin Spools

Your sewing machine will come with a few bobbin spools. Bobbin spools come in all sizes, and it is important to remember that you must use the correct size bobbin for your machine; the machine will not work correctly if the wrong size bobbin spools are used. Refer to the manual for guidance in fitting the bobbin spool into your sewing machine. Don't forget, you can always buy extra bobbin spools from a specialist dealer.

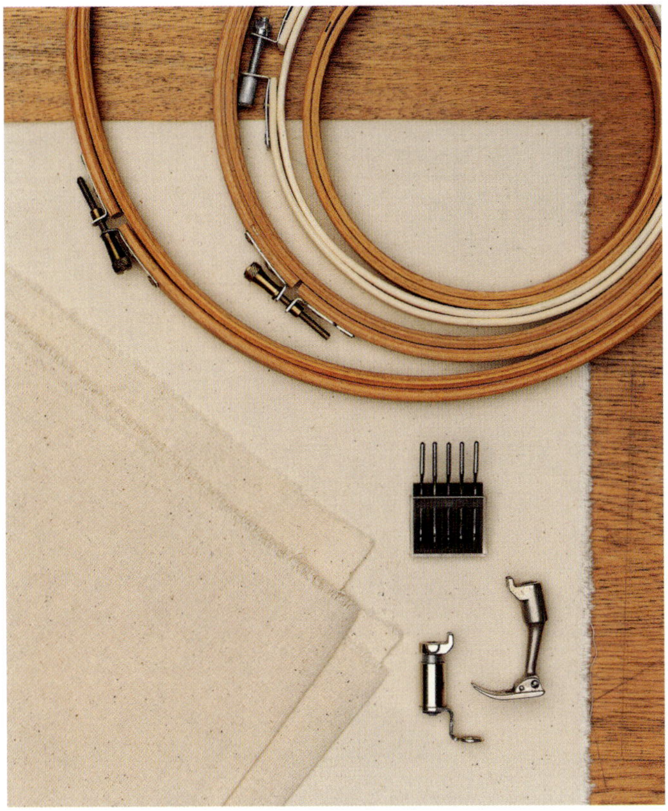

A selection of simple materials and equipment needed for free machine embroidery.

SEWING MACHINE NEEDLES

There are many different types of sewing machine needles and they come in varying sizes. Each needle is designed to suit different types and thicknesses of fabric. You must choose the type and size of needle best suited to the project on which you are working. Universal sewing machine needles are recommended for general all-purpose sewing.

For specific fabrics like knitted cotton jersey, a ballpoint needle is required as this is designed not to puncture the fabric but to part the fibres gently. For heavier weight fabrics like denim or cotton drill, a thicker needle such as a jeans needle is required, which has a stronger shaft and a finer point to enable it to go easily through densely woven fabric. Quilting needles allow for precision sewing through single and multiple layers.

For machine embroidery you can use good-quality standard size 80 needles or a specific machine embroidery needle. These needles have an enlarged eye that protects the thread as the needle goes in and out of the fabric at high speed. Some machine embroidery needles are titanium tipped; this special metal coating resists adhesives (such as when fabrics have been fused together in fabric appliqué) and prolongs the life of the needle.

Generally speaking, more expensive branded needles are superior to cheap needles, which should be avoided as they are of poorer quality and can lead to frustration when sewing. Problems such as missed stitches, tiny rips in the fabric and crumpling in the stitch line are just three setbacks that can be avoided by using a quality needle. Needles are one of the cheapest pieces of equipment you can buy for your machine, so if you are going to spend time and effort on a sewing project, the smallest luxury you can afford is a new needle. If you buy a packet of assorted sizes, you will have a wide selection to choose from. It is always a good idea when embarking on a sewing project to start with a new needle, so if you encounter a problem early on it will not be that straight and sharp needle you have just put in.

Fitting a New Needle in your Sewing Machine

It is important when fitting a new needle to refer to your sewing machine manual and to use the correct tools provided with the machine, as recommended by the manufacturer. It goes without saying that if the needle is not correctly fitted, the sewing machine will not work properly and the new needle may break.

Have a look at a new machine needle closely and you will find it has a rounded front and a flat back. When you fit the needle, ensure the rounded front is facing you. Push it up into the machine as high as it will go and ensure the needle clamp screw is tightened securely, as the vibration of the machine may loosen the clamp and the needle may fall out while you are sewing.

HANDY HINT FITTING A NEW NEEDLE

When fitting a new needle, place a piece of paper underneath the foot, so that when you loosen the needle clamp screw and the old needle falls out, it will be caught by the paper and not disappear into the machine mechanism, thus avoiding a fiddly and time-consuming search.

Needle Sizes

Machine needle sizes are indicated on the packet. There are usually two numbers denoting the size: the first is the European (metric) size and the second is American (imperial). The European sizes range from 60 to 110 and the American sizes are from 8 to 18. The smaller the needle size, the finer the needle, so a size 70 is 0.7mm in diameter and a size 80 is 0.8mm in diameter.

You can use standard universal machine needles for the picture projects in the chapters ahead and I recommend size 80 sewing machine needles for free machine embroidery and working with layered fabrics. Of course, if you wish you may use a specific machine embroidery needle or a thicker needle if you are working with heavier weight fabrics such as denim.

MACHINE EMBROIDERY AND GENERAL SEWING THREADS

The two types of thread used in the projects in this book are sewing machine threads and machine embroidery threads. Both these types of thread are easily available from any good sewing shop or haberdashery department. Sewing machine threads are used for general sewing projects – the most common ones being cotton and polyester. Cotton thread is made from 100 per cent cotton fibres and is most suited for use on cotton and linen fabrics; it is not recommended to be used on jersey fabric as it has little elasticity and can snap when the fabric moves and stretches. Polyester thread is a strong sewing thread with a slight stretch to it, which makes it a good all-rounder, suitable for use with both stretch and cotton fabrics. Both cotton and polyester threads are suitable to use in all the picture projects in this book.

The most popular machine embroidery threads are made from rayon, viscose and polyester. These are purely decorative threads and should only be used with a sewing machine as they are too weak for general-purpose sewing. Machine embroidery threads come in a variety of weights; the two most popular weights being a 40 and a 30 (40 weight is slightly thinner than 30 weight). Both weights are good to use, however the 30, being slightly thicker, does fill in areas more quickly. The weight of thread, along with the meterage, is listed on each spool.

Machine embroidery thread comes in a wide variety of texture, weight and colour. It can be a solid blocked colour or multicoloured, as well as having a matt or sheen finish. A multicoloured thread is a single spool of thread that has been space dyed in different shades of the same colour or a random selection of colours. Metallic machine embroidery thread is also available in different colours. This is made from a core wrapped with metallized threads – this type of thread can give a sparkly finish to a project and is best used with a specific metallic sewing machine needle.

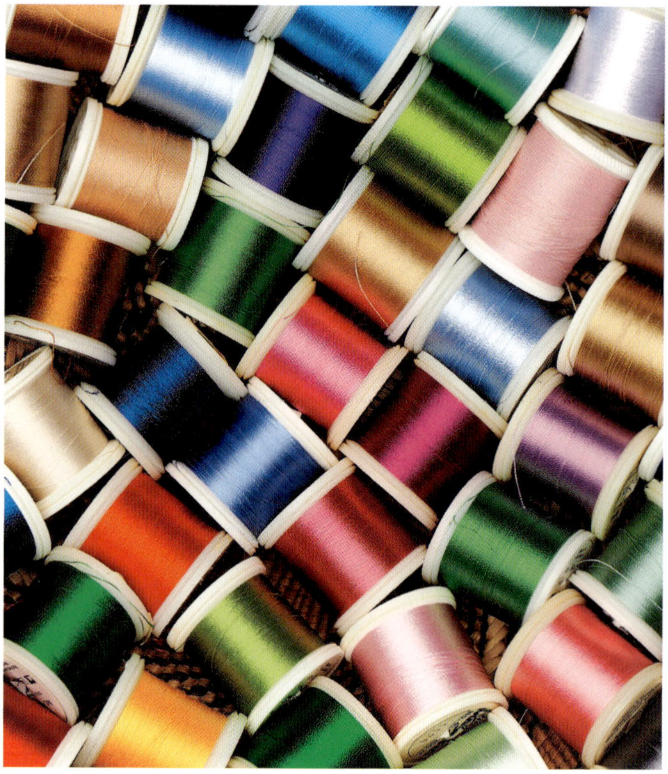

A basket of machine embroidery threads, ready and waiting for the textile artist.

A good-quality thread will be a pleasure to work with; it will smoothly embroider onto your base fabric and over your design. Avoid cheap thread as it will be of poor quality and will be more likely to snap, causing you frustration as you will need to rethread your machine multiple times. In addition, it could damage your sewing machine and your project will feature frayed thread, which you will need to keep cutting off.

If you are new to machine embroidery or do not have any machine embroidery threads, buy a selection pack or choose a small variety of colours. You can easily add to your collection as you progress. You can also use good-quality general-purpose sewing threads for machine embroidery. A mixture of different types can look very attractive in projects and, as a good rule, if you like the thread and your machine likes it, use it.

SEWING MACHINE TENSION AND EFFECTS

Helpfully, the sewing machine tension required for free machine embroidery is the same as that used for dress or curtain making, that is a normal or regular sewing tension. Although, altering the tension can create some different effects on the top surface of the machine embroidery with which you may wish to experiment. For instance, if you use a different colour thread in your bobbin and increase the top tension, little spots of the bobbin colour will appear on the top surface of your picture; this is a great way to mix colours and can look very attractive. If the top tension is decreased, then loops will appear on the top surface, which creates interesting texture. Both techniques can be used in any project as they can add interesting visual effects and variety to the top surface of the work.

Do not be afraid to experiment with these techniques within your work. if you are unsure of how the effect will look then try it out on a separate piece of fabric placed within another wooden embroidery hoop (outlined in Chapter 3, Step 2). If you like the result, you can use it in your work and if you do not, nothing will have been spoilt. Check your sewing machine manual to locate the tension dial – usually it will be on either the top or the front of the machine.

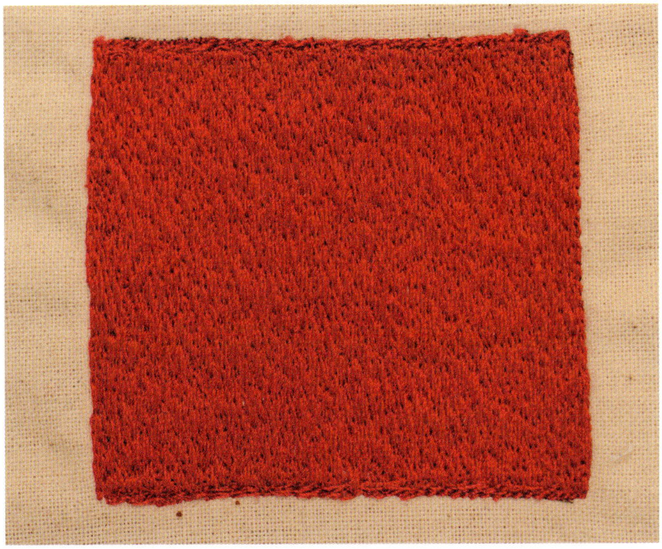

A machine embroidery sample made using the tension setting set to normal/regular.

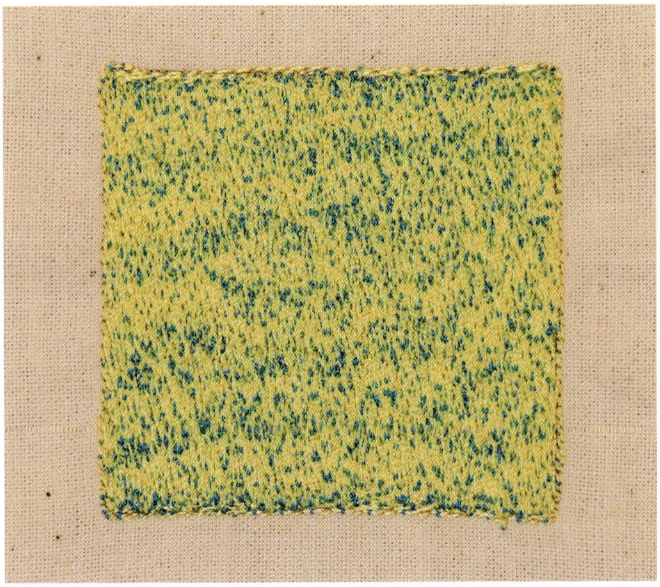

Increasing the top tension brings the bobbin thread through onto the thread surface.

GETTING TO KNOW YOUR SEWING MACHINE

If you have not used your machine for a while or if it is new to you, it is advisable to sit in front of it with the manual and a waste piece of fabric, thread up your machine and try out a few stitches. If your machine has a selection of fancy stitches, try these out too. Sometimes a new machine can be a little daunting, but after a while and with some use it will become a wonderful working companion. Together, you and your machine will make a wealth of textile projects.

When using your machine for free machine embroidery it is you that directs the stitch line because once the feed dog teeth are lowered you have the freedom to draw with the needle in any direction you wish. When the feed dog teeth are raised, it is the sewing machine that commands the direction and length of stitch.

HANDY HINT PROBLEMS WITH THREAD BREAKING

If you find that your top thread is constantly breaking, either replace your needle or loosen off the top tension. This will make the top thread slightly slacker and should prevent it from snapping.

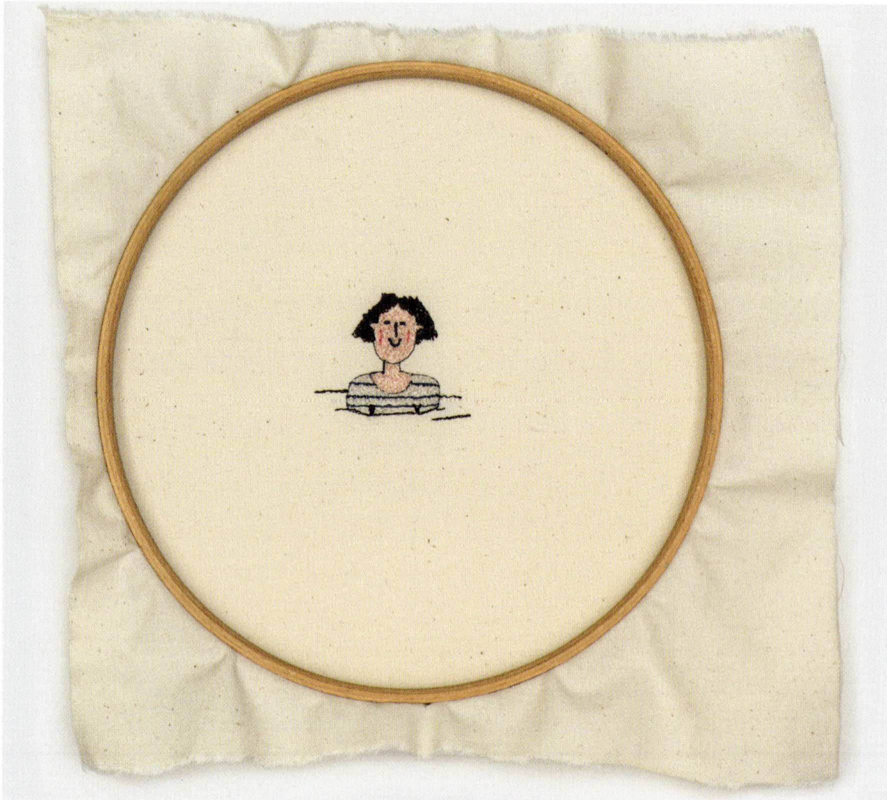

Lowering the feed dog teeth allows freedom to draw with the sewing machine needle.

When first using free machine embroidery it may feel a little awkward, but no doubt after some practice this technique will soon feel quite familiar. In no time at all your confidence and ability in using this new medium will develop into a skill you can use on numerous projects, giving you the opportunity to be as creative as you desire.

SEWING MACHINE HEALTH AND SAFETY

No matter how many years you have been sewing, there are a few simple safety precautions to remember:

- Make sure that your sewing machine is earthed and wired correctly.
- Tie back long hair and tuck in scarves or floaty garments. You do not want to sew yourself into your work!
- Protect your fingers – every time you stop sewing, take your foot off the foot pedal. Leaving your foot down increases the risk of it slipping, which may engage the machine, causing the needle to move whether fingers are near or far.
- Avoid creating trip hazards – watch out for cables and leads. You may wish to invest in a length of cable cover.
- When you finish sewing, switch off your machine and disconnect it from the wall socket.
- All broken or used needles and bent pins should be kept safely in a protective sharps container until they can be disposed of responsibly.

Red Tulips by Linda Miller, 20 × 20cm (8 × 8in), fabric appliqué and free machine embroidery.

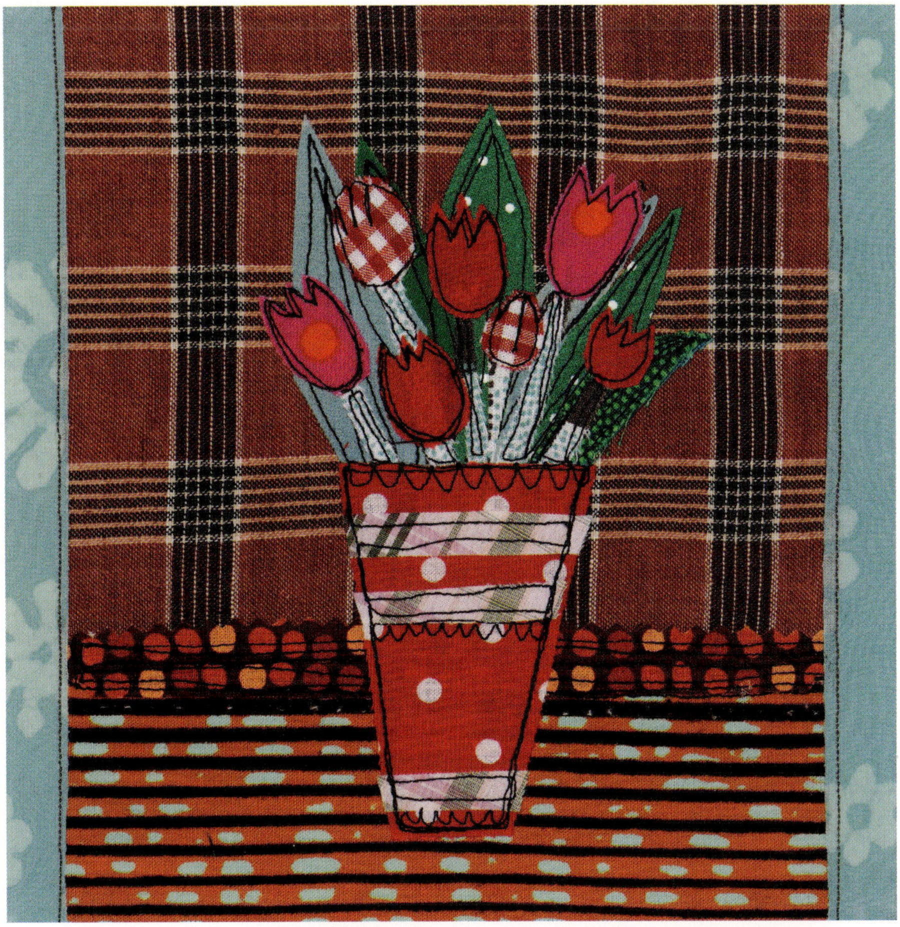

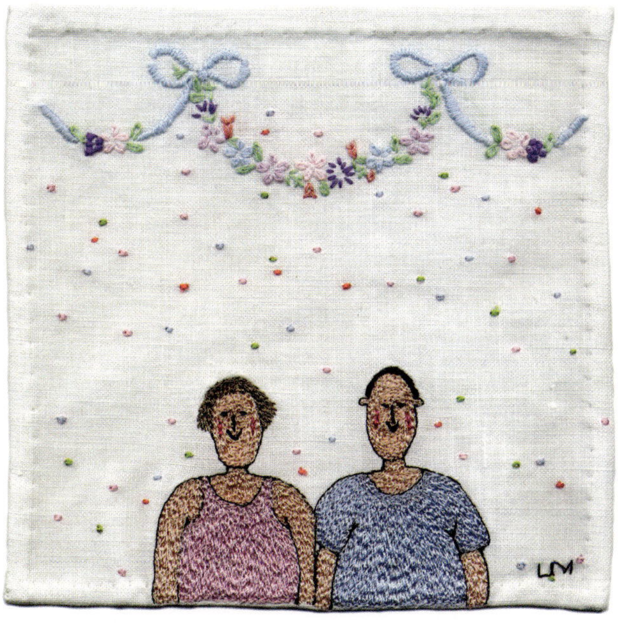

Blossom Canopy by Linda Miller, 16 × 16cm (6¼ × 6¼in), free machine embroidery and hand embroidery onto a linen cloth. (Photo: Michael Jennings)

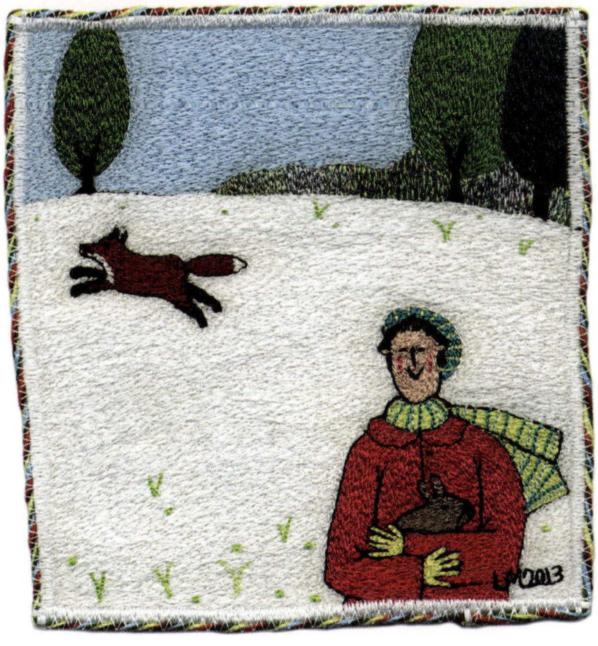

Hillside Fox by Linda Miller, 15 × 14cm (6 x 5½in), free machine embroidery. (Photo: Michael Jennings)

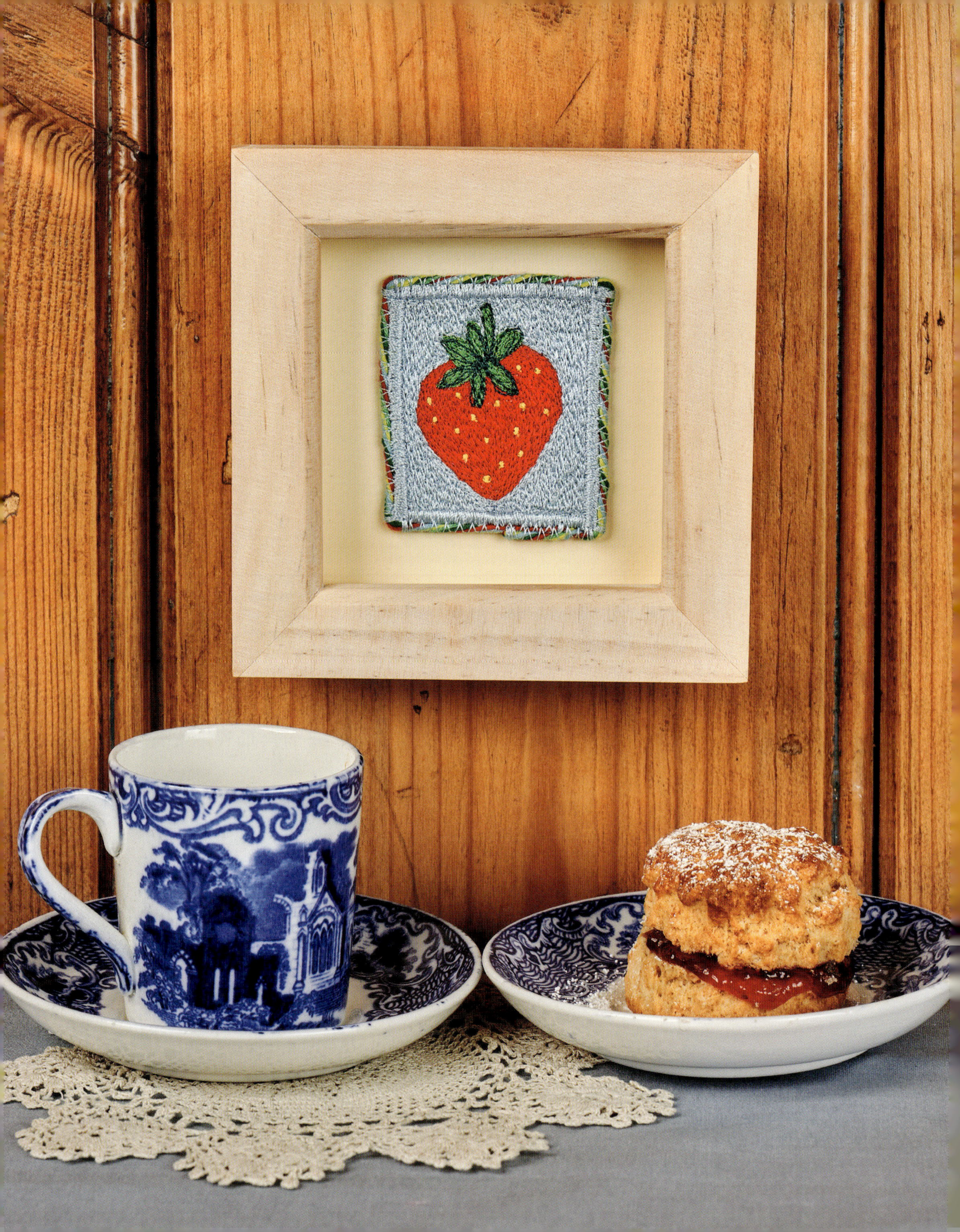

CHAPTER 3

USING THE SEWING MACHINE AS A DRAWING AND PAINTING TOOL

PICTURE PROJECT
Strawberry Delight – Solid Stitch Free Machine Embroidery

Undertaking this simple project of a solidly stitched picture of a strawberry will provide you with all the fundamental skills and knowledge you require for using your sewing machine as a drawing and painting tool through the medium of free machine embroidery. Once completed you will have the essential knowledge to enable you to complete the other projects in the chapters ahead.

You will be guided through how to lay out a simple motif, how to begin to free machine embroider using a minimum selection of colourful threads and then how to finish off your picture using satin stitch and hand embroidery threads to make a border with a stylish twisted edge. This strawberry delight will enchant any sewer!

Finished strawberry motif picture measures 6 × 5cm (2½ × 2in).

Finished picture will fit a frame that measures 12 × 12cm (4¾ × 4¾in).

With this project you will be sewing on the front.

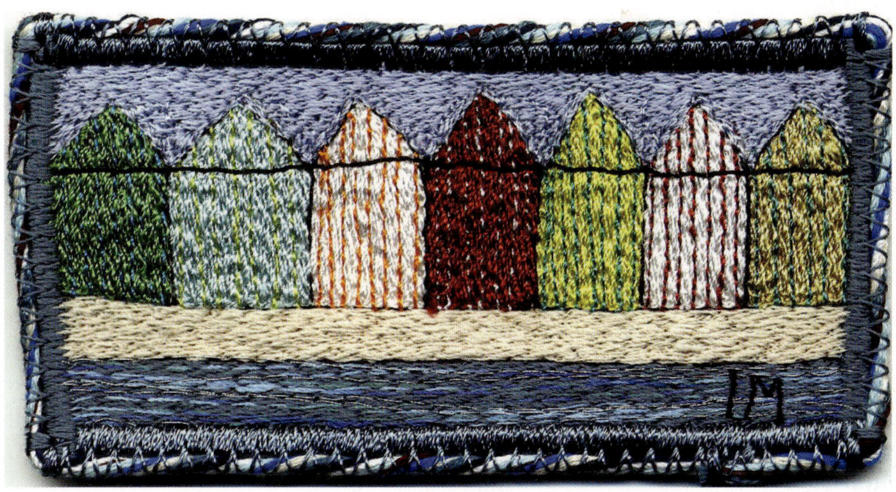

Beach Huts by Linda Miller, 5 x 10cm (2 x 4in), free machine embroidery. (Photo: Michael Jennings)

◀ *Strawberry Delight,* presented and framed in a wooden box frame.

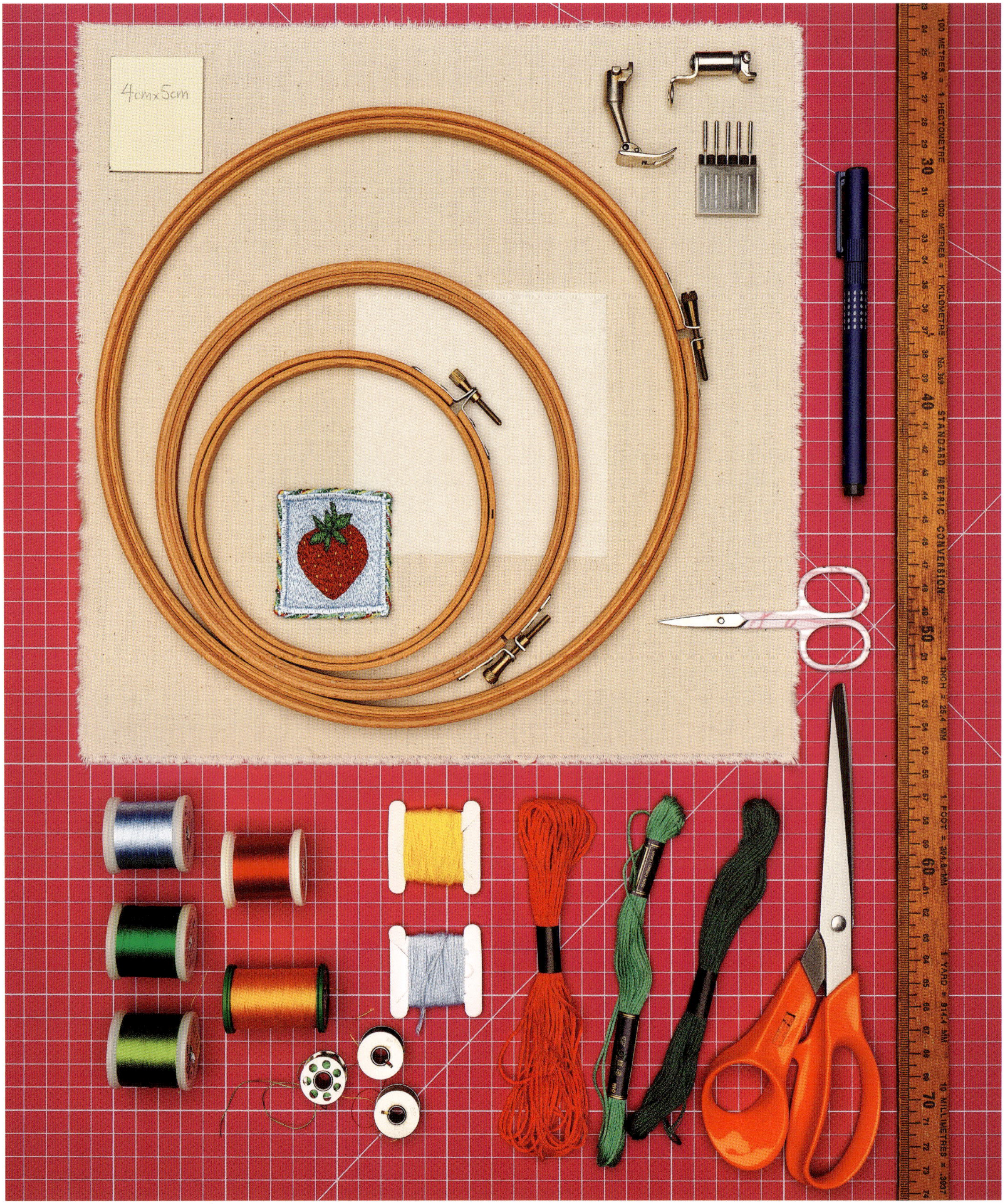

A selection of materials needed to make the picture project, *Strawberry Delight*.

YOU WILL NEED

Items from the basic tool kit, as listed in Chapter 1 Tools and Equipment, and the following materials:

- Piece of heavyweight calico measuring 25 × 25cm (10 × 10in)
- 15cm (6in) wooden embroidery hoop
- Piece of stabilizing fabric measuring approximately 12 × 10cm (4¾ × 4in)
- Selection of either machine embroidery threads in the weights of 30 or 40 or machine sewing threads in the following colours:
  - Red
  - Mid green
  - Dark green
  - Yellow
  - Pale blue
- Five colours of six-stranded hand embroidery threads in the following colours:
  - Red
  - Mid green
  - Dark green
  - Yellow
  - Pale blue
- Piece of good-quality mount board in a neutral colour, cut to the size of the frame's recess
- Unglazed box frame measuring 12 × 12cm (4¾ × 4¾in)

HANDY HINT TENSION

To create an even tension throughout this machine embroidery, you will be working from the centre of your picture to the outside edge. If you continue to follow this simple advice in all your solidly stitched work this will maintain an even surface, reduce puckering and prevent unnecessary undulations in your embroideries.

HANDY HINT TRUE AND EVEN COLOUR

To ensure you have a true and even colour throughout the top surface of your picture, make sure you use the same colour for the top thread and the bobbin spool. If you use a different colour in your bobbin there will always be a suggestion of this colour appearing on the top surface.

1 GETTING STARTED

Fit a new size 80 needle into both your sewing machine and the free machine embroidery foot. Lower the feed dog teeth or fit the plate that covers them (refer to your machine's manual). Alter the sewing machine tension to ordinary sewing tension (refer to your manual for where to find the top tension dial and adjust if required). Referring to your sewing machine manual, ensure your machine is set to a running stitch and alter the stitch length to 0.

Wind up four bobbins in the colours of red, mid green, yellow and pale blue. Insert the red threaded bobbin into your machine (bobbin thread). Thread up your sewing machine in the same red thread (top thread).

2 PLACING FABRIC INTO A HOOP

Separate a 15cm (6in) wooden embroidery hoop and put the outer hoop with the screw mechanism on a table, then place the piece of heavyweight calico over the top of this hoop. Lay the inner part of the hoop over the fabric and push the two hoops together. The fabric will now be sandwiched between the two hoops. Carefully tighten up the screw on the outer hoop, either by hand or with a screwdriver, if applicable; take care not to overtighten and be mindful of your fingers.

Place the fabric-filled hoop back on the table with the fabric resting on the table. While holding down the hoop with one hand, use the thumb and forefinger of your other hand to pull the outside of the fabric taut in the hoop and do this all the way around. This creates a tight, drum-like surface and enables the needle of the sewing machine to bounce in and out of the fabric. This side of the fabric will be the top side (the front); the reverse, with the hoop screw showing, will be the underneath (the back).

3 DRAWING YOUR DESIGN

On a piece of paper, and using either a HB pencil or a drawing pen and ruler, draw a box that measures approximately 6cm (2½in) deep by 5cm (2in) wide. On another piece of paper draw a simple strawberry shape. Once you are happy with the shape, draw it as big as you can within the box.

Place the finished drawing on a lightbox and put the calico-filled hoop over the top. Using a pencil, an air-soluble fabric pen or a fine-tipped permanent marker, trace the box and strawberry shape onto the calico, making sure it is in the middle of your fabric. It is important to ensure you are drawing on the correct side of the fabric (see Step 2). If you do not have a lightbox then stick your drawing onto a windowpane with some masking tape and lay the fabric-filled hoop over the top. Trace the shapes onto the fabric, again making sure the drawing is in the middle of the hoop.

HANDY HINT **HOW TO DRAW A STRAWBERRY**

If you are unfamiliar with or lack confidence in drawing, then follow these simple steps to draw a strawberry. First draw a heart shape, then in the dip at the top draw six oval-shaped leaves. Finally draw a stalk. Voila – a strawberry!

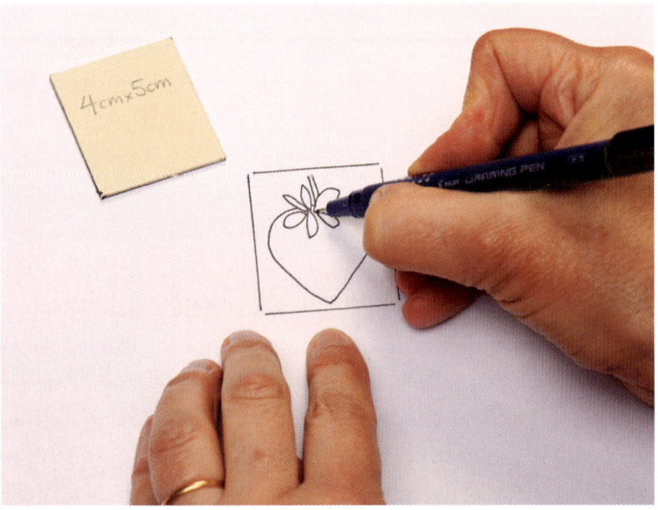

Draw a rectangle measuring 6 × 5cm (2½ × 2in) and then draw a strawberry to fit into this box.

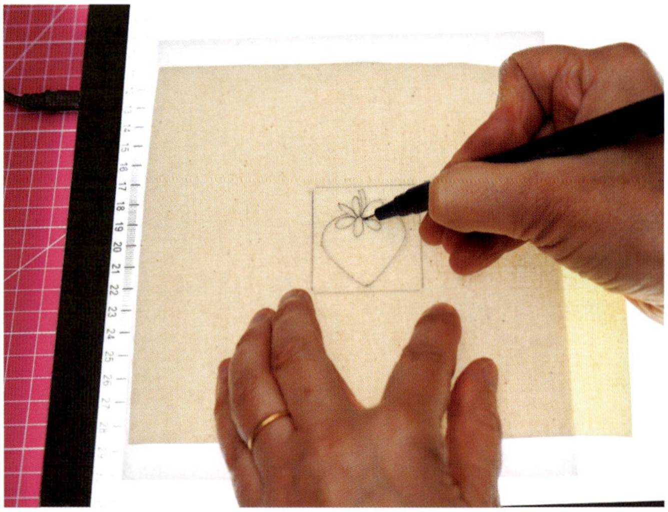
Place the strawberry drawing onto a lightbox and trace it through onto a piece of calico.

4 LEARNING TO FREE MACHINE EMBROIDER

Slide the fabric-filled hoop with your drawing on it under the free machine embroidery foot, lining up the drawing with the foot and needle. Check first that the sewing machine needle is as high as it will go and is therefore out of the way. If the foot is too low, preventing the hoop from fitting underneath, place your index finger under the free machine embroidery foot and push upwards, being careful to avoid the needle point. The foot will rise, and you will then be able to slide the hoop underneath it.

Bring up the bobbin thread onto the top surface of the fabric – this stops the threads from becoming knotted underneath the embroidery and enables trouble-free and easy sewing. To do this, hold the top thread in your left hand, and with your right hand lower the presser foot down. Then place your right hand on the wheel of the sewing machine. Turn the wheel anti-clockwise, enabling the needle to pierce the fabric, and keep turning the wheel towards you slowly until the needle stands proud of the fabric.

With your left hand, gently pull on the top thread. The bobbin thread will appear through the fabric. If it doesn't, turn the wheel a little more and again gently pull with your left hand on the top thread and the bobbin thread will appear. If you do this simple procedure every time you start to embroider, it will enable trouble-free sewing.

To begin to machine embroider, pull the two threads (top thread and bobbin thread) with your left hand until you have approximately 20cm (8in) of thread. Then, with your right hand, turn the wheel once more towards you until the needle of the sewing machine is in the fabric on the outside line of your drawing. Now place your right hand on the right side of the hoop and put your foot on the foot pedal. Very gently, as you slowly engage the foot pedal, move the hoop away from you with your hands.

The combination of feed dog teeth being lowered and the needle going up and down through the fabric enables you to draw with your machine. It is you that creates the stitch line with a constant pressure on the foot pedal. The quicker you push the hoop, the bigger the stitch line will be; and the slower you push, the smaller the line will be. It may seem a little confusing at first working in this way, but like most things, the more you do the easier and more familiar it will become. Remember, practice makes perfect!

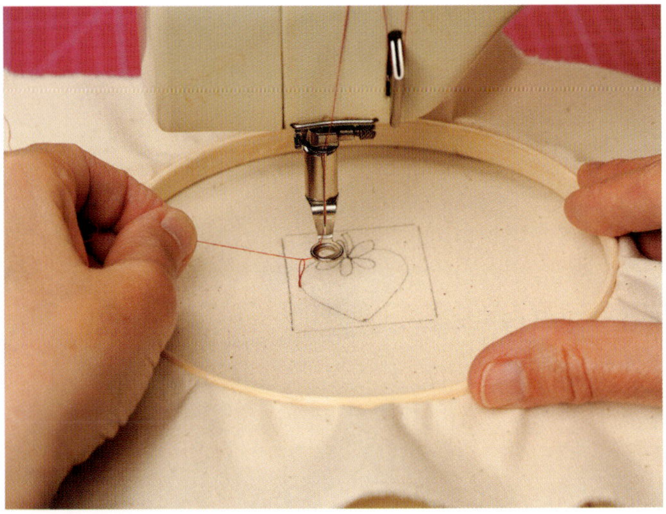

Bringing up the bobbin thread will reduce any knotting on the back of the embroidery.

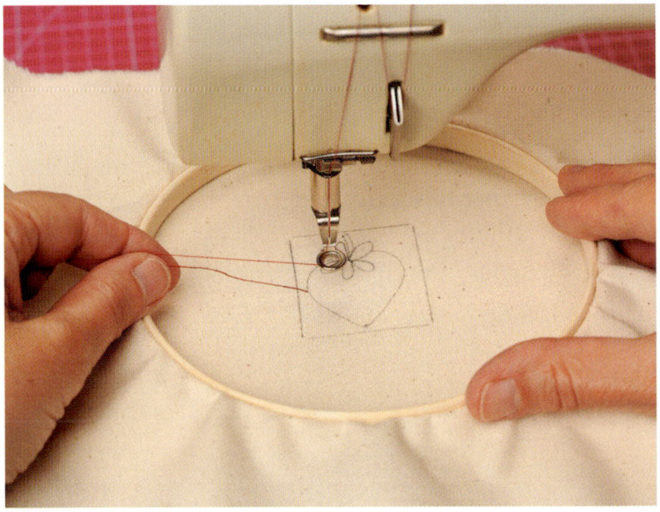

Hold the two threads and then place both of your hands on the outside of the hoop.

Follow the outside line of your strawberry drawing with the running stitch line of thread. Embroider all the way round the outside of the shape while still holding on to the two threads. When you have gone around the outside edge once, cut off the two threads at the base of the fabric where you first started using the embroidery scissors. Note: the stitches will not come undone as they are very small, and you will be going over this area again.

Now go around the outside edge once more, building up a thicker border. This will be good practice for following an outside edge line. Once this has been achieved, fill in the whole of the strawberry with the red thread. Try to take this stitch line in a vertical direction from the top of the strawberry to the bottom, following the contours of the strawberry to give it form and structure. As you sew and embroider, try to relax your shoulders and remember to breathe!

Cover as much of the base fabric as possible with thread, using a little shading motion by going over the area a couple of times. But don't be tempted to stay in one place sewing, as you will create lumps or knots of stitch underneath (on the back of your work). Such lumps will make it difficult to move the hoop and they will catch on the holes where the feed dog teeth usually sit, so try to keep moving in order to create an even covering of stitch, both on the front as well as on the back.

Once all the strawberry has been filled in with the red thread, stop sewing, take your foot off the pedal and put your right hand back on the sewing machine wheel. Turn the wheel towards you until the needle is out of the fabric and is high up. Lift the presser foot and slide the hoop out from under the embroidery foot. Cut off the top thread, close to the fabric surface, and then turn the hoop over and cut off the bobbin thread, again close to the thread surface. Admire your work and give yourself a pat on the back – well done!

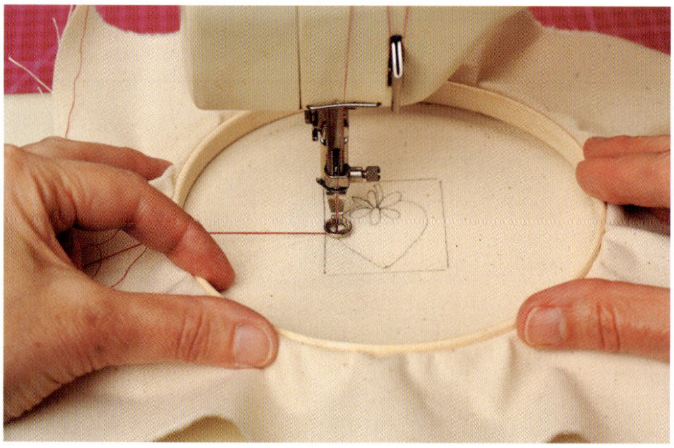

Position the needle on the strawberry drawing, then apply pressure to the presser foot.

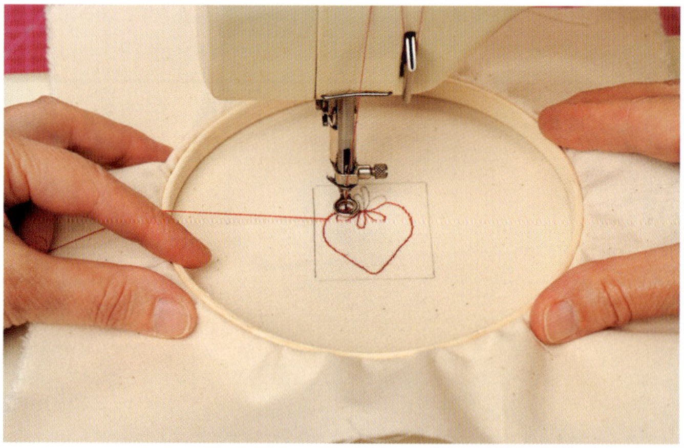

Follow the outline of the strawberry drawing with the red thread.

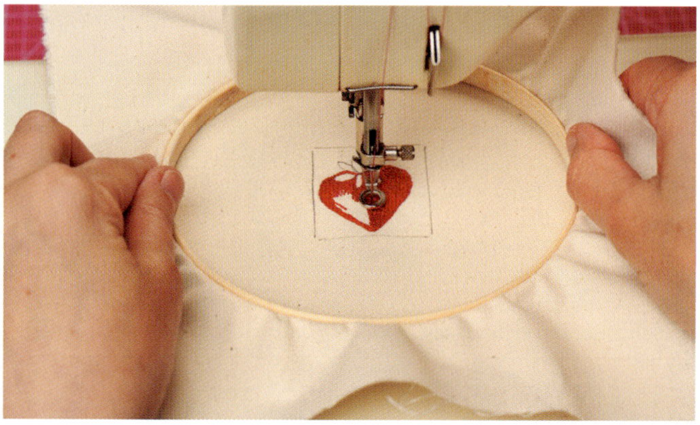

Cut away the two waste threads and follow the outline again before filling in the middle.

5 FOLIAGE

Unthread the machine both top and bottom and rethread with the mid green thread, ensuring you use a threaded bobbin in the same colour. Slide the fabric-filled hoop under the foot of the machine as before and lower the presser foot before you bring up the bobbin thread. Start at the top of the strawberry, where the leaves and stalk are, and repeat the process of bringing up the bobbin thread onto the top surface.

Follow the drawn line of the leaves and stalk with your stitch line filling in the six leaves and the stalk. Again, try to follow the contours of the shapes as this will give your picture a three-dimensional feel. To increase this effect, you could use threads with a sheen as the light will catch these, creating highlights and shadows.

To add definition to these elements, take the stitch vertically for the stalk and then from where the leaves meet in the centre out to the leaf tips. As you will be embroidering a much smaller area, you will automatically create smaller stitches, but be mindful to avoid those lumps on the back of your work. Do not worry if you cannot fill up all the base fabric as you will be adding another colour onto the leaves, so less stitching is fine.

Once again, when all the desired stitching has been achieved, stop sewing, take your foot off the pedal, and with your right hand turn the wheel towards you, which will remove the needle from your work. Lift the presser foot, slide the fabric-filled hoop from under the foot and cut off the top and bottom thread close to the embroidered surface.

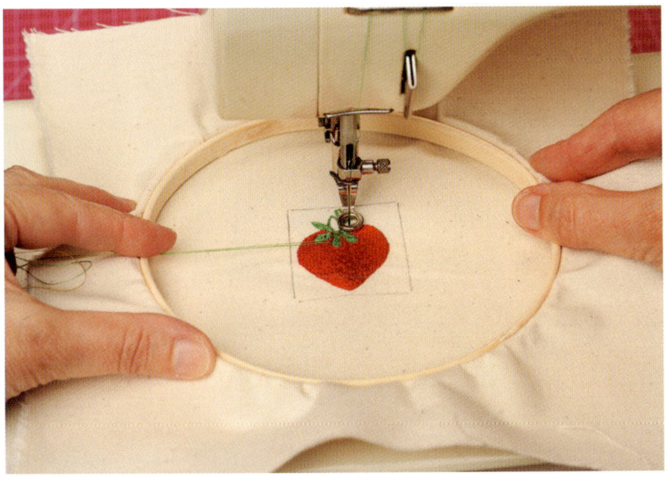

Thread up with the mid green thread and begin to embroider the strawberry's little leaves.

6 BACKGROUND

Unthread the machine top and bottom and rethread, this time with pale blue, which is the background colour. Slide the hoop under the foot and needle and repeat the process of bringing up the bobbin thread onto the top surface.

With the pale blue background colour, start following the outside edge of your strawberry, the leaves and stalk. Go around the outside a few times, creating a thick border line, then take your direction of stitch over to the outside edge of the box and do the same here. When you have completed this, start to fill in all the background, taking the direction of stitch horizontally from the top to the bottom in little filling-in sketch motions, as if you were using a pencil to shade. Remember to keep the needle moving over the base fabric. When all the base fabric has been covered, stop sewing and finish off as before.

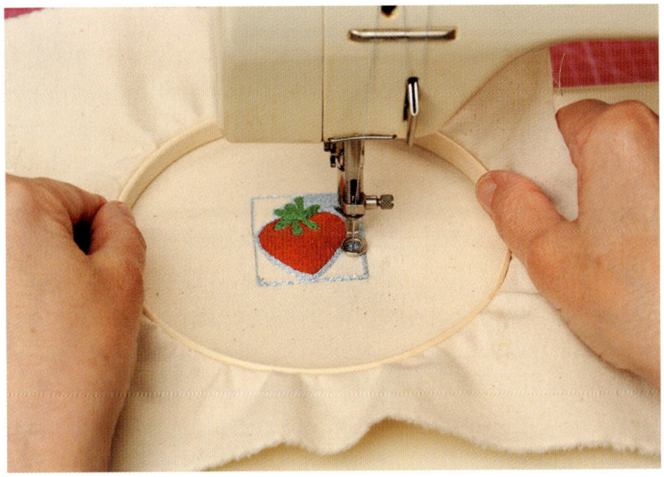

With the background colour, follow the strawberry's outline before completely filling in.

7 DEFINING THE LEAVES

Unthread the background colour from your machine and thread up with the dark green. Begin by bringing up the bobbin thread in the middle of the leaves. You are now going to draw an outline with the dark green thread around the outside edge of the leaves and stalk by carefully following the outside line of these shapes. Do not worry if your thread line has a wobble to it or keeps moving towards the centre of a leaf or the stalk as this outline is a mere suggestion. Having a darker outline on the greenery provides more definition.

When you have gone all the way round the foliage and arrived back in the middle of the leaves, stop sewing, take your foot off the pedal, raise the presser foot, slide out the hoop and cut off the threads.

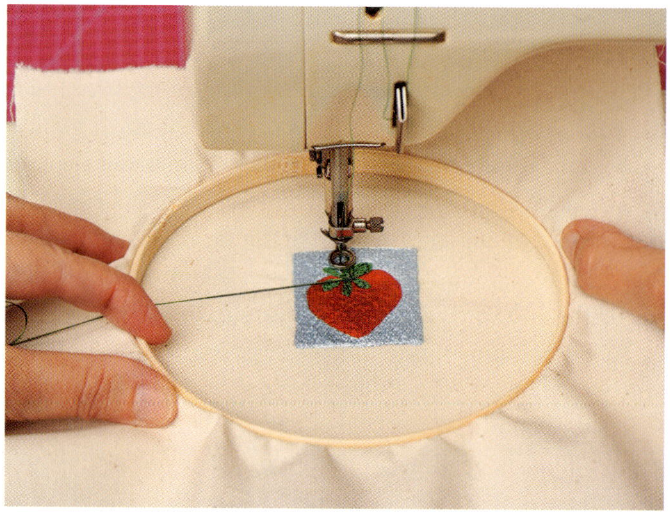

Use a dark green thread to draw veins and an outline on the strawberry's leaves.

8 STRAWBERRY SEEDS

The area of fabric around your strawberry can be used to experiment or practise with colour combinations and drawing stitch lines, as this fabric will eventually be cut away from the motif. To create the little strawberry seeds on the fruit, unthread the dark green thread from the top and the bobbin, and rethread both top and bottom with the yellow thread.

You now need to select a zigzag stitch on the machine, which needs to be 3–4mm wide. Once the stitch width has been selected, slide your hoop under the foot and needle and choose an area on the surrounding fabric not too near your strawberry. Lower the presser foot and bring up the bobbin thread as before. Hold the hoop still when you press on the foot pedal as the needle will go up and down and from side to side, creating a small zigzag stitch that will resemble a tiny dot. Try out a few zigzag dots on the surrounding calico fabric first, and when you are happy with the size of the dot, move the needle over to your strawberry and embroider a dot. Then, making sure the needle is out of the work, lift the presser foot up and move the needle over to another area of the strawberry (the top thread will carry over). Lower the presser foot and make another zigzag dot.

Repeat this technique about ten to fifteen times over the red area of the strawberry and when you feel you have achieved enough dots, take the needle out for the last time and raise the presser foot. Using the embroidery scissors, cut away the thread, close to the embroidered surface, both on the front as well as on the back. Then carefully cut away all the yellow threads that have been carried over onto the front of the work by snipping them as close to the stitched surface as possible. The carried-over threads on the back of the work can be left.

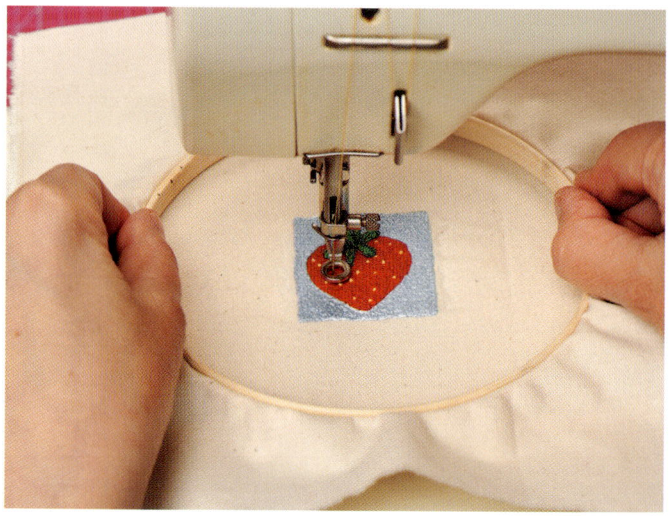

By setting the sewing machine to a zigzag stitch, dots can be achieved and used as seeds.

9 PRESSING YOUR WORK AND CUTTING IT OFF THE FABRIC

Loosen the screw on the wooden hoop and separate the two parts. Remove the base fabric containing your motif. Using a hot steam iron and a dampened linen cloth, press out the picture, remembering to press ever so gently on the back of your work. This is just to flatten the picture a little and lessen any puckering or unevenness within the embroidery.

Taking a pair of sharp dressmaking scissors, cut off the strawberry picture from the base fabric, leaving a 5mm fabric border around the outside edge of the blue background; use a ruler to get an accurate measurement. If the border is too wide, the zigzag will not be able to incorporate all the fabric into the width of stitch.

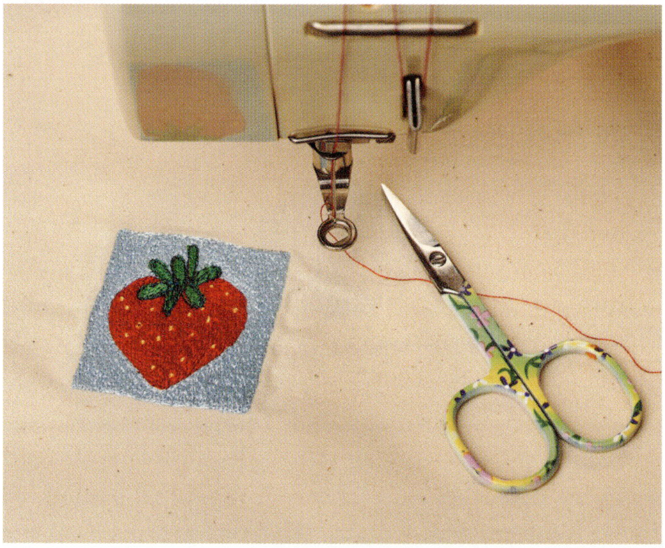

Remove the hoop and, using a steam iron, press on the back of the machine embroidery.

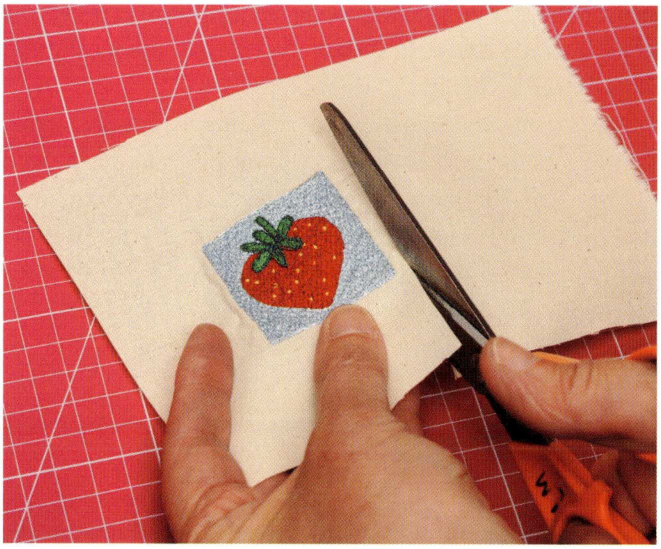

Cut away all the excess calico, leaving a 5mm border around the strawberry motif.

10 STABILIZING YOUR WORK AND RAISING THE FEED DOGS

Cut a piece of stabilizing fabric measuring approximately 12 × 10cm (4¾ × 4in) and place the strawberry motif on top. Put this to one side. It does not matter which side of the stabilizing fabric you place the strawberry on.

Refer to your machine's manual to see whether you should fit a general-purpose or zigzag foot for zigzag and satin stitching. Remove the free machine embroidery foot and fit either a general-purpose sewing foot or zigzag foot as appropriate. The size 80 needle can remain in the machine and the sewing tension can stay on 'general sewing mode'. Unthread the yellow top and bottom and rethread with the pale blue thread that was used for the background.

Raise the feed dog teeth. Note: if your machine has a plate that covers the feed dogs, you will need to refer to the end of this chapter for instructions on how to finish off. You may find the teeth will fully engage once one or two stitches have been achieved and you will most likely hear a little click when this happens.

11 SETTING YOUR MACHINE TO SATIN STITCH

Set your sewing machine to the widest zigzag stitch setting. The stitch length dial was set to 0 for the machine embroidery so you will now need to adjust it a little so that although the stitches are very close together, they are far enough apart to allow the fabric to be pulled through the machine without jamming. This is called satin stitch. Take a piece of the waste base fabric and try out the satin stitch until you are happy with it, before going on to edge your picture.

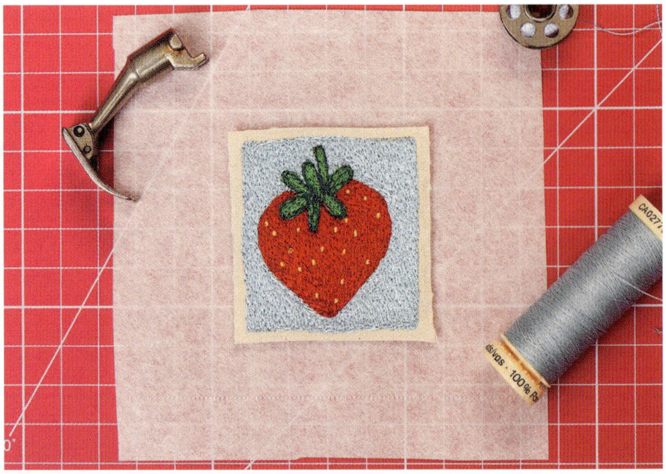

Lay the motif onto the stabilizing fabric and fit a sewing foot onto the sewing machine.

12 EDGING WITH SATIN STITCH

With the picture facing you, turn it 90 degrees anti-clockwise and place it under the machine foot. You are aiming to start sewing approximately 2cm (¾in) away from what is now the top on the right-hand side. Line up the edge of the picture with the middle of the foot and lower the presser foot onto the fabric border. The needle should catch the edge of the pale blue background and then the very outside edge of the base fabric.

Begin stitching slowly at first until you feel at ease with the technique, then if desired you can increase your speed a little. Sew satin stitch around the outside edge of the strawberry motif twice, securing the stabilizing fabric to the work. To do this, sew all the way along the first edge until you come to the end (corner of fabric) where you should stop with the needle in the outside edge of the border, thereby allowing the corner to be turned ready to stitch down the second side. Lift the presser foot and turn the picture anti-clockwise. Now lower the presser foot and line up the edge of the picture once more, so that the edge is in the middle of the foot, and you will see that underneath the foot is the very end of the first line of satin stitch. This will be present every time you turn a corner. Start sewing all the way along this second side until you come to the very end of the fabric border. As before, stop with the needle in the border and lift the presser foot.

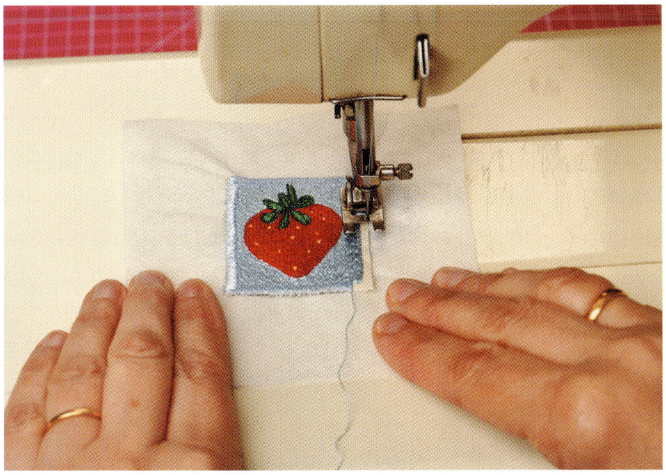

With the feed dog teeth raised, sew around the edge of the motif with a satin stitch.

Turn the picture again 90 degrees anti-clockwise and lower the presser foot, lining up the edge of the fabric with the middle of the presser foot. Proceed in this way until you reach the fourth side. When you are halfway down, stop with the needle in the embroidery. Cut off the two threads (top and bobbin threads) where you first started sewing, avoiding cutting the zigzag – you do not want these stitches to come undone. Complete the last corner and repeat the whole process again.

When you reach where you first began, stop, lift the presser foot and take the needle out of the embroidery. Cut off both the top and bobbin threads close to the zigzag border, avoiding cutting into the satin stitch once again. A few of the satin stitches may unravel but do not worry as they will be covered up with the open zigzag stitch described in Step 14.

13 REMOVING THE STABILIZING FABRIC

Remove the stabilizing fabric from the strawberry motif picture by gently tearing it away. If necessary, use the embroidery scissors to cut it off, being careful not to cut any of the satin stitch. Put the picture to one side.

14 A TWIST OF COLOURFUL STRANDED COTTON

Keeping the zigzag stitch wide, increase the depth of stitch a little so that there is about 3mm between each zigzag stitch. Practise this open zigzag stitch on the waste fabric and, once you are happy with the stitch line, cut the threads and put the sample piece to one side.

Pull out 20cm (8in) lengths of sewing thread from the top of the machine and from the bobbin spool. Lay them at the back of the machine before lowering the feed dog teeth and raising the needle. Place the strawberry picture under the presser foot in the same spot where you started with the satin stitch, approximately 2cm (¾in) in from the right-hand side. Line up the outside edge of the satin stitched piece with the middle of the presser foot and lower the foot onto the embroidery; this will secure it in place.

Take all five colours of the stranded hand embroidery cottons and give them a twist. Holding the end of the stranded cottons in your left hand at the back of the machine, with your right hand slide them under the presser foot so that they lie by the first edge of the satin stitch. The aim with this open zigzag stitch is for the needle to catch in the middle of the satin stitch and then to catch the outside edge of the twisted stranded cottons. This will attach the twist to the side of the satin stitch border.

Sew three or four zigzag stitches to hold it in place then raise the feed dog teeth and slowly sew over the twisted cotton strands. Ensure the needle catches in the middle of the satin stitch and reaches over to the outside edge of the twisted

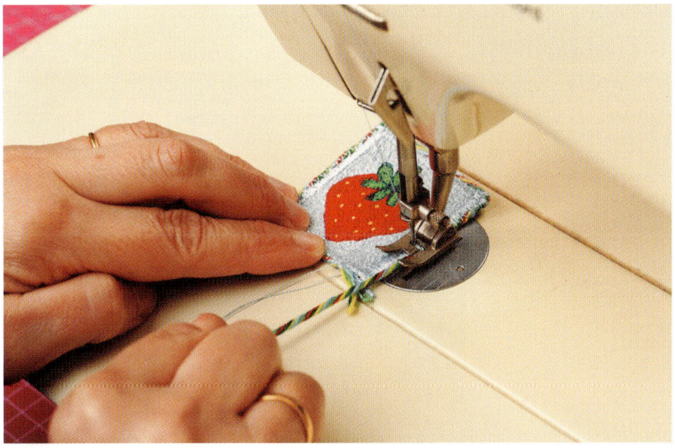

Place the twist by the side of the satin stitch and use a zigzag stitch to sew around the edge.

strands. Sew all the way along the first edge until you come to the end (corner of fabric) and stop with the needle still in the embroidery.

Lower the feed dog teeth and take the zigzag stitch over three or four times, stopping with the needle in the satin stitch border. Raise the presser foot lever and turn the embroidery 90 degrees anti-clockwise before lowering the presser foot lever once more.

Take the zigzag stitch over this side of the corner three or four times again, stopping with the needle in the border, and raise the feed dogs. Twist the stranded cotton threads and continue to sew over them and half of the satin stitch. Repeat until you reach halfway down the fourth side, making sure the needle rests in the satin stitch border when you stop sewing. Tuck the long sewing threads from the start of the twisted border under the motif to keep them out of the way.

Continue stitching to where you first began and stop approximately 1cm (⅜in) after this point, completing the last corner in the same way as the previous three corners. Lower the feed dogs and take the stitch over three or four times. Then raise the needle, lift the presser foot and pull out the long machine threads, cutting them approximately 20cm (8in) away from the twisted border.

15 FINISHING OFF

Cut off the two sets of twisted threads close to the border edge, being careful not to cut the machine threads or the zigzag stitch, as they may unravel. Using a hand sewing needle, darn the four machine sewing threads into the back of the border to secure them, then cut off the waste thread. Stand back and admire your finished *Strawberry Delight*!

Instructions for Sewing Machines with a Plate that Fits Over the Feed Dog Teeth

Follow the instructions from Steps 1 to 10, then remove the plate and continue to follow the instructions on how to edge the strawberry motif. Do not refit the plate to cover the feed dog teeth. When the instructions refer to lowering the teeth, simply turn the dial for the length of stitch to 0 on your machine as this action will reduce the stitch depth to almost nothing. With the zigzag stitch, this will enable you to secure the twisted strands to the satin stitch border at the start of the twist and at the corners and the twist finish.

When the instructions refer to raising the feed dog teeth after a specific action has been completed, open out the stitch length once more and continue sewing until the feed dog teeth need to be lowered. Turn the stitch length dial to 0 and continue in this manner.

At Step 14, because the feed dog teeth on your sewing machine are exposed, it will not be possible to slide the twist of stranded cottons beneath the presser foot as they will catch on the exposed feed dog teeth. Simply raise the presser foot, place the twist on the edge of the first side and lower the foot, which will hold the twist to the edge of the strawberry picture, before you start to sew with the open zigzag stitch.

For framing and presentation, see Chapter 9.

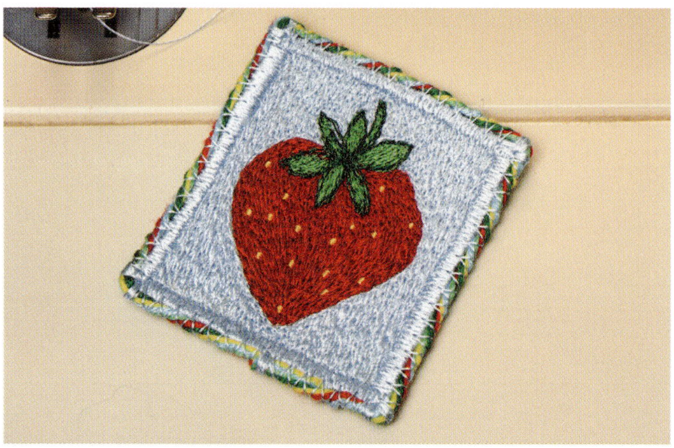

The completed *Strawberry Delight*. Time to stand back and admire all your hard work!

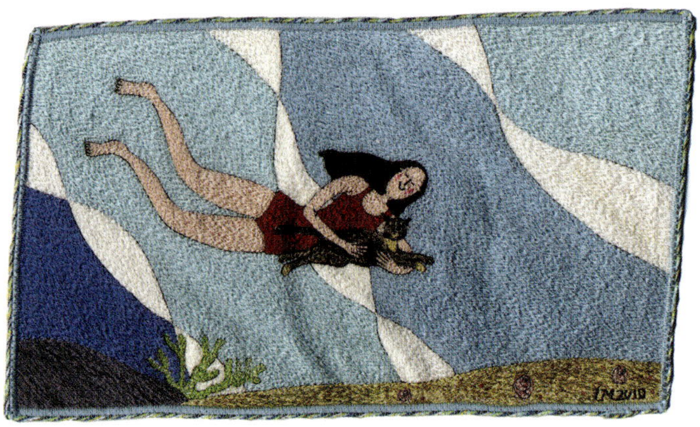

Under the Sea by Linda Miller, 20 × 30cm (8 × 12in), free machine embroidery. (Photo: Michael Jennings)

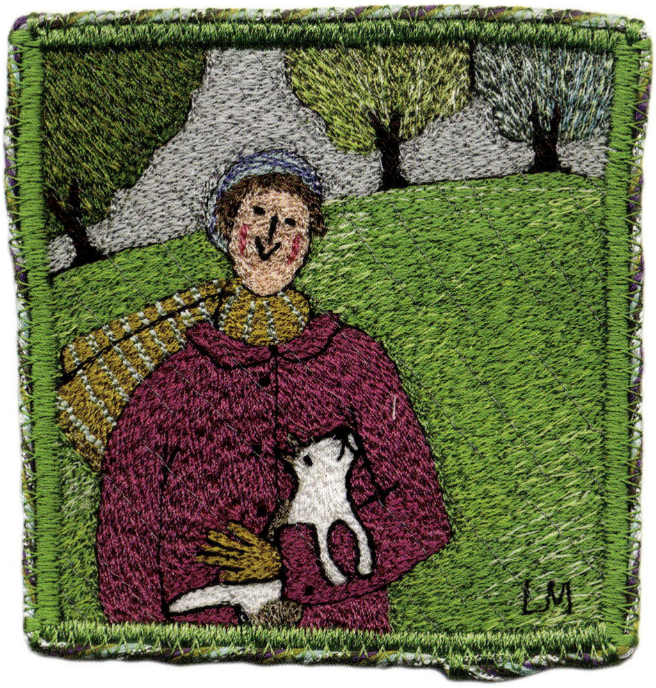

A Lady and her Dog by Linda Miller, 10 × 10cm (4 × 4in), free machine embroidery. (Photo: Michael Jennings)

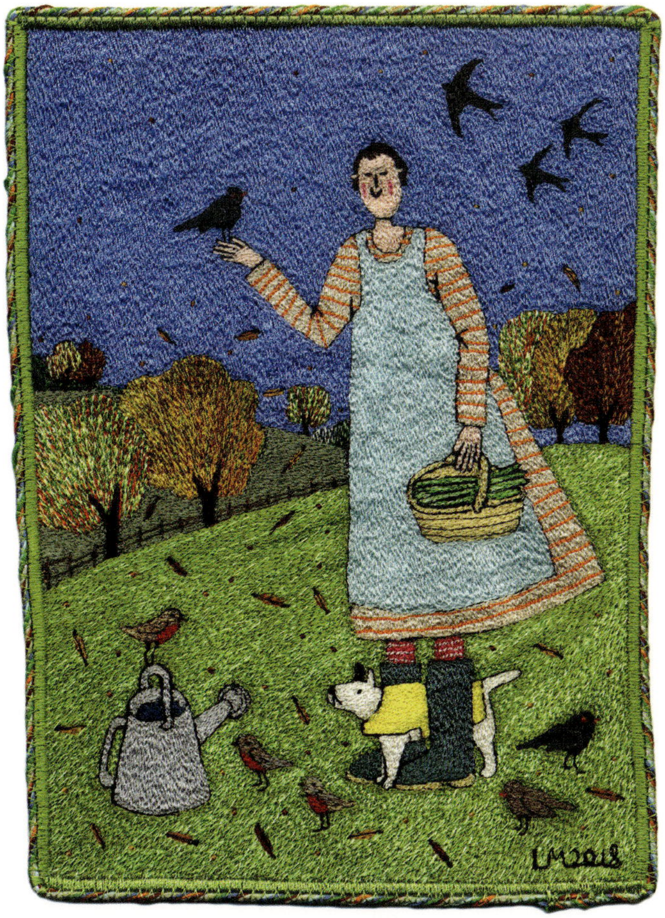

The Birds Sing Your Name by Linda Miller, 25 x 19cm (10 ×7 ½in), free machine embroidery. (Photo: Michael Jennings)

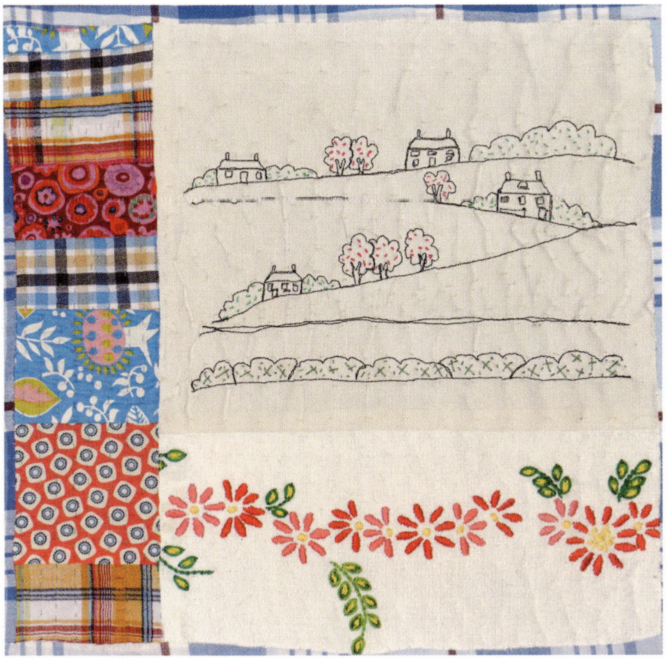

Hillside View by Linda Miller 30 × 30cm (12 × 12in), free machine embroidery and hand embroidery on linen cloth.

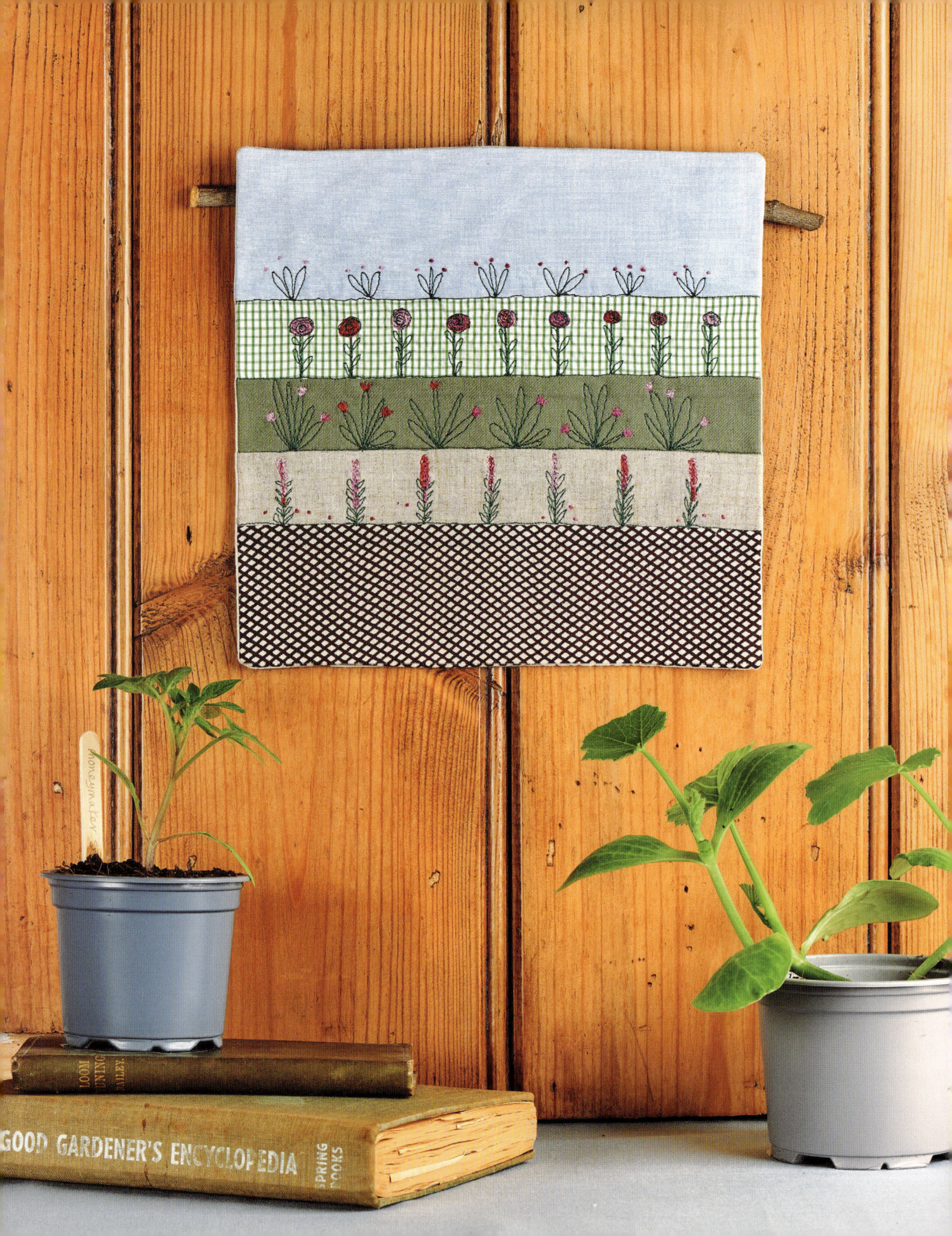
GOOD GARDENER'S ENCYCLOPEDIA
SPRING BOOKS

CHAPTER 4

FABRICS GALORE!

PICTURE PROJECT

Spring Greens – Free Machine Drawing onto Pieced Fabrics

As sewers we are very lucky to have so many different fabrics to choose from: florals, plains, cottons, man-made materials with stretch, heavyweight, lightweight, sheer, silky, textured, jersey and linen, to name a few. Sometimes it can be difficult to know where to start, especially if you are new to sewing. However, after a little time experimenting with your sewing and working your way through your growing fabric stash, you will quickly identify what kind of materials you enjoy working with and those you feel respond well, giving the most favourable results. In addition, experience will reveal those fabrics that are rather more challenging, which perhaps need a little more energy and technical ability to work with. Someone else may find these materials much easier to work with, so fabric swapping with friends is a great way to catch up with sewing colleagues as well as updating your collection.

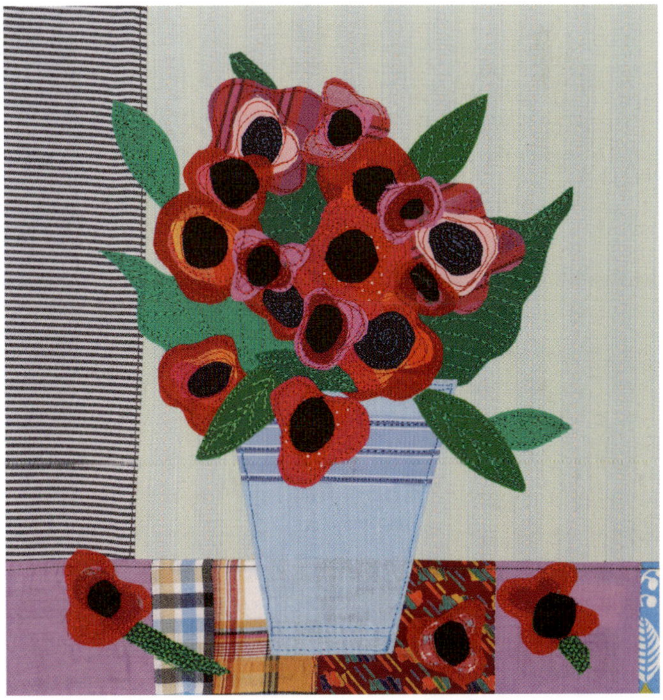

Poppies by Linda Miller, 30 × 30cm (12 × 12in), fabric appliqué and free machine embroidery.

Buying fabric from a high-street store enables the buyer to both see and feel the cloth, which is generally a more satisfactory purchasing experience than trying to choose it from an online shop. Shopping online for fabric is a tricky and time-consuming task (unless you are already familiar with the exact material you are ordering). Fabric can look flat on-screen, colours are notoriously inaccurate and often you cannot see the intricacies of the pattern or design, so when it arrives it may not quite live up to your expectations, which can be disappointing and frustrating. Some high-street fabric shops include a café, which is an additional advantage of this way of shopping for fabric: while having a good browse amongst the fabrics and haberdashery you can have a coffee, cake and contemplation, before making your purchases and hurrying home to begin your new project.

◀ *Spring Greens*, presented and displayed using a garden twig.

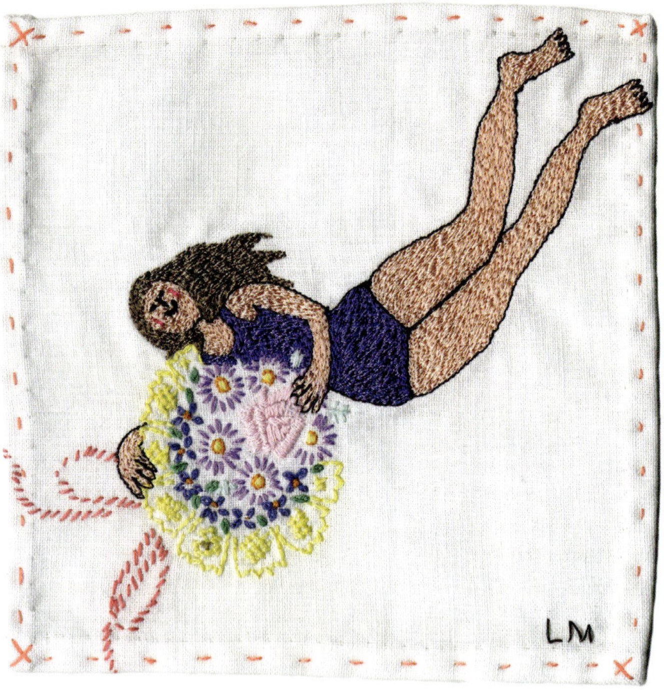

Ocean Flowers by Linda Miller, 20 × 20cm (8 × 8in), free machine embroidery and hand embroidery on linen cloth. (Photo: Michael Jennings)

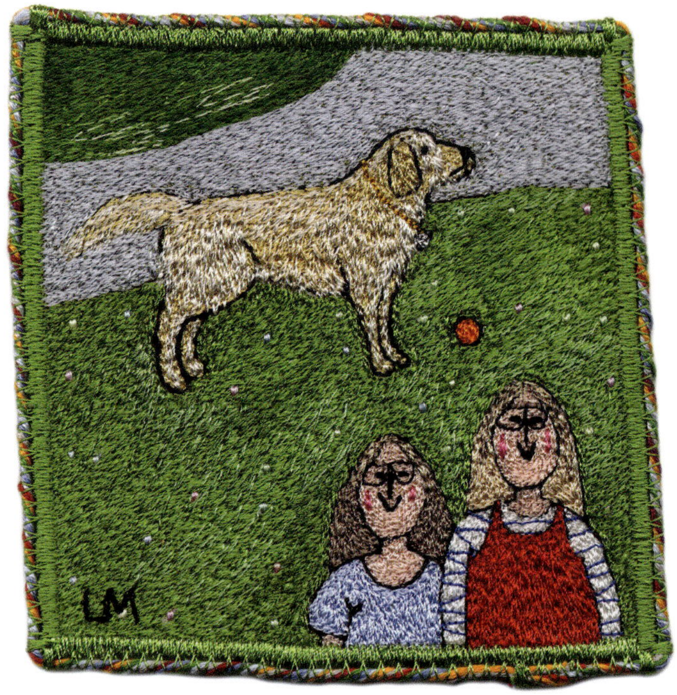

Don't Go onto the Road! by Linda Miller, 10 × 10cm (4 × 4in), free machine embroidery. (Photo: Michael Jennings)

The pieced and assembled fabric projects and the appliqué techniques featured in this book utilize different types of colourful and decorative fabrics. Try using fabrics in different weights to give your picture projects depth and texture. Cotton dressmaking and patchwork materials are ideal as they are easily found, lightweight and good all-round fabrics to work with.

Although polycottons are generally inexpensive and widely available, they are not as desirable to work with as 100 per cent cotton fabrics – they will fray, they cannot withstand high heat from the iron and visually they are not as pleasing to the eye. Note: synthetic fabrics, although attractive in colour and price, are unsuitable for use in appliqué techniques, as due to their chemical compound, like polycottons, they will not tolerate a hot iron and therefore will not work alongside natural fibres such as linen and cotton. Equally, stretch fabrics, which can be challenging to work with, will not be suited to this type of project, so are best avoided.

A word of warning about furnishing fabrics, which are heavier weight and tend to have more of an open weave: for the projects in this book they may not be suitable as they can require more work and will tend to fray when working with fabric appliqué. You could always consider reusing or repurposing clothes that you or your family no longer wear.

Reusing and upcycling is a good way to help to combat overuse of the earth's resources and, if the colour and weight is right for your project, then what could be a better way to give old fabric a new life? The same goes for domestic textiles such as tablecloths and bed linen – there is a lot of fabric in a duvet case. Try them all and see what happens! By combining different textures with plain and patterned fabric, one can achieve striking and colourful results.

Fabrics for Projects: What Works Well Together

Once you have chosen the type of fabric you are going to use in your project, you need to consider colours and patterns that work well together. Where colour and pattern are concerned it is a completely individual choice and it is always worth taking the time to make sure you choose wisely.

Firstly, spend a bit of time playing around with different fabric combinations by laying them together and then mixing them up again. The camera on your phone can be a useful aid here – by taking photographs you can create a record of the different fabric arrangements. Sometimes, looking at your photographs after a little time, you can see more clearly which fabric groupings you prefer, and you can save them for future reference for other potential projects. If you don't have a camera phone to hand, you can always leave the possible combinations of materials out on your worktable and return to them after a while with fresh eyes to make your decision.

Remember, you want the fabrics to complement each other and not fight, and you don't want patterned fabrics to be so busy that your overall embroidery stitch line gets lost in the design. You will find that the more you work with textiles you will build knowledge and experience of this generous medium, and in time your confidence will grow. Taking the time to get the best possible combination of fabrics, textures, colours and patterns will pay off in the long run.

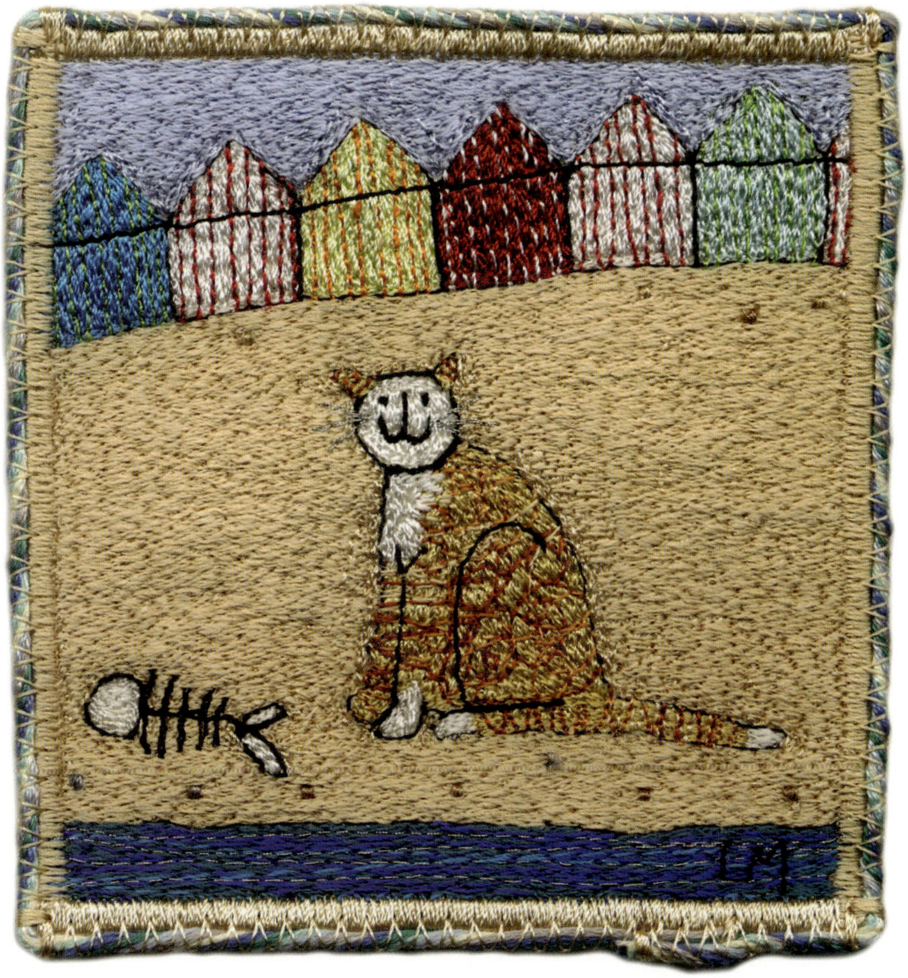

Beach Snack by Linda Miller, 10 × 10cm (4 × 4in), free machine embroidery. (Photo: Michael Jennings)

PICTURE PROJECT: *SPRING GREENS*

This project consists of piecing together a selection of patterned and plain fabrics to create a background ready for drawing with free machine embroidery stitch. Working with your own selection of fabrics and garden-inspired imagery, you will create this simple but effective collection of 'spring greens'. A garden twig makes an unusual feature from which to hang the finished picture. It would make a lovely gift for a keen gardener.

This project combines the techniques of assembling fabrics and free machine embroidery drawing with threads.

Finished picture measures approximately 22 × 22cm (8¾ × 8¾in).

With this project you will be sewing on the front of the work.

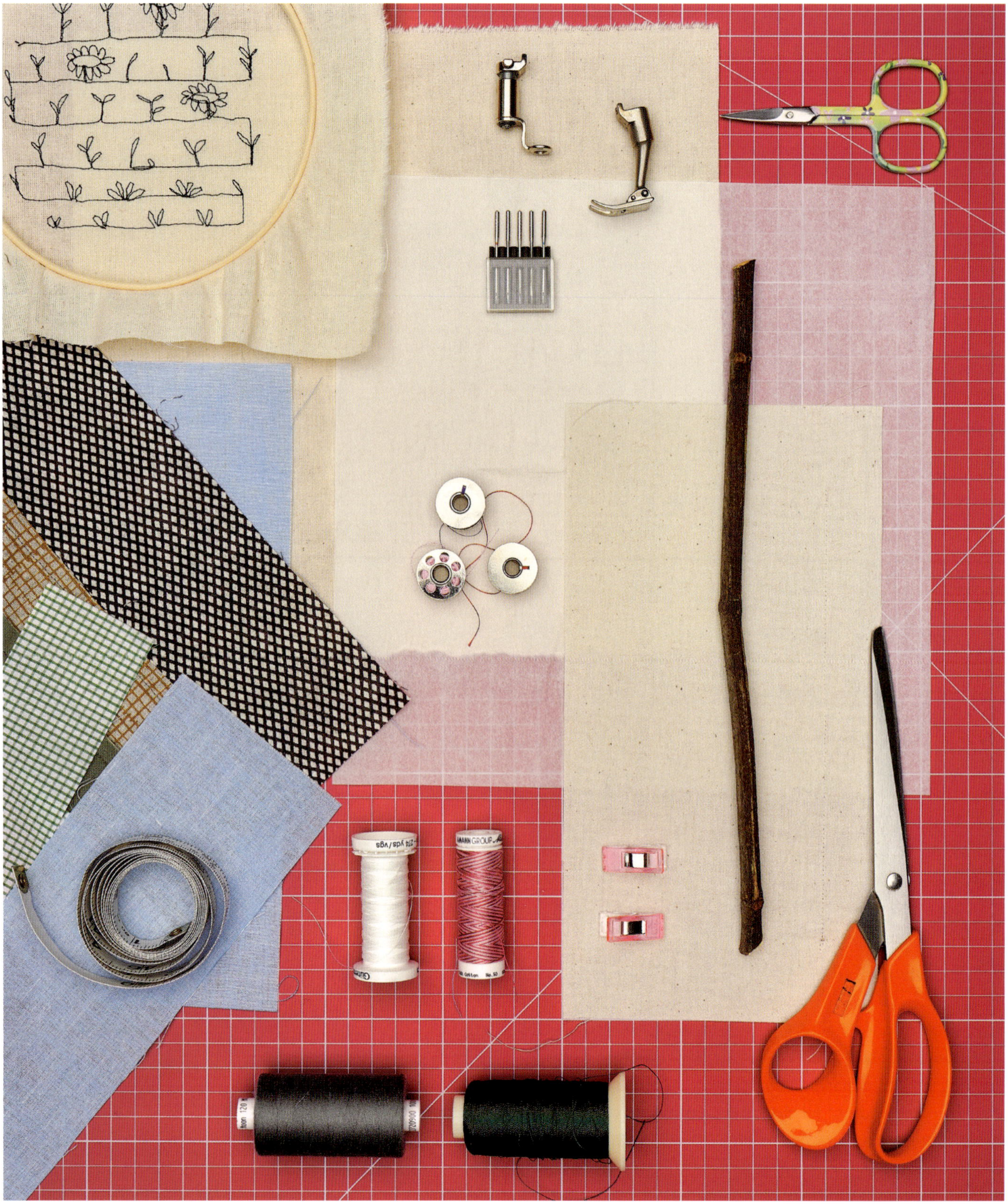

A selection of materials needed to make the picture project, *Spring Greens*.

YOU WILL NEED

Items from the basic tool kit, as listed in Chapter 1 Tools and Equipment, and the following materials:

- Piece of medium weight calico fabric measuring 25 × 25cm (10 × 10in)
- Piece of plain coloured cotton fabric measuring 25 × 25cm (10 × 10in) to back the finished picture
- Piece of fusible fabric measuring 25 × 25cm (10 × 10in)
- Spool of mid grey machine sewing thread
- Two spools of coloured thread (either machine embroidery thread in the weights of 30 or 40 or machine sewing thread), for example:
  - Dark green
  - Multicoloured pink
- Five pieces of cotton fabric in a selection of plain and patterned designs of your choice, for example:
  - Piece of mid blue fabric measuring 8 × 26cm (3¼ × 10¼in)
  - Piece of light green fabric measuring 5 × 26cm (2 × 10¼in)
  - Piece of mid green fabric measuring 5 × 26cm (3¼ × 10¼in)
  - Piece of mid brown fabric measuring 5 × 26cm (3¼ × 10¼in)
  - Piece of dark brown fabric measuring 8 × 26cm (3¼ × 10¼in)
- Piece of plain coloured cotton fabric measuring 6 × 22cm (2½ × 8¾in) for the sleeve on the back of the finished picture (as described in Chapter 9)

HANDY HINT NEW FABRIC

If you have purchased new 100 per cent cotton fabric for your project, you may wish to wash and iron it first to allow for any shrinkage – a hot iron with a lot of steam can shrink your material.

HANDY HINT TENSION

An embroidery hoop is not required to make this picture. Instead, the top pieced fabrics are adhered to the heavyweight calico using the fusible fabric. This creates a solid fabric base, which is ideal to work on. To keep the pieced fabric from puckering, loosen off the top tension on your sewing machine slightly. This will reduce the tension in your stitch line – refer to your machine's manual for instructions on how to do this.

HANDY HINT TRUE AND EVEN STITCH LINE COLOUR

Always make sure that your bobbin thread matches your top thread. This will ensure the free machine stitch line is clean and clear, true in colour and stands out beautifully on the pieced fabric background.

GAINING CONFIDENCE WITH FREE STITCH LINE DRAWING

If you have not used your sewing machine for drawing before and want to be prepared for the project ahead, where you will be drawing simple botanical motifs, then have a practice stitching session or two.

Take a piece of heavyweight calico, approximately 25 × 25cm (10 × 10in), place it in a wooden embroidery hoop measuring 15cm (6in) and pull the fabric taut. This will give you a stiff surface on which to practise.

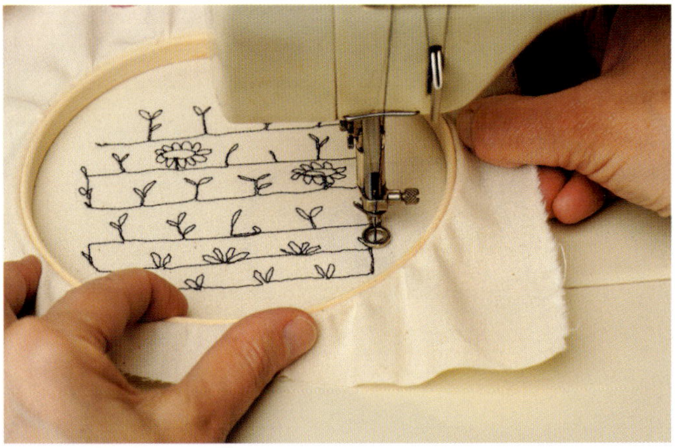

Practise drawing with the machine needle. This will give you confidence with the project.

Thread up your sewing machine in the dark green thread, fit the free machine embroidery foot and lower the feed dog teeth. Follow the instructions in Chapter 3, Step 4 to begin drawing with the thread.

Ensuring you keep your fingers clear of the needle and the free embroidery foot, start with a simple line drawing in the middle of the fabric and draw anything that comes to mind. You may want to start with a simple doodle such as a little row of daisies, small hearts, circles, straight lines, wavy lines… anything at all that inspires you to have a go and makes you feel more at ease with the medium. By the end of this exercise, you will feel more confident in drawing with the stitch line and once you are happy with your technique you can start on your project.

1 GETTING STARTED

Iron and cut your chosen fabric strips and place them right side up on a table in the order of the background composition, starting with mid blue at the top for the sky, then light green, mid green and mid brown, finishing off with dark brown at the bottom.

Pin or clip the first two pieces together along the longest edge with right sides facing. Thread up your sewing machine with mid grey machine sewing thread, fit your ordinary sewing foot and raise the feed dogs. Use a standard straight stitch and set the sewing tension to ordinary sewing.

Taking your pinned pieces of material, line up the fabric edge with the sewing foot to give a seam allowance of approximately 6mm, and sew the strips together. Using the steam setting on

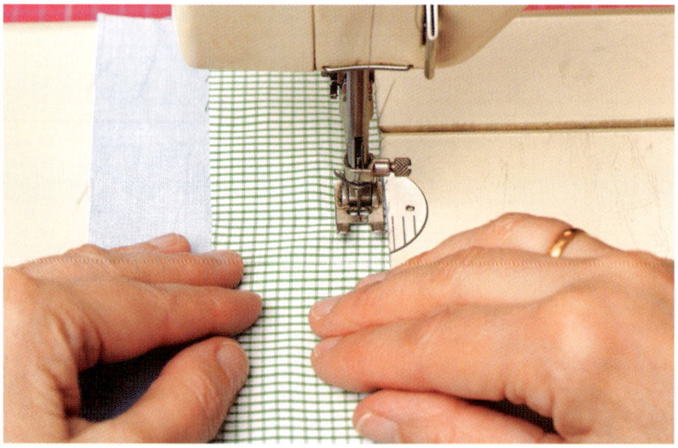

Sew all the strips of fabric together in sequence, using a seam allowance of 6mm.

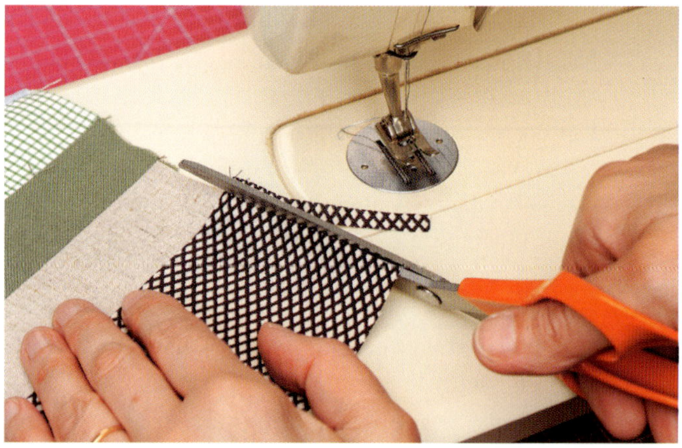

Trim up the background fabric, being mindful not to cut too much of the fabric away.

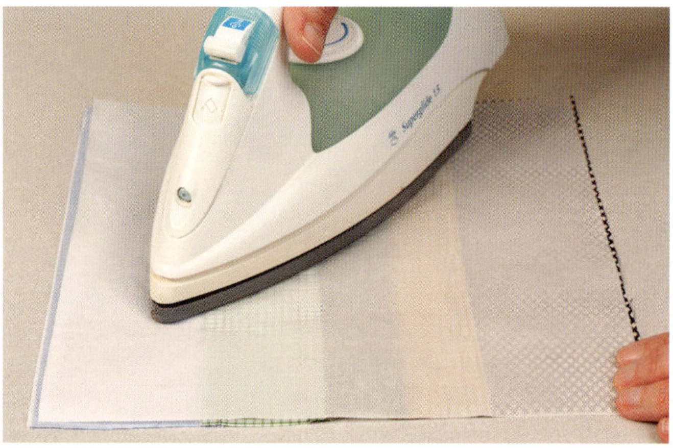

Cut to size a piece of fusible fabric and iron it onto the back of the pieced fabric strips.

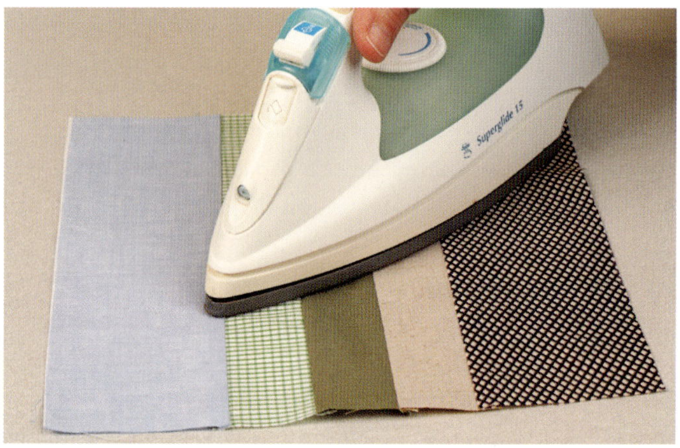

After peeling away the paper, iron the pieced fabric strips onto the heavyweight calico.

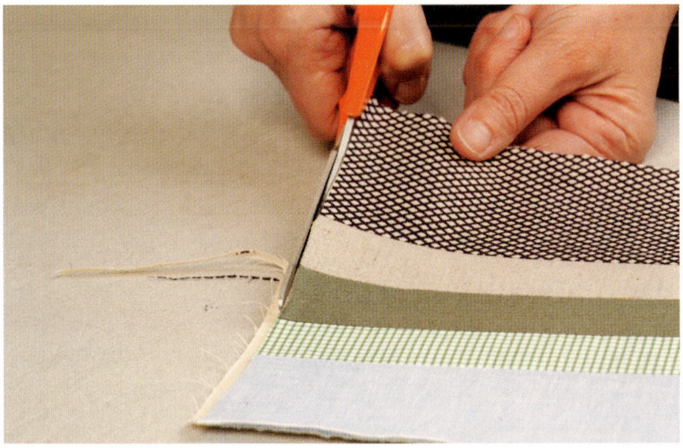

Cutting away any surplus calico with a pair of sharp scissors will create a neat edge.

the iron, iron out the seams – this is crucial to ensure a flat workable surface on which to embroider. Take the next fabric strip and pin and sew together in the same fashion, ensuring you have kept the pieces in background order. Continue until all the pieces are sewn together and pressed.

Carefully trim up the two sides to neaten, ensuring that you do not cut too much fabric away. Place the assembled fabric on the ironing board with the right side down so you are looking at the back of the work, and place the fusible fabric on top. Iron the fusible fabric onto the back of the pieced work, being careful only to iron the paper side of the fusible fabric. Allow to cool before peeling away the paper.

Lastly, lay the piece of calico over the top and iron together to form one stiff piece of fabric. Once cool, trim off a few millimetres from the side to neaten the edges, if required.

Set up your machine for the stitch drawing by exchanging the sewing foot for the free machine embroidery foot and lower the feed dog teeth. Decrease the sewing tension slightly. Wind a bobbin in the dark green thread and thread up the sewing machine in the same colour. To refresh yourself with how to begin to machine embroider, refer to Chapter 3, Step 4, and use this technique at the beginning of each row of flowers.

Note: the measurements for the stitch drawing of the plant motifs and spacing of each flower are an approximate guide size; you may choose to make your imagery slightly bigger or smaller. Whatever you decide, make sure that each image begins and ends approximately 3cm (1¼in) from the fabric edge. This will allow for a seam allowance when the backing fabric is sewn on.

2 FIRST ROW: YUCCA LEAVES AND STITCHING IN THE DITCH

Stitching in the ditch is a quilting term used to describe the technique of stitching along the seams of a quilt, either by hand or machine. This technique will be used to apply the free machine embroidery stitching to the assembled pieced fabrics. The sequence of stitching is from the top to the bottom row, while working along each seam and decorating each piece of fabric as the stitch line continues from left to right.

To begin, start off at the top left-hand side on the seam of the blue and light green fabric, place the needle in the seam about 5mm in from the edge and bring up the bobbin thread. Lower the presser foot, make a couple of small stitches to secure your work and then cut away the two waste threads close to the fabric surface. Then, begin to slowly draw with your needle, following the line of the seam – the 'ditch' – as close as possible.

Stitch a 3cm (1¼in) line, then take the stitch line in a vertical direction and draw three little oval-shaped leaves onto the blue fabric with the base of the leaf motif attached to the ditch line; the leaves should measure approximately 1cm (⅜in) from base to tip.

After the third leaf, take your stitch line back into the ditch, sew on the seam line for 3cm (1¼in) more, then once again create three oval-shaped leaves on the blue fabric and take your stitch line back into the ditch. Continue repeating this line and leaf drawing until the last leaf cluster is approximately 3cm (1¼in) away from the right-hand side. Do not worry if you find that your line has a wobble to it; this will all add to the charm of your drawing!

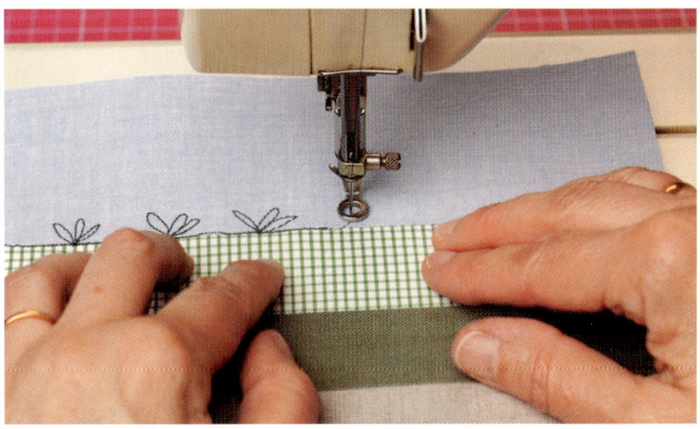

Stitching in the ditch and using free machine embroidery to make clusters of leaves.

Continue to draw with the stitch line in the ditch until the needle is at the edge of the fabric. Finish off using the stitch securing technique that you began with, and cut off the top thread and bottom thread as close to the fabric surface as possible.

3 SECOND ROW: RUBY SUNFLOWER STEM AND LEAVES, SECOND STITCH IN THE DITCH

Starting on the left-hand side of the second seam, place the sewing machine needle in between the light green and mid green fabrics. Secure the first couple of stitches then cut away the waste threads. Stitching in the ditch again, sew a horizontal line of stitches for 3.5cm (1½in) then take the stitch line in a vertical direction upwards towards the blue fabric for 2cm (¾in), creating a stem.

At the top of the stem, draw a small circle about 1cm (⅜in) in diameter, then as you follow the stem back down towards the seam, create little oval-shaped leaves on alternate sides of the stem, similar in shape to the yuccas above but a little smaller. Again, don't fret if they have a wobble or are uneven.

On completion of the stem, flower and leaves, take the stitch line back onto the seam and stitch in the ditch for 2.5cm (1in). Repeat the above steps until you have a row of ruby sunflowers. The last sunflower should be 3cm (1¼in) from the right-hand side. Continue stitching in the ditch to the edge, finish off with the securing technique and cut off the waste threads top and bottom.

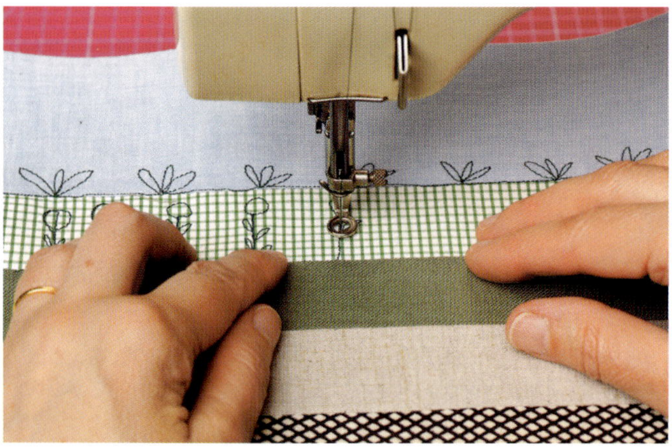

Drawing tall sunflower stems will give impact to the second strip of pieced fabric.

4 THIRD ROW: CANNA PINK SPARKLER LEAVES

Place your needle on the third seam, in between the mid green and mid brown fabric. Secure the first couple of stitches then cut away the waste threads. Stitch in the ditch for 3cm (1¼in), then using the seam line as a starting point, create five or six large oval-shaped leaves in a fan silhouette measuring approximately 2.5cm (1in) high from the base of the leaf to the tip.

On completion of the last leaf, take the stitch line once more back onto the seam. Draw horizontally for 3.5cm (1½in) and then repeat the fan-shaped leaf motif. If you like, you may draw different numbers of leaves on each plant to vary the design and add an additional element of interest. The last flower motif should be 3cm (1¼in) from the right-hand side. Continue stitching in the ditch to the edge, finish off with the securing technique and cut off the waste threads top and bottom.

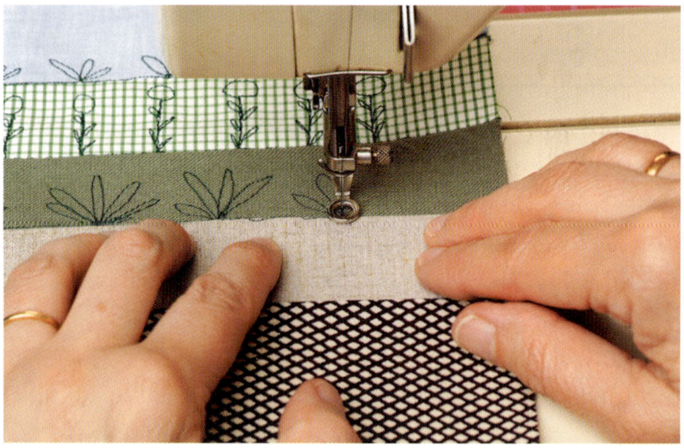

Celebrate any wobble the drawn stitch line has; this will make your work unique to you.

5 FOURTH ROW: HOLLYHOCK STEM AND LEAVES

Beginning on the left-hand side of the fabric in the last seam between the mid brown and dark brown fabric, secure the first couple of stitches then cut away the waste threads. Stitch in the ditch for 3cm (1¼in) before taking the stitch line vertically, creating a stem. After 2.75cm (1⅛in) turn and come back down the stem for approximately 1cm (⅜in), then begin to create small oval-shaped leaves on either side of the stem in a parallel formation until you reach the bottom.

Follow the seam for 3cm (1¼in) and continue to create the hollyhock stems and leaves until the last is approximately 4cm (1½in) away from the right-hand side of the fabric. Take the stitch line along the seam to the edge and finish off as before. With the right side of the fabric facing, and using your iron, gently press.

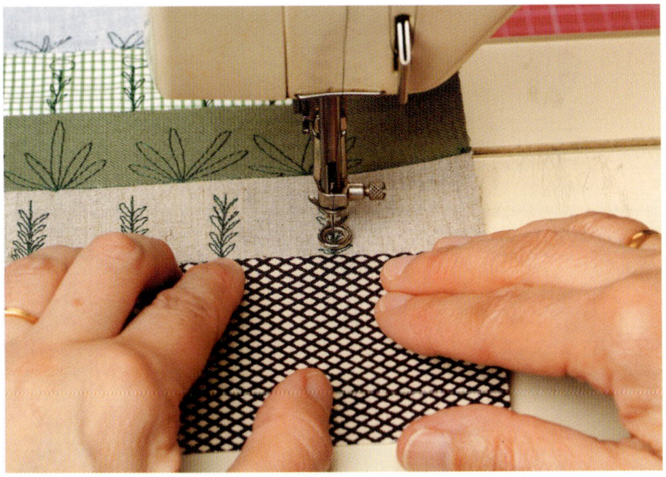

The last row of plants has small leaves evenly placed either side of the flower stem.

6 YUCCA FLOWERS, ZIGZAG STITCHED TINY DOTS

Now we return to the first row of yuccas to create the little flowerheads by creating tiny dots in a selection of multicoloured pink zigzag stitches on each of the plants. Start by threading up the sewing machine in the multicoloured pink and wind up a bobbin spool to match. Set the sewing machine to a small zigzag stitch, approximately 3–4mm wide. Keeping the feed dog teeth lowered, slide the fabric under the embroidery foot and bring up the bobbin thread a few millimetres away from one of the little leaf clusters on the row of yucca plants.

Proceed to free machine embroider a row of three tiny dots (for this technique, see Chapter 3, Step 8). Continue to embroider three or four little dots above each of the yucca plants on this row, carrying over the top and bottom threads from plant to plant until the last flowers have been completed. Cut off the top and bottom threads and then cut away the threads that have been carried over from dot to dot. Turn the stitch dial back to a running stitch.

7 RUBY SUNFLOWER HEADS, VERTICAL AND SPIRAL STITCHES

Starting on the left-hand side, bring up the bobbin thread in the middle of the first sunflower head. Fill in the circle of the flower head, firstly using a few stitches in a vertical direction, and then on top of these vertical stitches in a spiral direction create a circular multicoloured flower head. Note: it is important to follow this instruction to avoid puckering the work. Once completed, cut off the top and bottom threads before using the same technique on all the flowers in the row.

8 CANNA PINK SPARKLER BLOOMS

On the third row, bring up the bobbin thread on the tip of one of the leaves of the first canna pink sparkler flower. Embroider small fan-like shapes that mimic the canna leaves onto either one, two or even three of the leaf tips, aiming to make each bloom 4–5mm high.

9 HOLLYHOCK FLOWERS

Starting at the top of the first hollyhock stem, draw a series of small tight spirals down the left-hand side in a circular motion, stopping about halfway, then continue back up the right-hand side. If the flowers look a little sparse then repeat once more over the top, making the flowers richer in colour and depth.

Repeat this technique on all the hollyhock stems in this row and once more cut off the waste thread close to the fabric surface. If you like, make some tiny zigzag dots at the bottom of the stems to represent blooms that have fallen off of the top of the flowering hollyhocks (for this technique, see Chapter 3, Step 8).

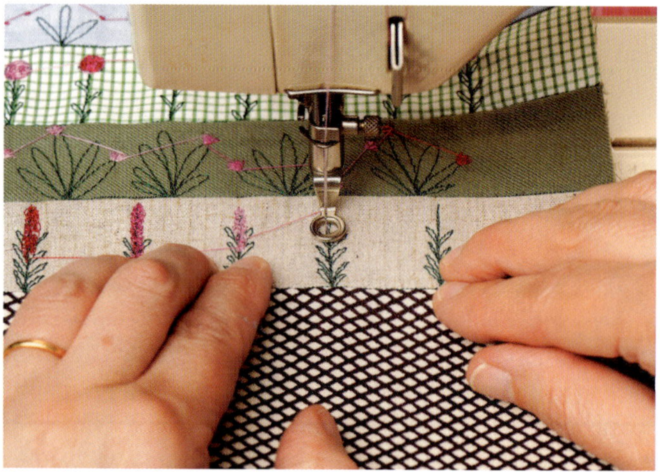

Use a series of spirals in pink thread to create blooms for the hollyhock flowers.

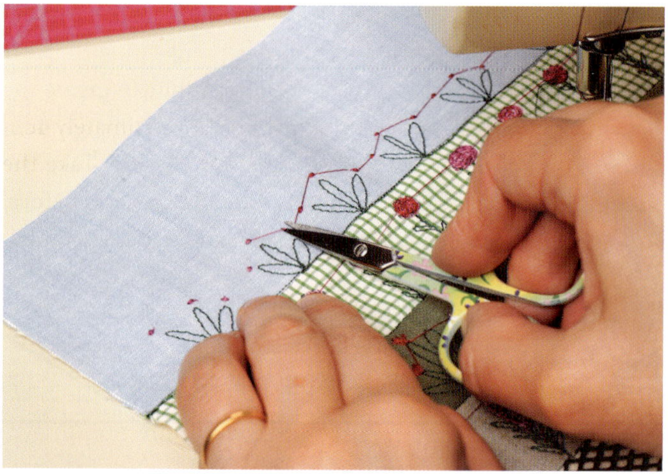

Embroidery scissors are designed for cutting away threads close to the fabric surface.

10 FLOWER SPIRALS ON THE RUBY SUNFLOWERS

Thread up the sewing machine in the dark green thread, ensuring you have the bobbin colour to match. Place your needle on the outside edge of the first sunflower and stitch in a spiral direction to create a swirl working into the middle of the flowerhead. Repeat for each sunflower and then cut away the waste threads. With the right side of the fabric facing, gently press.

Now you have finished all the embroidering you can trim your picture to neaten off the edges as required, being mindful not to cut away too much fabric.

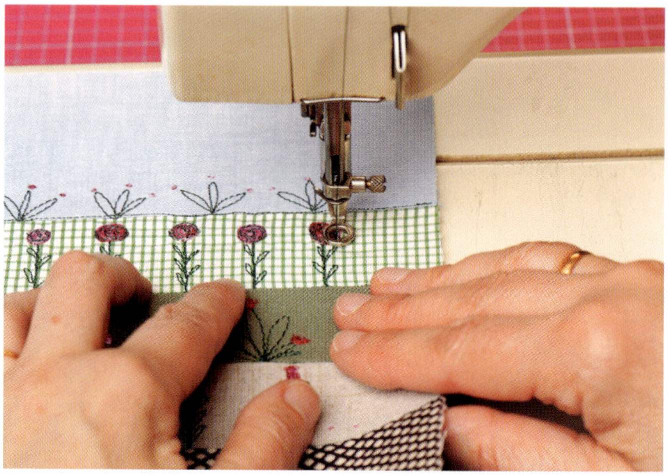

After stitching the tiny dots in the multicoloured thread, fill in the sunflower heads.

11 BACKING THE PICTURE

Fit the ordinary sewing foot and raise the feed dog teeth. Thread up using the mid grey sewing thread, ensuring you have the same colour in the bobbin. Alter the sewing machine tension dial to a general sewing setting. Place the picture onto the backing fabric, with the right sides together, and pin or clip in place. Line up the side of the foot with the side of the fabric and, using a seam allowance of approximately 6mm, sew around all the edges, leaving an opening of 10cm (4in) at the bottom to allow for turning the work the right way around.

To reinforce the seam opening where the picture will be turned, sew forwards and back over a couple of centimetres at both ends of the opening. Once sewn, snip off any waste

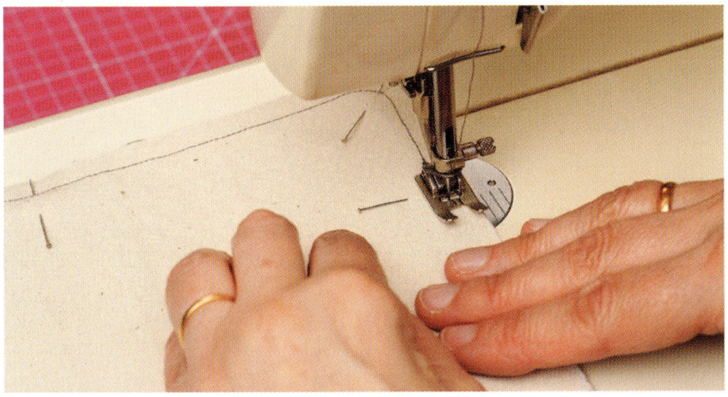

Sew on the backing fabric, remembering to leave an opening of 10cm (4in) at the bottom.

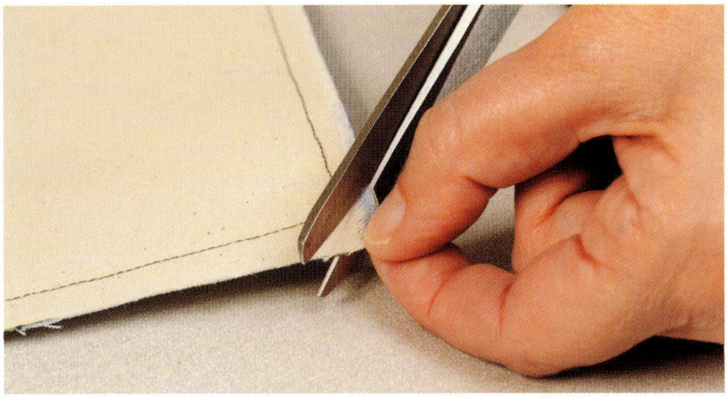

Cutting away the corners and along each edge will help to reduce the bulk of the fabric.

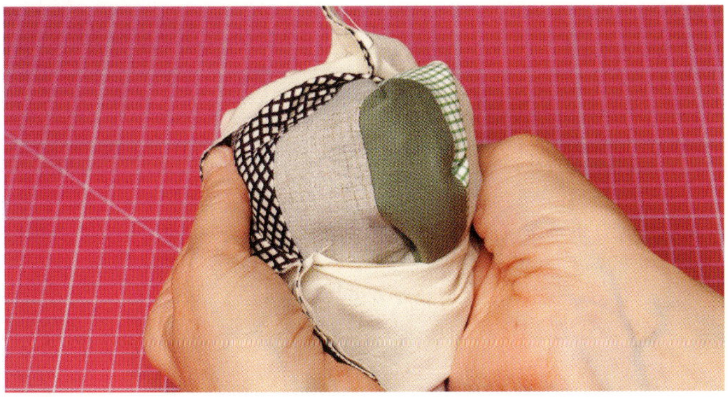

The fabric will be stiff to turn out; a corner and edge shaper will push out the seams.

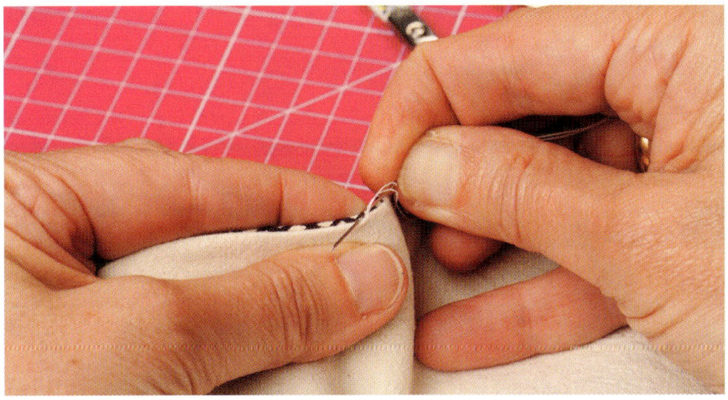

Thread up a sewing needle in a neutral colour and whip stitch over the opening.

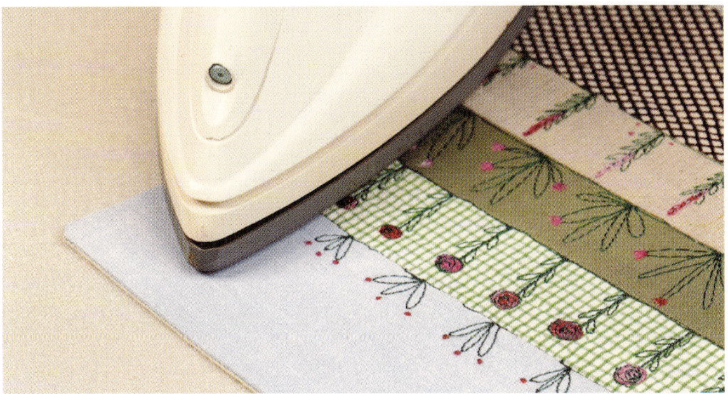

Press your picture with a steam iron, first on the back and then carefully on the front.

threads, clip the corners to minimize the bulk of the material, trim off the excess fabric from the outside edge and then turn out. The fabric picture will be quite stiff, so you will need to use a corner and edge shaper to gently push out the corners and side seams.

Gently press and then hand sew the opening closed with a whip stitch. Give your work a final pressing before admiring the new techniques that you have mastered in this *Spring Greens* picture project!

For instructions on sewing the sleeve in place, finishing off, presentation and framing, see Chapter 9.

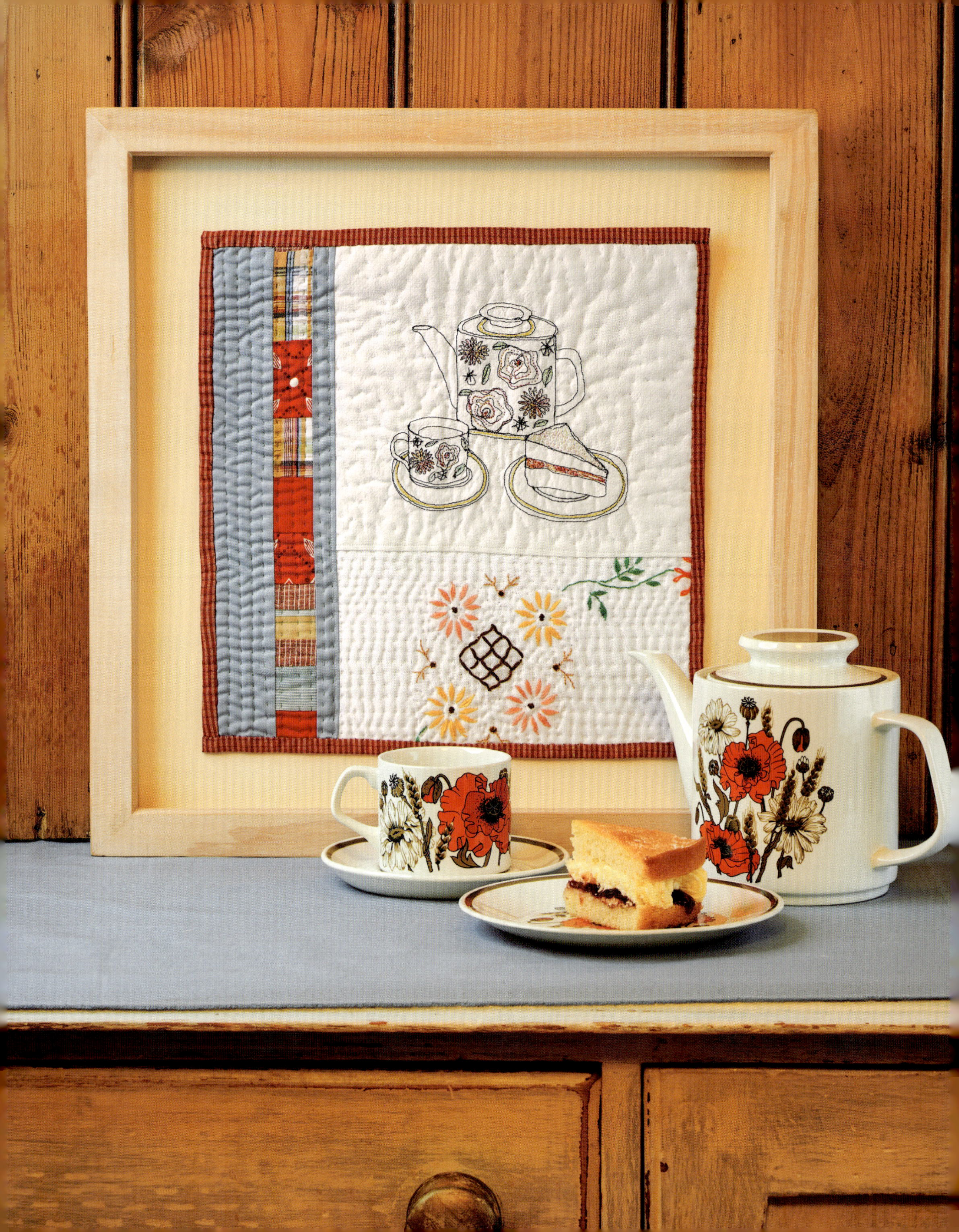

CHAPTER 5

FINDING INSPIRATION FOR YOUR IMAGERY AND DESIGN

PICTURE PROJECT
Embellishing a Vintage Cloth

NARRATIVE CLOTH

We all have stories to tell. Themes and narratives can emerge quite easily from our day-to-day lives: everyday chores, tasks and pastimes in which we participate can provide a wealth of ideas to reproduce onto cloth. For hundreds of years, we have been telling our stories and histories, and the craft of hand stitching has long been used to illustrate our narratives: from embroidering small samplers to stitching huge banners and tapestries. After a move away from the popularity of hand sewing in the second half of the twentieth century, the new millennium has seen an international renaissance of interest in stitch and textiles.

Across the globe, stories have been told through textiles, from well-known historical events such as the Norman Conquest stitched into the famous Bayeux Tapestry to domestic family histories that have been sewn lovingly into beautiful quilts. Quilts, which were a functional necessity before central heating, become family heirlooms handed down from one generation to the next, treasured not only for the skill in the making of them but for the family history that they hold.

In the twentieth century, stitched banners were often used by campaigning groups, such as the suffragettes and the temperance movement, to illustrate their slogans and messages of conviction as they marched to promote the wants of the rally and demands for social change.

In the Victorian era it was very common for children to learn needlecraft techniques by embroidering samplers; these small pieces of cloth demonstrated hand stitch skills while preparing girls for their future married lives. Looking at these samplers gives us an insight into the importance of teaching and learning a domestic craft and shows us how different our world is now, providing a reflection of society's ever-changing values.

These examples of using stitched and embellished cloth to commemorate, illustrate and celebrate events, causes and the everyday, powerfully show the history of people's lives across the world through stitch and textiles.

The making of domestic textiles for the home has been an extremely popular pastime for many years. Hand-embroidered cotton and linen cloths became very popular in the early 1900s, providing a time-consuming occupation that was undertaken by women and girls. For many years, women were encouraged to demonstrate their homemaking abilities with examples of needlecraft adorning the home on the tea table, chair back and pillowcase, where their needlework skills could be admired. However, later in the twentieth century saw the arrival of mass-produced machine-manufactured household textiles for the modern home. These items were much more affordable and readily available, which in turn meant the pastime of hand stitching textiles lost their appeal and became less fashionable for some.

◀ *Embellishing a Vintage Cloth*, presented and framed in a wooden box frame.

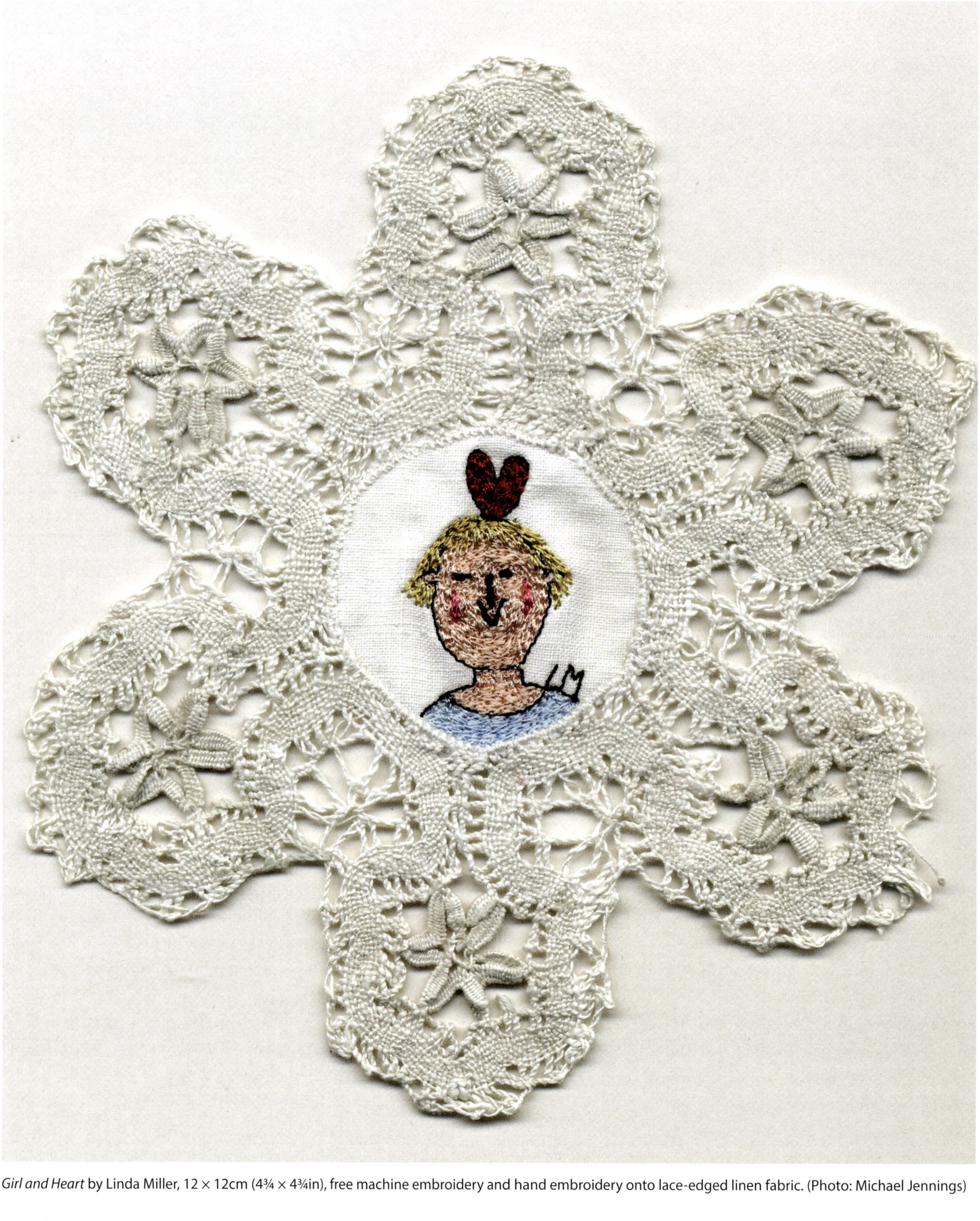

Girl and Heart by Linda Miller, 12 × 12cm (4¾ × 4¾in), free machine embroidery and hand embroidery onto lace-edged linen fabric. (Photo: Michael Jennings)

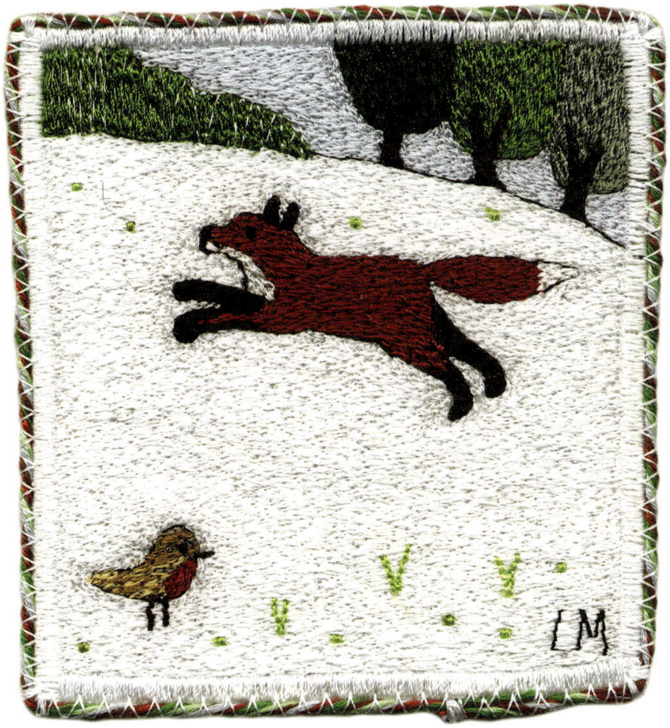

Fox in the Snow by Linda Miller, 10 × 9cm (4 × 3½in), free machine embroidery. (Photo: Michael Jennings)

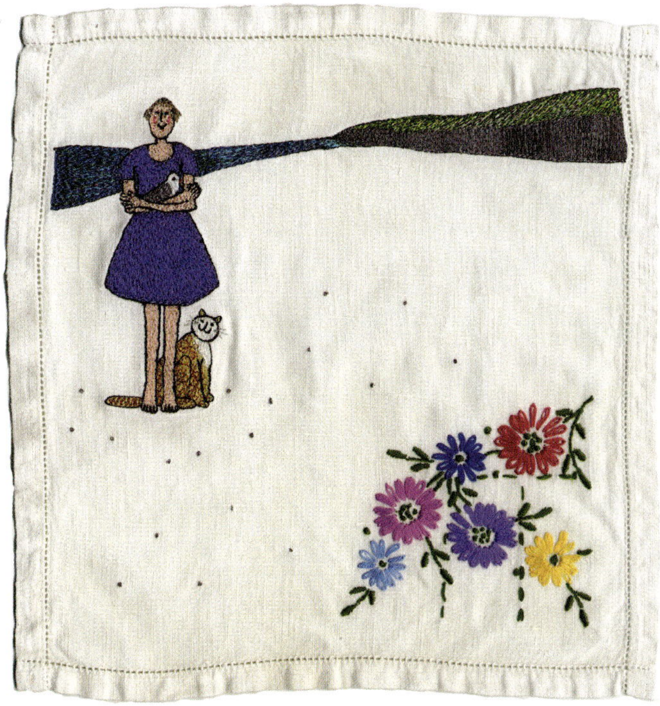

Beach Flowers, 30 × 30cm (12 x 12in), free machine embroidery and hand embroidery on linen cloth. (Photo: Michael Jennings)

This changing social and economic landscape led to a devaluing of the homemade and contributed to the breakdown of the years-old handing down of domestic sewing knowledge and techniques through generations. The domestic textile perhaps unfairly began to acquire labels such as fussy and old fashioned, and yet for some devotees the lure of the craft and the opportunity it presented to tell stories proved too strong to abandon and they continued to celebrate their narratives in cloth.

The twenty-first century has seen a welcome resurgence of the craft of making, with digital technology providing us opportunities to discover, learn and share new stitching techniques through our textile narratives. We can seek refuge from our sometimes overly fast-paced modern life, where we have everything at the touch of a button, to take time for ourselves and enjoy the simple occupation of making and telling our story within the world through working with cloth. Slow stitching has become fashionable once more and has been reinvented and slotted into our modern world alongside ideas such as mindfulness, encouraging us to slow down and enjoy the present moment. However, the internet, together with the popularity of global travel, has introduced us to different traditional stitching techniques from across the world, such as Japanese sashiko and Indian kantha, which have been used for centuries in decorative textile making. The addition of these culturally different stitching methods to our existing realm of needlecraft knowledge allows us to engage with varying styles and practices and to express ourselves creatively as individuals by making pieces of work with an intrinsic value. In the twenty-first century the handmade has once more become valued for its skill and inherent craft; unlike the mass-produced, the handmade celebrates the unique personality of the maker, encapsulating their own emotions and stories.

Giving old clothing a new life by using it in a narrative project, such as *Embellishing a Vintage Cloth*, can be a powerful and unusual way of capturing memories of family and the past, while simultaneously making something new to become an heirloom of the future. Treasured memories are often evoked when touching and working with reused cloth, such as a piece from a worn cotton shirt, apron or a child's dress; we are reminded of those who wore the fabric and it can bring back happy recollections of days gone by. In addition, worn cloth can add to the narrative through its very pattern – designs, fashions and materials change throughout the decades and

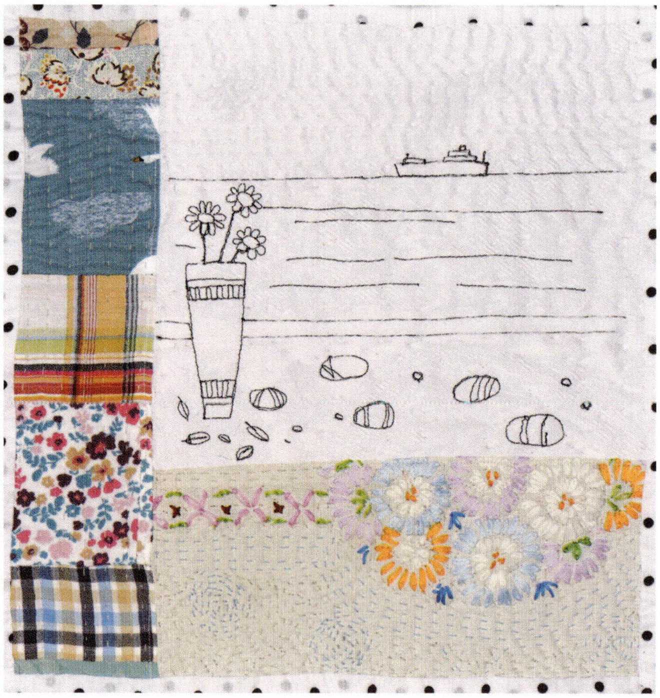

The View from Alan's Window by Linda Miller, 30 × 30cm (12 × 12in), pieced fabrics, free machine embroidery, hand embroidery and hand stitch.

fabric can be very evocative of a particular era, reinforcing memories and connections and bringing feelings of nostalgia for the time in which the cloth was made and worn. Using fabric in this way can create a piece of absolutely unique work with a very personal story, which can be prized by its ultimate recipient, whether it is received as a gift, an heirloom or indeed bought to add to a textile collection.

As fabric lovers, many of us keep a collection of garments that are no longer worn but which may hold precious memories alongside treasured pieces of vintage hand- or machine-embroidered textiles such as tray cloths, pillowcases, antimacassars or quilt tops, which we have collected, inherited, or been given by relatives and friends. If you are a fabric enthusiast then you will recognize how compelling the opportunity can be to collect precious pieces of printed and stitched textiles, often thinking that each piece will one day surely be put to good use. However, more often than not we put these cherished pieces away and our collection of memory fabric grows, but also with it sometimes a resistance to use any of it because we do not want to break the spell of times gone by as we revel in nostalgia. Now is the time to break into that wonderful stash for this project!

PICTURE PROJECT: *EMBELLISHING A VINTAGE CLOTH*

Making a piece of simply framed textile art from a collection of assembled and embellished cloths, and drawing our visual story upon it through stitch is a way of turning the everyday fabric into a treasured kaleidoscope of personal memories and emotions.

A hand-embroidered tray cloth and pieces of patterned and plain fabric are required for this project. Small scraps of cloth that hold memories from different eras of our lives can be used, and these can be from clothes such as old shirts or dresses or vintage household textiles like tablecloths – ideally something that has meaning or significance to you. You can replace the hand-embroidered linen with a section of a quilt or a crazy patchwork piece, making it more unique and personalized to you and your memories. Working on worn and washed cloth creates a different sewing experience than using new fabrics – the softness of the old material as it is hand sewn can be delicate and sensuous to the fingertips and the slowness of hand stitching enables the sewer to succumb to the gentle rhythm of the stitched line. Adding in quilting techniques and mixing machine embroidery with hand stitch changes the look of the fabrics used.

The memory image I have chosen to use for the drawing on this piece was part of a vintage tea service that I had inherited. The hand-embroidered tablecloth and the 1970s china were very much entwined in my memory and conjured up recollections of many happy family gatherings, drinking tea and eating cake. The assembled fabric is a collection of worn cloth and pieces of material I had been given by friends, chosen for their similarity in colour to the china. Each fragment is very personal to me and as I pieced and sewed it together, I had a strong sense of loved ones being very close once more.

If you prefer not to use a piece of material that holds too many precious memories, then you can always use a selection of both new and found fabrics. Charity and second-hand shops are a good way to source textiles such as men's cotton shirts and children's clothes in both patterned fabrics and muted colours and will still give that lovely worn look to your assembled picture.

For the assembled strip I used six pieces of different fabric in total, which I cut into various sizes, keeping the width approximately the same. I then edged either side of the pieced strip in a contrasting colour and cut the assemblage to the required size.

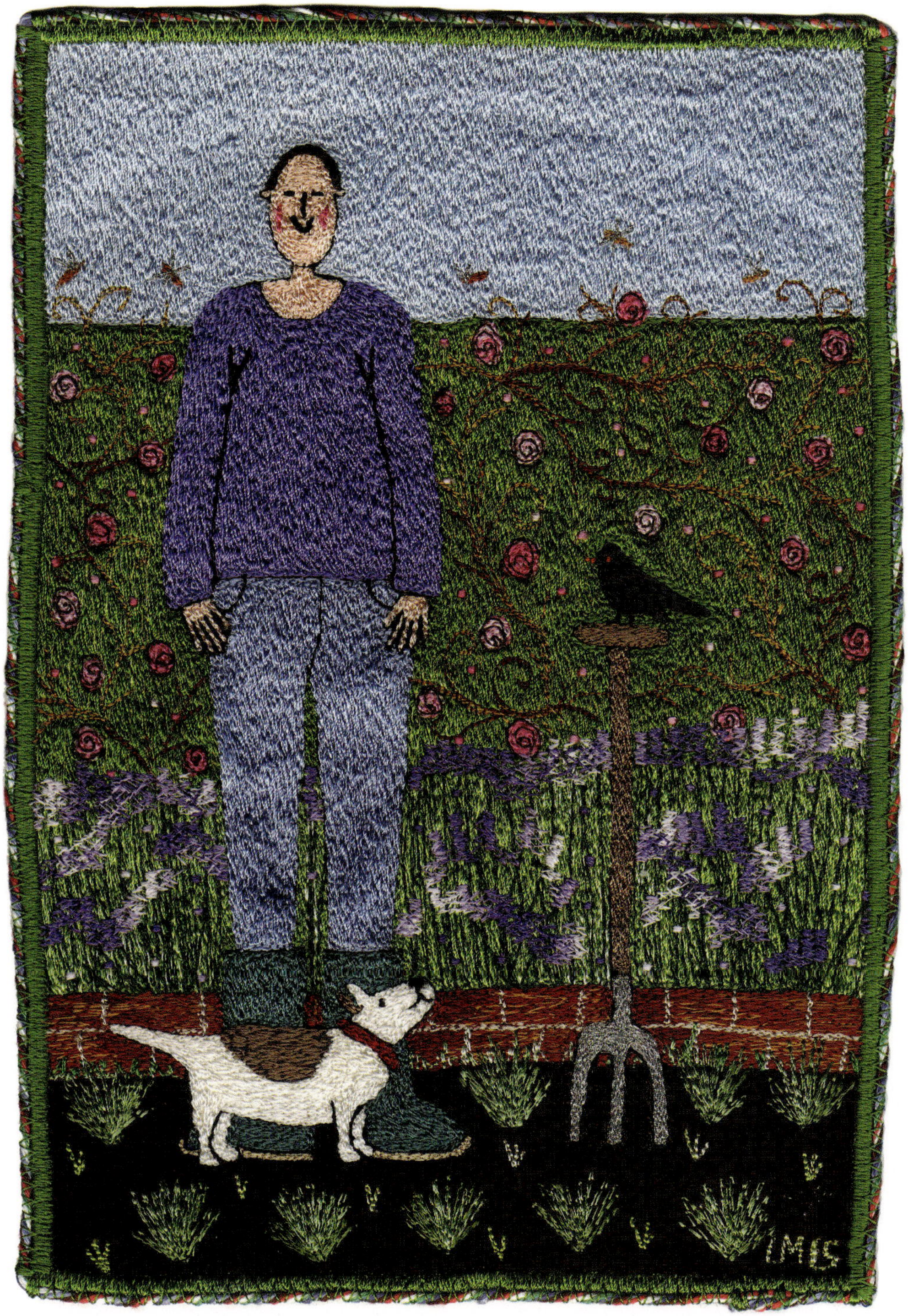

Lavender Garden by Linda Miller, 16 × 23cm (6¼ × 9in), free machine embroidery.

As this project combines these assembled fabrics with free machine embroidery drawing, it is essential to stabilize the back of the piece. This can be achieved easily by ironing a piece of interfacing fabric on to the reverse of the assembled piece in order to make the structure of the entire work much stiffer. This will create an ideal surface on which to free machine stitch without having to use an embroidery hoop, which can feel restrictive at times. The finished framed piece can then be hung alongside treasured family photographs to keep memories together.

Finished picture measures approximately 31 × 31cm (12¼ × 12¼in).

With this project you will be sewing both on the back and front of the piece.

The measurements for this project piece are an approximate guide size. You may choose to make your image slightly bigger or smaller. Whatever you decide, make sure that your image finishes 3cm (1¼in) from each side of the fabric edge to allow for a seam allowance when the picture is completed. Remember, if you choose to alter the size of your piece you will require a different size frame than that recommended here.

The seam allowance used is 6mm.

HANDY HINT WORN EMBROIDERY AND OLD QUILT TOP PIECES

When working with vintage fabrics it can be challenging to know which sections to use. Rather than trying to maximize the whole piece of fabric by using every scrap of cloth and not being completely happy with the finished article, choose the piece that talks to you; you will find that by being selective you will enjoy the visual effect of the placing much more. Rely on your gut feeling – which part do you like best? It is a personal choice so take a bit of time and play about with it.

It can help to make a viewfinder to look through. To do this, cut out a window from a piece of paper and move your viewfinder over the fabric. You can then select the area that you wish to use without being distracted by the piece in its entirety. If the vintage fabric you wish to use for this project has age spots, holes or is worn thin in places, then you can always hand sew a small patch on to it first to cover these imperfections if you want to – if the fabric used for the patch itself has an important meaning to you then this will make the cloth picture even more special.

YOU WILL NEED

Items from the basic tool kit, as listed in Chapter 1 Tools and Equipment, and the following materials:

- Piece of A4 copier paper, 80gsm
- Piece of heavyweight linen/cotton fabric measuring 21 × 24cm (8¼ × 9½in)
- Piece of hand-embroidered fabric, for example from a tray cloth/tablecloth, measuring 13 × 24cm (5¼ × 9½in) or a part of a quilt top
- Piece of thin quilting wadding/thin fleece fabric measuring 37 × 37cm (14½ × 14½in)
- Pieces of cotton fabric in a selection of plain and patterned designs of your choice, such as little scraps of memory cloth, to make a strip which when assembled and sewn together should measure 32 × 9cm (12½ × 3½in)
- Piece of cotton fabric for the back and quilter's hem measuring 38 × 38cm (15 × 15in)
- Piece of lightweight iron-on interfacing fabric measuring 33 × 23cm (13 × 9in)
- Spool of mid grey machine sewing thread
- Spool of white machine sewing thread
- Spool of hand quilting thread in a colour of your choice
- Spool of hand sewing thread in the colour of your backing fabric
- Spool of tacking thread (any colour)
- Spool of black machine embroidery thread or a black machine sewing thread
- Three or four spools of either machine embroidery thread or machine sewing threads in colours of your choice
- Piece of good-quality mount board in a neutral colour, cut to the size of the frame's recess
- Unglazed box picture frame measuring 44 × 44cm (17½ × 17½in)

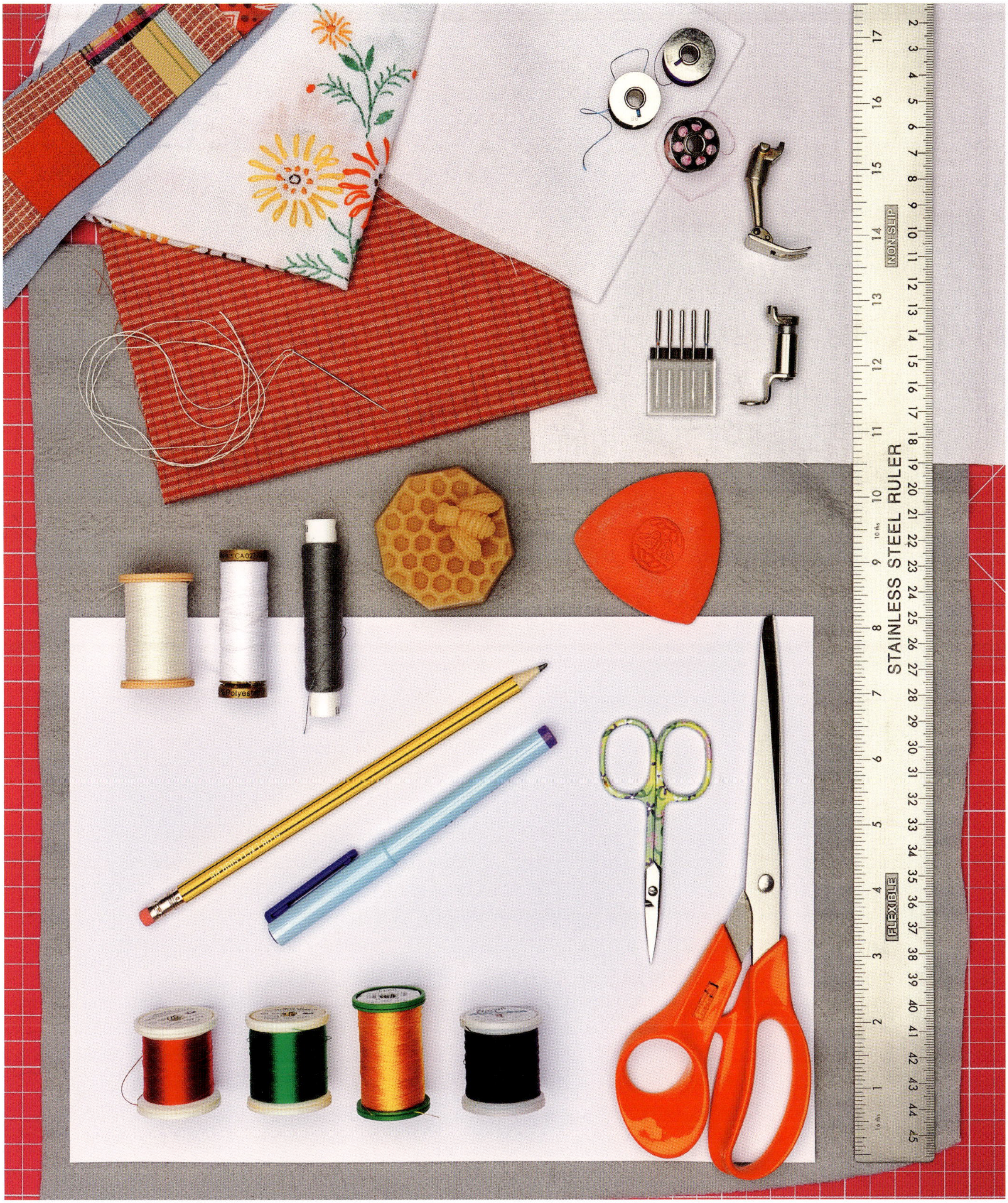

A selection of materials needed to make the picture project, *Embellishing a Vintage Cloth*.

1 GETTING STARTED

Draw your memory image onto paper. This could be any number of objects or scenes that have significance for you: it may be a domestic article such as a teacup, baby's first shoe, musical instrument, favourite landscape or garden flowers. Spend some time sketching and drawing out your image. When you are happy with your picture, write 'front' at the top of the paper.

If you find the challenge of drawing too much, it may be easier to use a family photograph. To do this, place the photograph either on a lightbox or windowpane and trace the image through onto the paper. Once your image is complete, remove the photograph turn the paper over and using the same method, trace the drawing through so that you have a reverse image. Write 'back' at the top of this side of the paper.

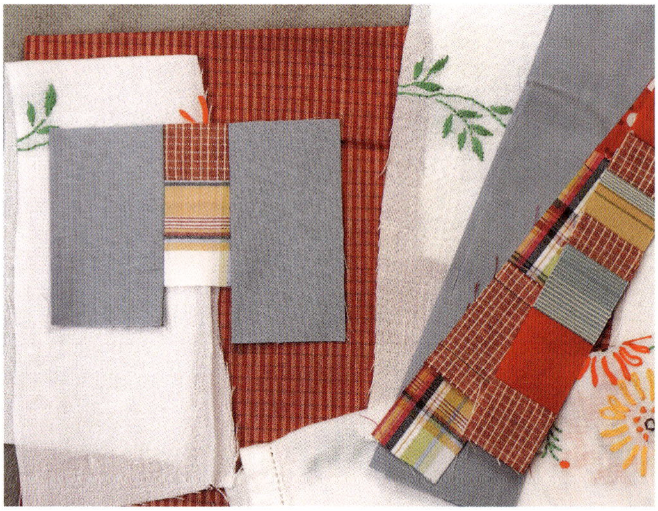

Select a mixture of hand-embroidered linens, new cotton fabric and worn cloth.

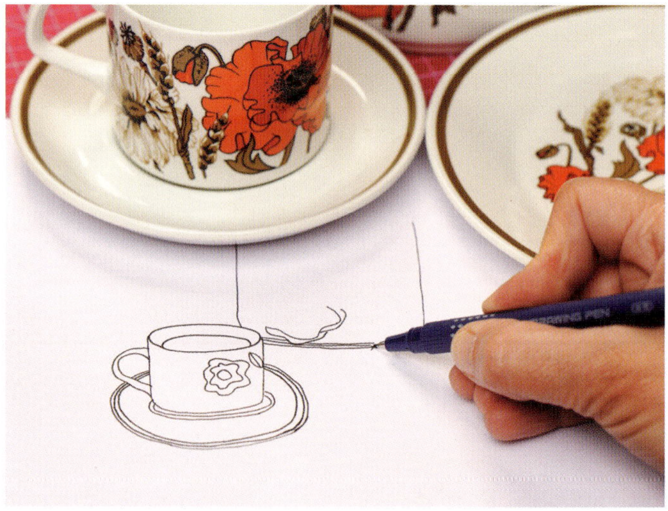

Once the image has been drawn onto paper, write 'front' at the top of the sheet.

2 FABRIC PIECING

Iron all your chosen fabrics and lay them out on a table, positioning the pieces as follows: the little fabric pieces for the assembled vertical strip on the left; the plain piece of heavyweight linen/cotton fabric on the right; and the hand-embroidered tray cloth/tablecloth below this.

Thread up your sewing machine with the white machine sewing thread and, with right sides facing, sew together the heavyweight piece of linen/cotton and the hand-embroidered fabric along the widest side of the fabric, using a seam allowance of 6mm. Press the seam flat with a steam iron and, if desired, sew a line of top stitch along the flat seam, then place to one side.

Lay out the ironed pieces of memory fabric in your preferred order and then sew the pieces together in a strip formation using the mid grey sewing thread. Cut the strip to measure 32 × 9cm (12½ × 3½in). Iron and press out with a steam iron.

With right sides together, pin and then sew the assembled strip to the left-hand side of the already joined linen fabrics. Once sewn together, iron flat and, again if desired, finish with a top stitch on the right side of the assembled pieces of cloth.

With the wrong side of the fabric facing, iron the piece of lightweight iron-on interfacing fabric onto the heavyweight cotton/linen and hand-embroidered linen fabrics only (it does not need to be ironed on to the assembled strip).

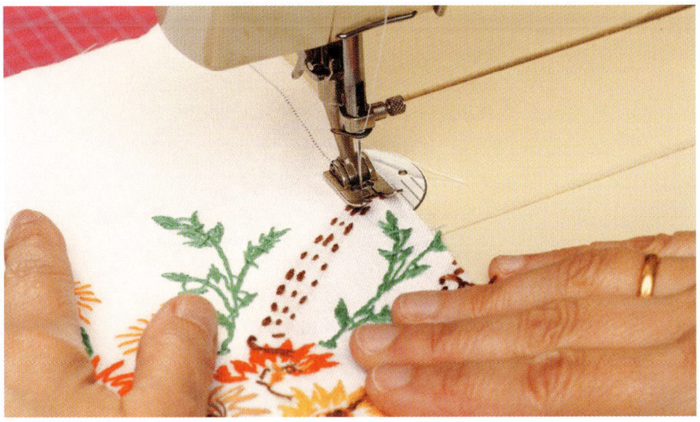

Sew the chosen linen and cotton fabrics together using a seam allowance of 6mm.

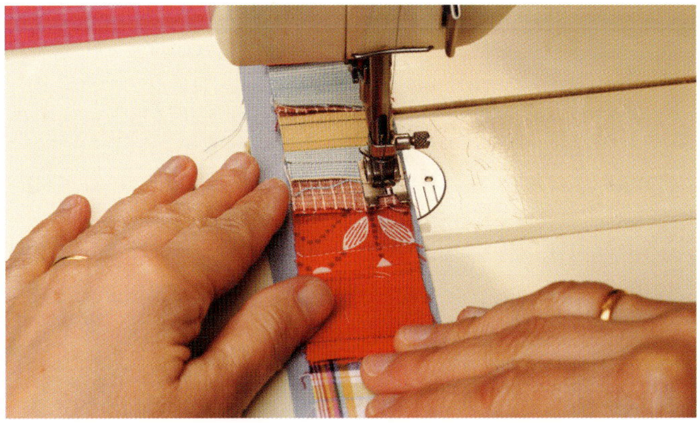

Assemble the pieces of memory fabric and sew them all together to form a strip.

HANDY HINT **PIECING FABRIC**

Fabric that is going to be placed and pieced is much easier to work with if it is ironed first. Ironing out creases allows the fabric to lay flat and, if the fabric is patterned, the full design can be seen and cut accordingly before being sewn into place.

As sewers, it can be easy to make fabric and colour selections. However, sometimes it can be daunting, especially when faced with a large quantity of different patterns, colours and textures, to make what you think is the right selection. One way to overcome any difficulties you may be experiencing with piecing is to sew strips of fabric together in a random manner. This way, happy accidents can appear with colour and pattern combinations that would not necessarily be first thought of.

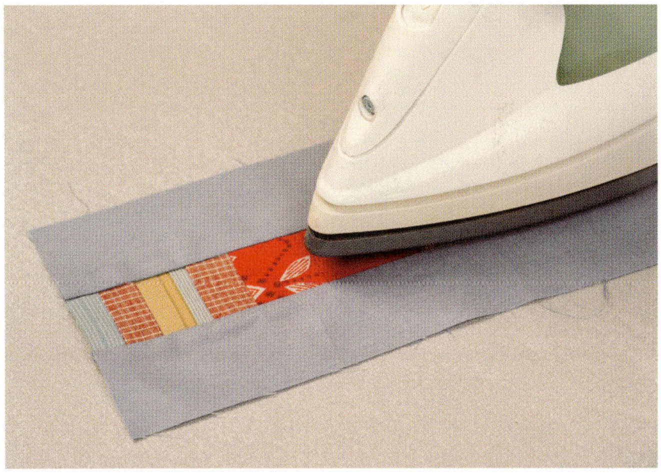

Thoroughly press the strip of memory fabric before trimming to measure 32 × 9cm (12½ × 3½in).

3 DRAWING THE IMAGE ONTO THE FABRIC

Using masking tape, stick the paper with the drawing right side down onto a lightbox, then place the fabric – again with the right side down – onto the drawing. Position it so that the drawing is centrally placed on the heavyweight linen/cotton fabric section of the pieced fabric, and trace the drawing through using either an air-soluble pen, a fine point permanent marker pen or an HB pencil. You will be drawing onto the back of the fabric and drawing directly onto the interfacing fabric in preparation to sew over this drawn line.

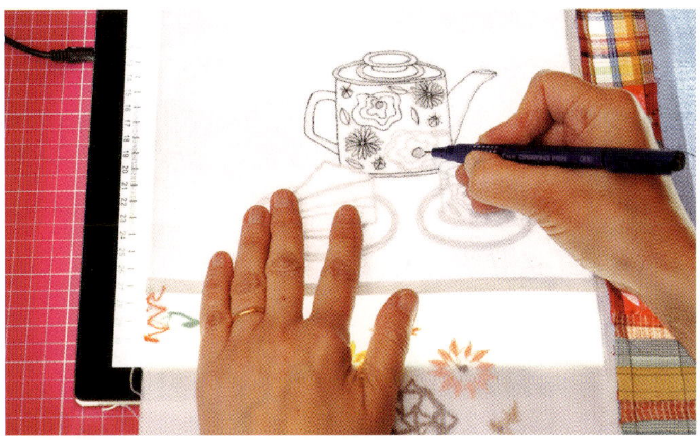

Use the lightbox to the trace the drawing onto the 'back' of the assembled fabrics.

HANDY HINT DRAWING ON FABRIC WITH A PENCIL AND FOLLOWING WITH STITCH

By drawing onto paper and then translating the drawn image onto the back of the fabric, the correct positioning of the outline can be achieved simply by moving the sketch around the plain piece of fabric until the most complementary position is found.

The most convenient tool to use for drawing onto fabric is an air-soluble pen, as the drawn line disappears after approximately eight hours, leaving no trace. However, if you do not have an air-soluble pen then either a fine point permanent marker pen or an HB pencil can be used. If using a pencil, it is important to ensure that it is an HB, which is a hard pencil. The drawn line needs to be visible but if the pencil used is too soft (such as a 2B) then the graphite from the pencil may bleed either into the fabric or into the thread line, and this can make it appear dirty. Whatever drawing tool you choose to use, try it out first onto a piece of fabric to see how it marks the fabric surface.

When using a machine-stitched line as a focal point on the plain fabric, it is easier if both the pencil and stitching lines are made on the back of the work first. This way no evidence of pen or pencil is left on the front of the fabric. The pencil-drawn line can be followed easily and simply with the stitch line before turning the fabric over and machine embroidering the image with an array of colourful threads (see Step 5).

4 STITCH DRAWING

Thread up the sewing machine with the black machine embroidery thread and place a bobbin of the same colour into the machine. Note: when using this reverse free machine embroidery stitch technique, it is the bobbin thread that will be on the right side of your fabric collage, so it is important to have the correct coloured thread in the bobbin.

Fit a free machine embroidery foot and lower the feed dog teeth, loosen off the top tension slightly and slide the pieced fabric collage under the foot with the line drawing facing you. Begin the process of drawing with the thread, as outlined in Chapter 3, Step 4.

Starting in the middle of your drawing and working outward to maintain a reasonable tension throughout, trace over the drawn line with your stitch line. Once all the desired sewing has been achieved, cut off both the top and bobbin threads close to the surface of the fabric. Lightly press the fabric. From now on, all sewing will commence on the right side of the picture.

5 ADDING COLOUR WITH MACHINE EMBROIDERY

Adding a splash of colour can bring your stitch drawing alive. The suggestion of colour enhances the monochrome image without saturating the narrative. You may choose to fill in key parts of your drawing with either machine or hand embroidery or you may decide that just having a black stitched drawing is enough. There is no right or wrong method when working on this piece; it is a personal choice. If you decide to keep the drawing purely in a line of machine stitch, remember that you can always add colour later with hand stitch when the piece has been assembled. It is important to go with your gut instinct and be true to yourself. Once you have completed your initial stitching, trim up the outside edges to even off the fabrics.

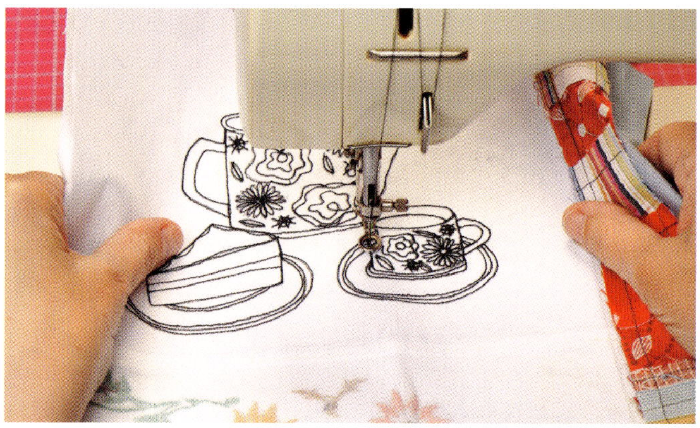

Thread up the sewing machine with black thread and wind a bobbin in the same colour.

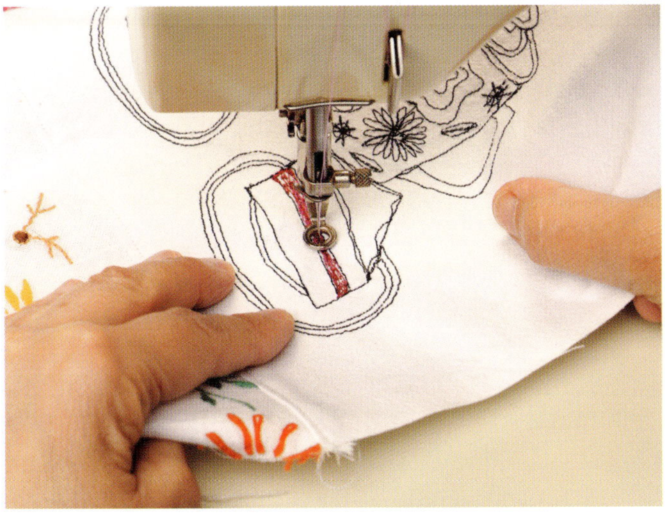

Adding a splash of colour to the stitched drawing can bring the impression to life.

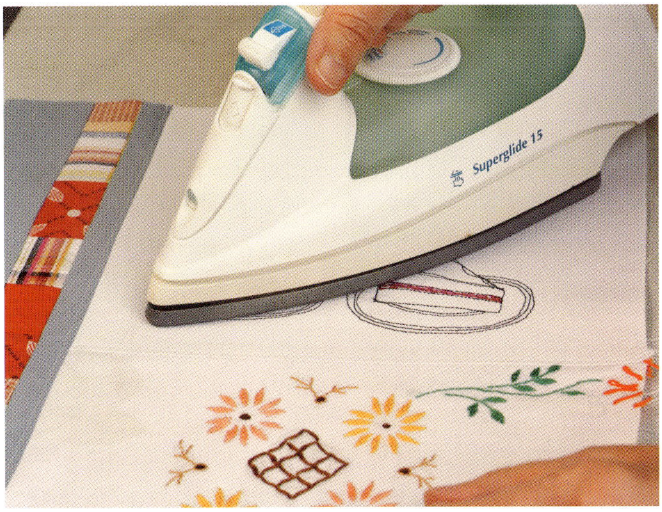

Press the finished assembled picture with a hot iron before trimming up the edges.

6 TACKING THREE LAYERS TOGETHER

On a cutting mat (to protect your work surface from being scratched) take your piece of cotton fabric for the back and place it right side down. Using masking tape, stick the four corners down, pulling out the fabric to make it taut Next, lay the quilting wadding over the top, positioning it in the centre of the backing fabric – again, make it taut by sticking it down at the four corners. Then, place the assembled fabric picture right side up onto the top of the wadding, once more making sure it is centred. Smooth it out with the palm of your hand and stick it down again at the four corners. Do not worry if there is puckering within the machine embroidery image; remember, it is a unique piece and it will all add to its charm.

Do not cut the backing fabric to fit, as the excess will be used to make a border around the outside edge of the completed picture (the quilter's hem). Thread up a hand sewing needle with the tacking thread and, starting at one of the centre edges of your piece, begin to tack using a long running stitch, making sure to sew all the three layers together. Work in rows about 4cm (1½in) apart to form a grid. At the start and end of each row, ensure the tacking thread is secured with a couple of repeated large stitches, which when required will be easy to undo. When the tacking grid is complete, remove the masking tape from each layer and your work is ready for the next stage.

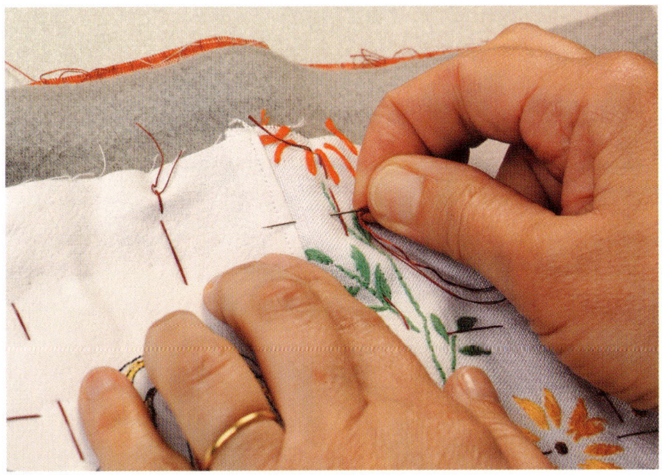

Use sticky tape to secure the three layers down on a cutting mat before tacking together.

7 SLOW STITCHING: QUILTING

Taking your chosen quilting thread, thread up a hand sewing needle and run the thread through a piece of beeswax – this will enable the quilting thread to run smoothly through the three layers of fabric, reducing knotting and snagging as you sew. Knot the end of the thread and push the needle through the edge into the middle of the layered fabrics. Aim for the needle to reappear near to the seam of where the three pieces of main fabric are joined, so that the knot is in the inside of the layered fabric and does not show on either the front or the back of the work.

Starting on pieced memory fabrics begin a running stitch, aiming to get each of the stitches 3mm or 4mm long and the same distance apart over the strip. The rows should be distanced approximately 5mm to 1cm (⅜in) apart. When the end of a row is reached, repeat a couple of stitches on themselves before pushing the needle in between the layers of wadding and cotton fabric in preparation of beginning a new row, turning the fabric accordingly.

When the length of thread is about to run out, make two or three small overstitches on the reverse of the work. Push the needle through into the middle of the three layers and then back out to the reverse of the fabric once more, before cutting the thread close to the surface; this will trap the end of the thread in the layered fabric, so the thread end does not show.

Rethread the hand sewing needle and repeat the hand stitching until all the desired rows have been completed. The last row of stitching should finish approximately 1cm (⅜in) from the outside edge. You may choose to continue with the slow stitching by putting some hand stitch across the plain background fabrics, around the machine embroidery image or upon the hand-embroidered section of the piece. Just be mindful to stitch no nearer than 1cm (⅜in) to any of the outside edges. When all the hand sewing has been completed, carefully take out all the tacking threads and gently press the back of the work.

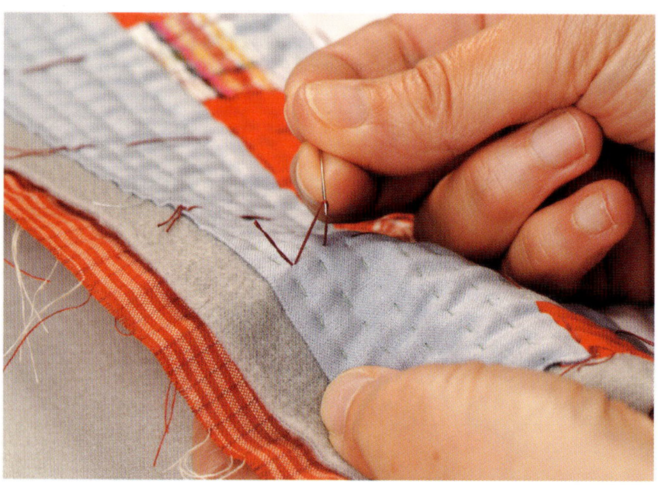

Once all the quilting has been achieved, used the needle to pull out the tacking threads.

8 TRIMMING UP

Lay the finished work on a cutting mat or worktable, right side up. Turn the top edge of the backing fabric back on itself, ensuring it is out of the way. Using a sharp pair of scissors,

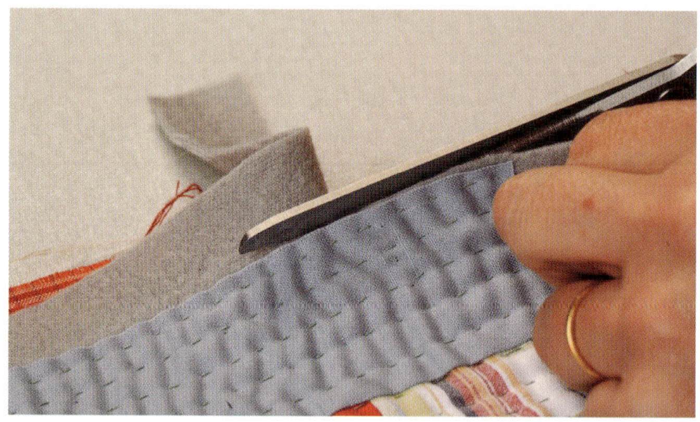

Tuck the backing fabric under the completed picture and cut away the thin wadding.

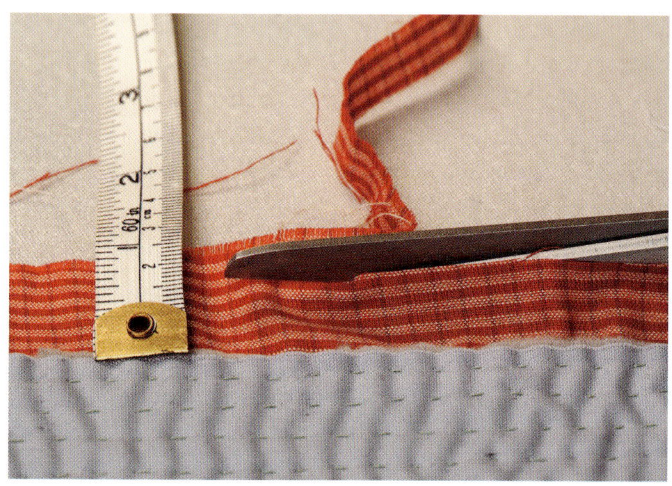

Open out the backing fabric and, using a tape measure, cut it away to a hem of 2cm (¾in).

neaten up the wadding to the size of the top fabric, making sure you do not cut any of your hand quilting stitches or the backing fabric. Continue in this way so that each side of the picture piece is neatened up. Open out all the sides of the backing fabric and then cut each side to leave a border of 2cm (¾in).

9 USING THE BACKING FABRIC TO MAKE A QUILTER'S HEM

Starting at one of the sides of the picture piece, turn 1cm (⅜in) of the backing fabric onto the picture, turn 1cm (⅜in) again to create a double hem and pin in place; then turn the opposite side and repeat. Next, turn the top edge of backing fabric in the same manner to create a double hem, ensuring each corner is folded neatly, and pin in place. Complete the bottom edge in the same way as the top.

Thread up a hand sewing needle in the same colour as the backing fabric and secure the border hem edge with a blind hem stitch, making sure that the knot is hidden in between the three layers. When a corner is reached, whip stitch the very outside edge (approximately 1cm, or ⅜in) to secure it, before continuing along the hem.

Continue in this manner until all four sides of the hem and the four corners have been stitched down, ensuring the end of the thread is knotted and secured as in Step 7 above. Remove all the pins, and with the right side down, gently press out the reverse with a steam iron. Turn the piece over and admire all your hard work!

For presentation and framing, see Chapter 9.

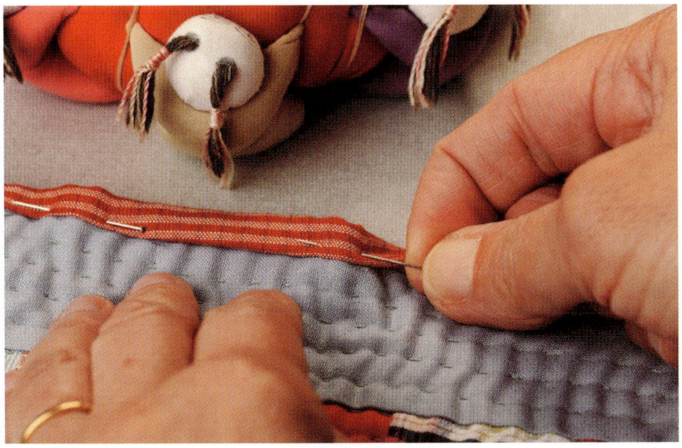

Fold a quilter's hem over the picture front, which measures 1cm (⅜in), and pin it in place.

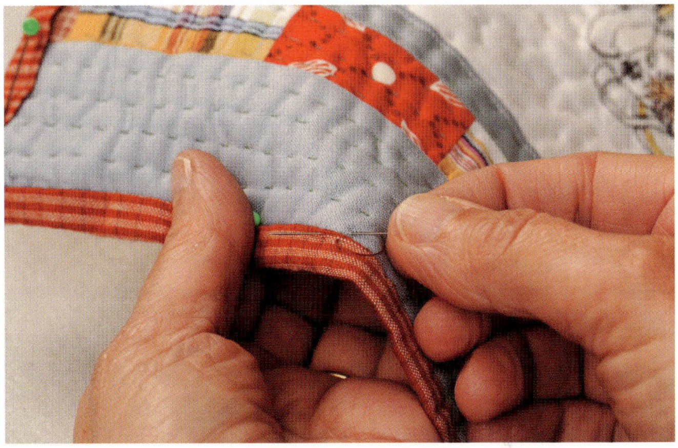

Thread a needle in a similar colour to the backing fabric and sew the hem in place.

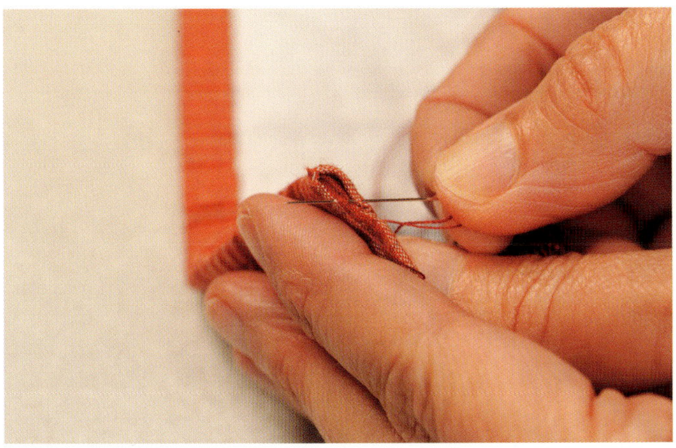

Sew each corner of the quilter's hem using a whip stitch before securing with a knot.

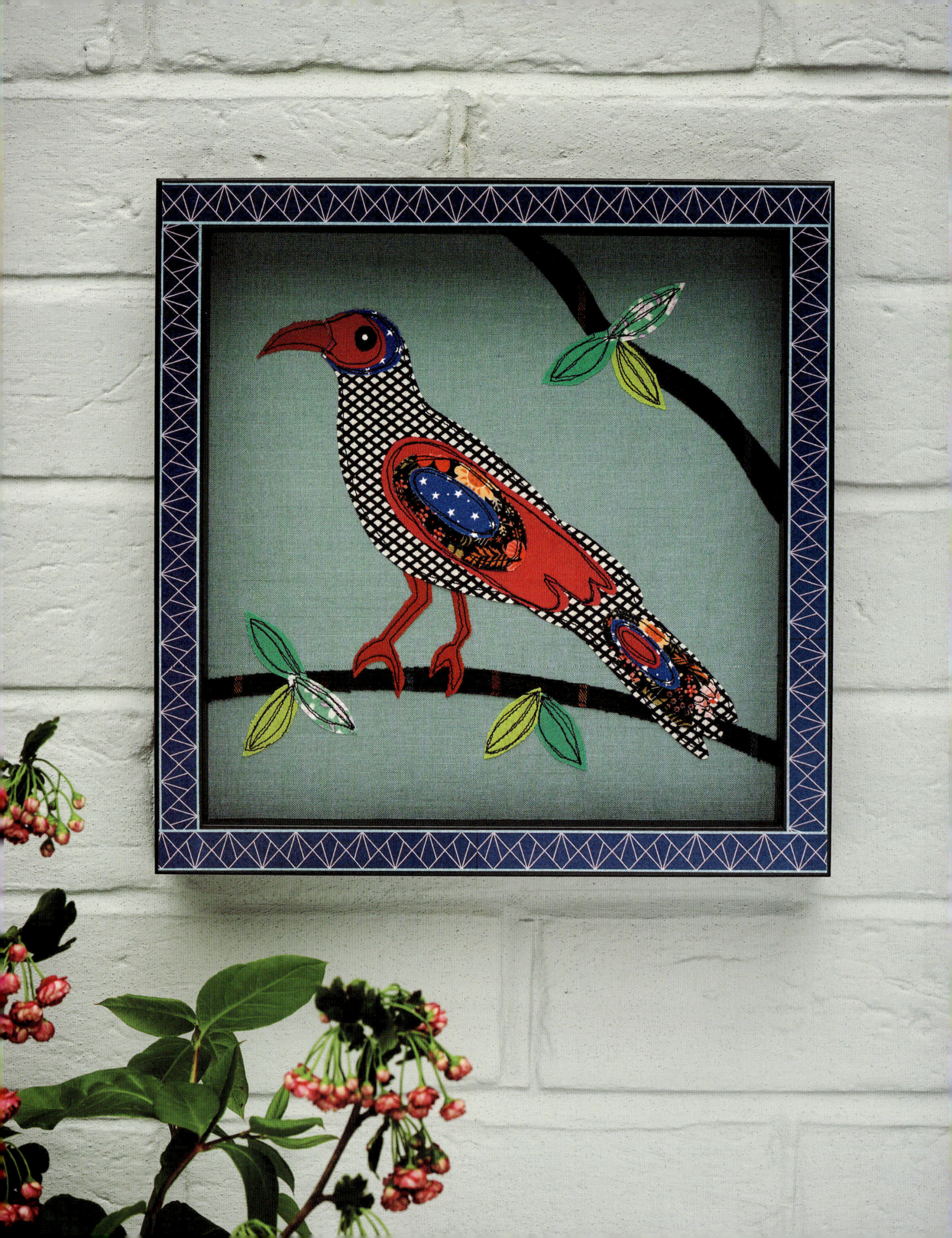

CHAPTER 6

COLOUR EXPLORATION THROUGH FABRIC APPLIQUÉ

PICTURE PROJECT

Bird of Paradise – Fabric Appliqué with Free Machine Embroidery

Fabric appliqué is a very old but versatile needlework technique that has long been used to decorate garments, quilts and other domestic textiles. The word appliqué comes from the French verb *appliquer*, which translates as 'to apply', and the technique involves sewing or sticking one piece of cloth over another larger piece to form a picture or pattern that can be decorated with stitch.

It is believed that appliqué was used by the ancient Egyptians and other early cultures, and evidence of early appliqué has been found during archaeological explorations. The technique was known in Britain from the later Middle Ages and examples of appliqué from around the world can be viewed in the British Museum and are included in the V&A collection.

Appliqué can be used to patch and strengthen worn areas in fabric and is a popular decorative technique in its own right, used commonly on household textiles such as cushion covers, runners, bags, purses and bed linen, as well as on clothing. In the twenty-first century, as we move away from mass production and consumerism and embrace more individual, eco-friendly lifestyles, this ancient medium is now very fashionable, particularly when employed as a decorative way of repairing and embellishing worn or frayed items.

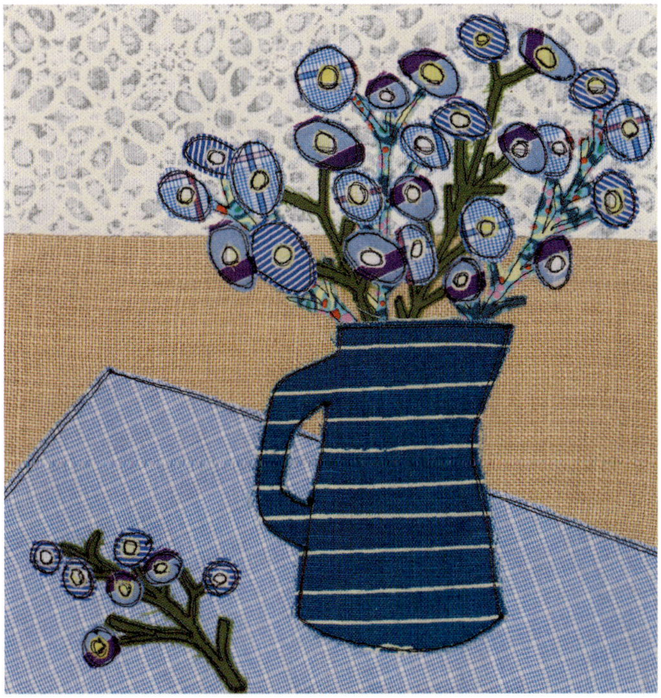

Cornish Mizzle by Linda Miller, 25 × 25cm (10 × 10in), fabric appliqué and free machine embroidery.

Appliqué has also long been used for picture making and storytelling. The traditional appliqué technique is to use little pieces of material cut into shapes – which may be abstract or figurative, such as people, flora and fauna – and the raw edges turned under by hand before being hand sewn into place onto a fabric background. In this way, a pictorial scene can be simply fashioned with little equipment – the only resources needed are cloth, thread and imagination.

◀ *Bird of Paradise,* presented and framed in a wooden box frame.

As indicated in the introduction to this book, the twentieth century saw the mass production of the electric sewing machine. This, together with the development of new fabrics and adhesives, allowed contemporary fabric appliqué techniques to emerge. Replacing the technique of hand turning raw edges for adhering pieces of material together using a fusible fabric, in collaboration with swapping hand stitch for machine stitch, has allowed the development of a different approach to fabric appliqué. These modern methods allow a painter's approach, where fabric and decorative machine stitch can be applied quickly, thus encouraging a spontaneity to the art of fabric picture making.

The contemporary and traditional techniques give a very different look to the finished article, but both can be equally beautiful. Finished contemporary appliqué is flatter in appearance when compared to the hand-applied and stitched technique, which has more of a raised surface. This exciting medium is very versatile, and the contemporary and traditional techniques, as well as being used separately, can also be used in conjunction with each other to produce inspiring and original images.

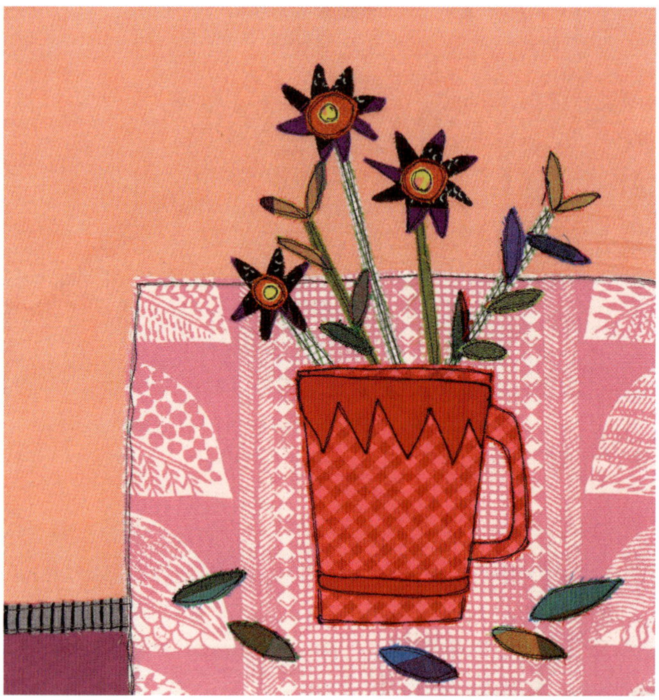

Star Flowers by Linda Miller, 30 × 30cm (12 × 12in), fabric appliqué and free machine embroidery.

Creating a visually pleasing composition from little pieces of cut fabric is all about placement, shape and colour. When placing cut pieces of fabric, it is important to get the balance right and to be happy with your own personal choice. Take your time with placing the different shapes and enjoy the process – you may find it rather therapeutic as you experiment with different arrangements. Indeed, it can be very satisfying to use up some of those scraps, especially when using fabric from well-loved but no longer worn garments. Remember, the collage pieces do not have to fit exactly and can overlap each other, allowing for the very quick creation of a distinct foreground and background. This is an ideal way in which to explore and work with a broad array of pieces of cloth, which differ in shape, texture and colour.

We all have our favourite palette of colours, which we return to turn time and time again. This range of colours and tones is revealed in the clothes we wear, the paints and furnishings we use to decorate our homes and, of course, in our creative endeavours. Often, when we attend a creative workshop or a class, we notice our contemporaries' colour choices in their work basket, jewellery and their own attire; indeed, we are often drawn to those who seem to share our own preferences. In our work, sometimes we find ourselves repeating the same colour choices. These can keep us stationary and, if we are not careful, our making can become stale. Therefore, it can be challenging but exciting to try out new ways of working with colour. For example, you may naturally avoid pairing cerise pink with scarlet, but why not try it and add a splash of hot orange and acid yellow to explore a riot of colour! It is only by experimenting that we discover, learn and understand how the colour spectrum works and how we can exploit this in our work.

Another way of refreshing your colour palette is to take inspiration from the natural world: a dark forest green against a cobalt blue sky or the dark grey blue of an ominous rain cloud against the lime green fields of summer. Inspiration can be gleaned from other sources too, by looking at the work of artists, designers and makers to see how they have used colour within their work. A relaxing hour or two of research flicking through interior design magazines, websites, art books or even exhibition catalogues, all of which can be accessed in your local library, can provide some wonderful new ideas for different colourways in a fabric appliqué project.

The medium of fabric appliqué is ideal to create a personal commission from a friend or family member, which can provide an excellent opportunity to open our eyes to new colours that we have not previously used within our work. Working to another's specifications means you may have to put your own preferences to one side and focus on the commissioner's likes and dislikes in terms of colour, texture and style to create a unique piece specifically for them. This experience can be invaluable in driving both our work and our confidence in colour arrangements forward. Indeed, if we stay open to new ideas, we may find our design capability develops naturally. Sometimes this development is only noticed when we look back onto earlier work and see for ourselves the progression that we have made. Another key way of learning is, of course, by making mistakes and sometimes our mishaps can lead to happy accidents that provide a new path of discovery. Remember, there is no right or wrong way to select colour; it is up to you, so be bold and don't be afraid to take a chance.

A word on the use of light. Good natural daylight is always the best to work in and to make your choices, so you can easily see how colours work together and play off each other. However, working in good daylight is not always possible. A good alternative is to work under a directional lamp with a daylight simulation bulb (these are easily available from the high street or online); these bulbs emit a very close approximation of natural daylight known as white light, giving a truer light to work under, which is not only kinder to our work but also to our eyes.

In this book, there are two projects using the medium of fabric appliqué. The project in this chapter, *Bird of Paradise* uses bonded fabric appliqué, whereas in Chapter 7 the reverse fabric appliqué technique is used to make the picture project, *Colourful Kites*. Both these techniques are very different: *Bird of Paradise* is a more controlled use of the medium, while *Colourful Kites* is a reverse fabric appliqué technique requiring a more intuitive approach to colour use. Both techniques use free machine embroidery to enhance the fabric outlines and define the fabric appliqué picture image.

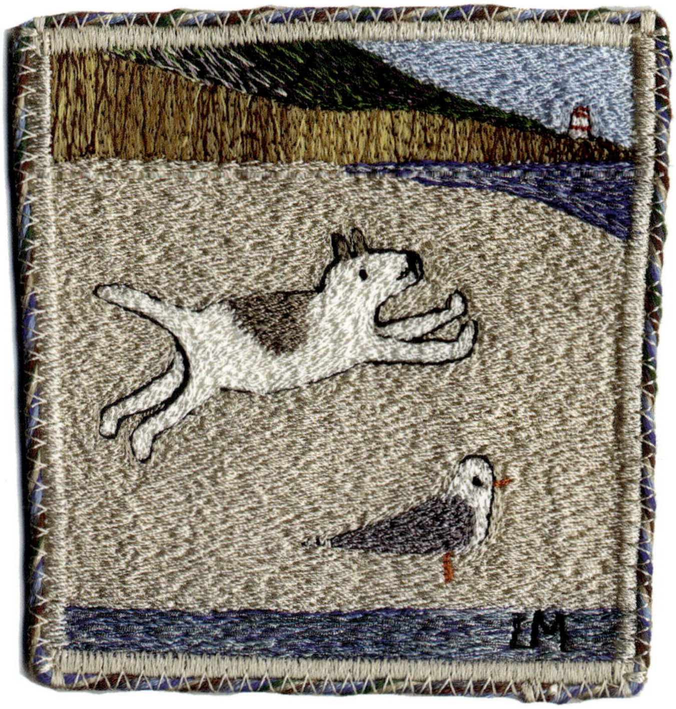

Beach Chase by Linda Miller 10 × 10cm (4 × 4in), free machine embroidery. (Photo: Michael Jennings)

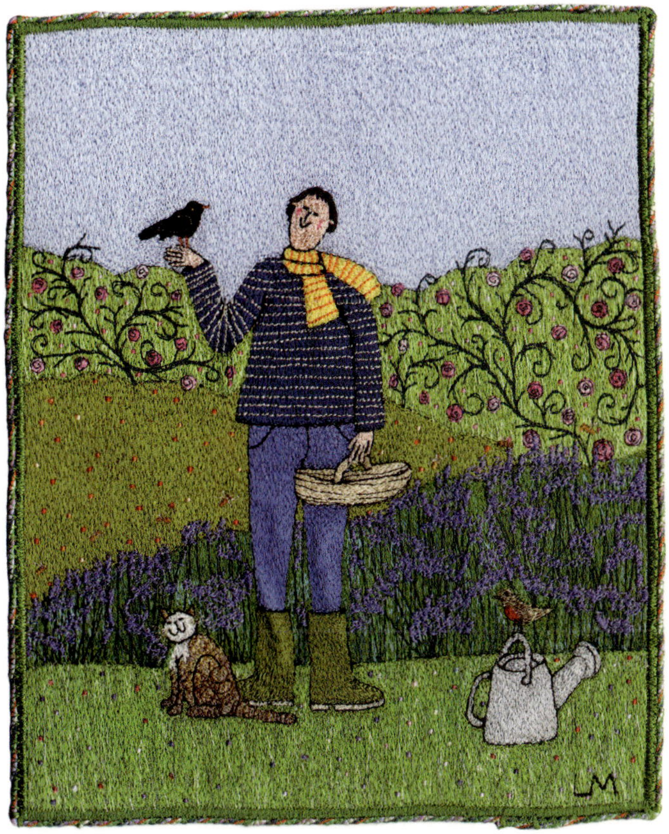

Gardener's Friend by Linda Miller, 27 × 22cm (10¾ × 8¾in), free machine embroidery. (Photo: Michael Jennings)

SCRAPS OF FABRIC IN VARYING COLOUR, PATTERN AND SIZE: WHAT TO USE

The imagery for this project features a striking bird of paradise sitting on a branch within its forest setting. It provides an excellent opportunity to use some of those colourful fabric scraps that we all have accumulated in our work baskets over time and we often simply cannot bear to throw away. Such saved fragments of material will provide the perfect source material from which to create the array of colourful feathers required for the subject of this picture. If you are not confident at drawing, the straightforward shape of the bird is easy to achieve, and using your colourful scraps to bring a simple drawing to life makes this a deceptively uncomplicated project that realizes a beautiful picture.

You can choose to use similar colours, as in the example here, or, of course, make your own choice of colour combinations using fabric scraps that can be bright, muted, patterned or plain. In fact, as the bird of paradise is such a colourful creature, any colour combination will work. One point to be aware of when making your selection is to be wary of using too many patterned fabrics – there needs to be a balance between the patterned and plain fabric to ensure the bird stands out sufficiently from its forest background.

As with all fabric that requires numerous pressings with a high heat, you will want to ensure you choose 100 per cent cotton fabrics to work with, as cotton material can withstand a higher heat when being ironed and therefore there is less chance of it being scorched or melted by the heat of the iron.

This project combines both bonded fabrics and free machine embroidery drawing with threads. The ironing onto the base fabric of an array of fusible fabric pieces, some in layers, to create fabric appliqué makes the whole fabric structure much stiffer and therefore an ideal surface on which to free machine embroiderer without using an embroidery hoop, which can limit the free flow of the stitch line.

PICTURE PROJECT: *BIRD OF PARADISE*

Finished picture will fit a frame that measures 25 × 25cm (10 × 10in).

With this project you will be sewing on the front.

The measurements for the *Bird of Paradise* drawing are an approximate guide size; you may choose to make your imagery slightly bigger or smaller. Whatever you decide, make sure that your imagery finishes at least 3cm (1¼in) from each side of the background fabric edge to allow the picture to sit comfortably without the frame cutting into the imagery.

If you choose to alter the size of your fabric appliqué picture you will require a different size frame than the instructions for this picture project recommend.

It is important that all drawn lines on the fabric do not smudge or bleed – to ensure this doesn't happen use a permanent marker pen, not pencil or biro.

HANDY HINT CHOOSING A PALETTE OF COLOURFUL FABRIC SCRAPS TO WORK WITH

It can sometimes be overwhelming trying to select colours for a particular project when you have such a vast array of fabric pieces to choose from, especially if you have accumulated material scraps over the years, inherited somebody else's work basket or indeed bought a bundle of fabric pieces with a specific project in mind.

For this *Bird of Paradise* picture project you will need a total of ten different fabrics to make the following: the background – a plain fabric in a colour of your choice; the bird's body – brown; the bird's head and wings – red and pink; the bird's beak and legs – orange; branches – brown; leaves – three different greens.

Start by selecting some potential fabrics in similar colours for each of the picture components and place them in three piles: a pile for the background, a pile for the bird and, lastly, a pile for the branches and leaves. Take one piece from each pile and lay them together until you have a collection of colours and patterns that balance well and that you are happy with. This simple exercise allows you to whittle down the choice of fabric colours and can also give you an alternative colourway to play with.

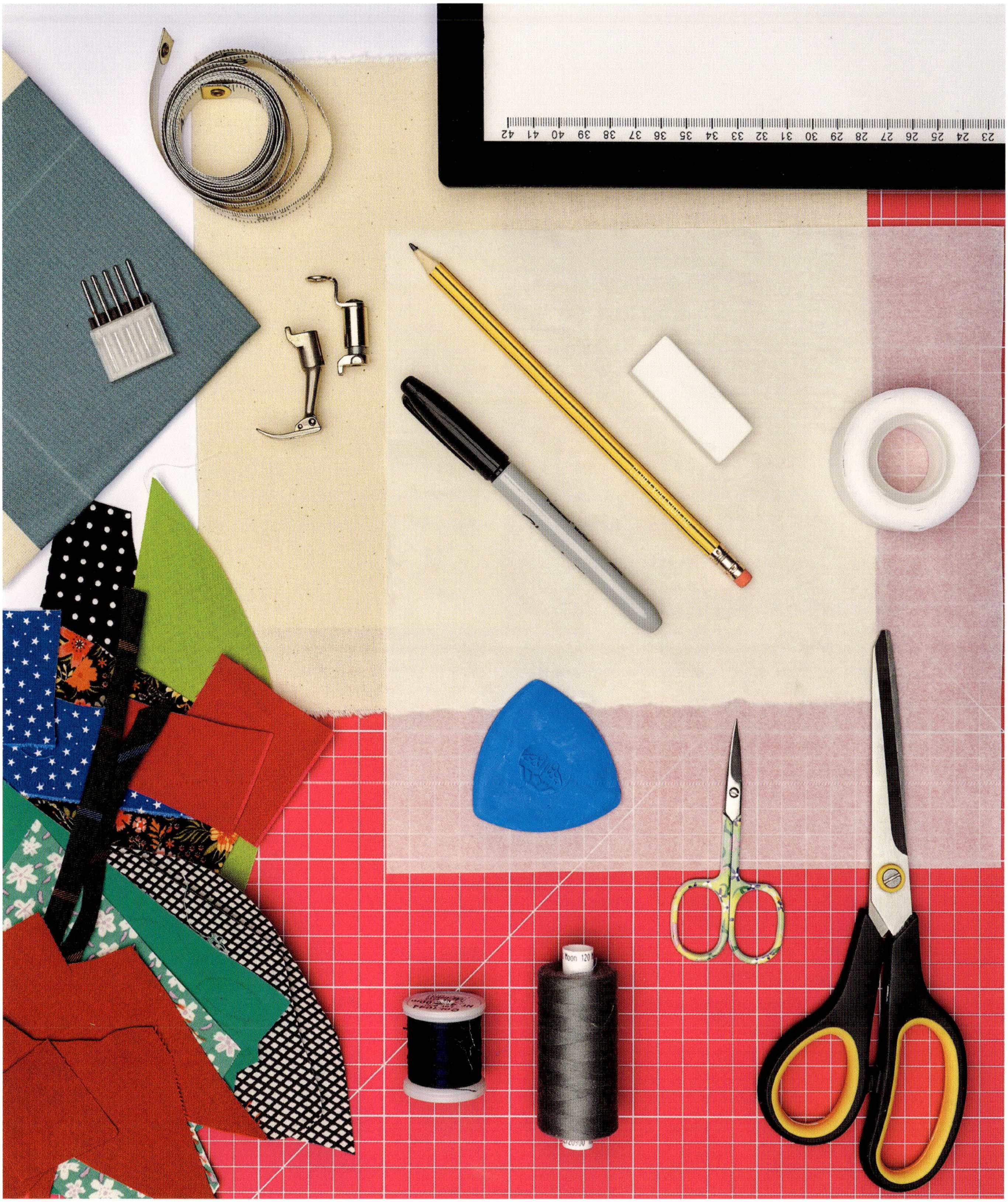

A selection of materials needed to make the picture project, *Bird of Paradise*.

1 GETTING STARTED

//

On a sheet of paper and using a pencil, draw out a square box that measures 24 × 24cm (9½ × 9½in). Take your chosen frame apart and carefully lay the front of the frame onto the drawn square so that the square is central. Using the pencil, mark the outside of the frame recess onto the paper. Any imagery drawn outside of this box will be hidden by the frame, but to avoid the abrupt end of the picture within the frame, allow a little of the background imagery to bleed into this box.

On a separate piece of paper, draw out your bird image. When you are happy with the bird drawing, trace over the initial pencil outline with a permanent black marker pen. Use paper scissors to cut out the bird drawing and lay it in the middle of the square box. To add balance to the composition, two branches are needed: one for the bird to perch on and the other in the distance. Both branches have a couple of little leaves on them – this gives a splash of colour and completes the background arrangement.

On a separate piece of paper, draw out the two branches. When the drawing is complete, go over the pencil lines with black permanent marker pen. Cut the branches out and lay these shapes in the box. Next, draw eight or so leaf motifs. Again, outline them in black and cut them out, then place them either singly or in groups of three upon the two branches.

YOU WILL NEED

Items from the basic tool kit, as listed in Chapter 1 Tools and Equipment, and the following materials:

- Packet of fusible fabric 1.2 × 1.75m (1¼ × 2yd)
- Piece of lightweight calico measuring 30 × 30cm (12 × 12in)
- Scraps of fabric in a selection of colours and patterns for the forest background and the bird image, either in your own choice of colours, or as a suggestion:
  - Background: light teal measuring 27 × 27cm (10¾ × 10¾in)
  - The bird's body: brown
  - Head and wing: red and pink
  - Beak and legs: orange
  - Eye: tiny piece of polka-dot fabric or a black sequin
  - Branches: pale brown
  - Leaves: three different greens: light, mid and dark
- Spool of black machine embroidery/machine sewing thread
- Spool of pale grey sewing thread
- Piece of good-quality mount board in a neutral colour, cut to the size of the frame's recess
- Unglazed box frame measuring 25 × 25cm (10 × 10in)

HANDY HINT PAPER SUITABLE FOR DRAWING

If you do not have drawing paper, a good alternative is A4 printer paper, which is used in a home printer; use 80gsm weight paper, easily found in any high street stationers or supermarket. Use sticky tape to stick together a couple of sheets, giving you the freedom to express your drawing of whatever size.

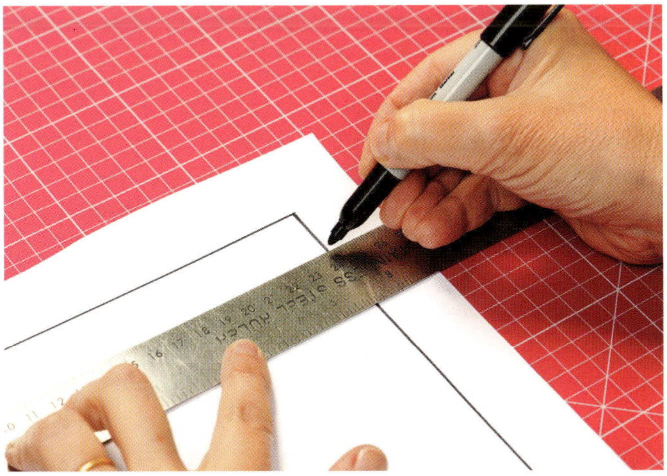

On white paper and with the aid of a ruler, draw out a box that measures 24 × 24cm (9½ × 9½in).

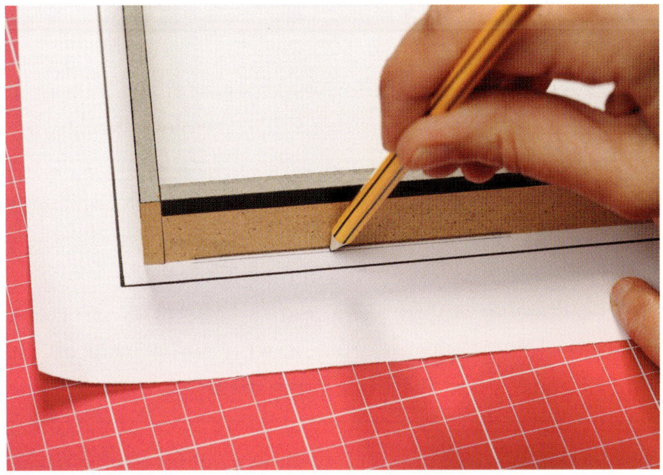

Centrally place the frame's recess in the drawn box and mark with a pencil.

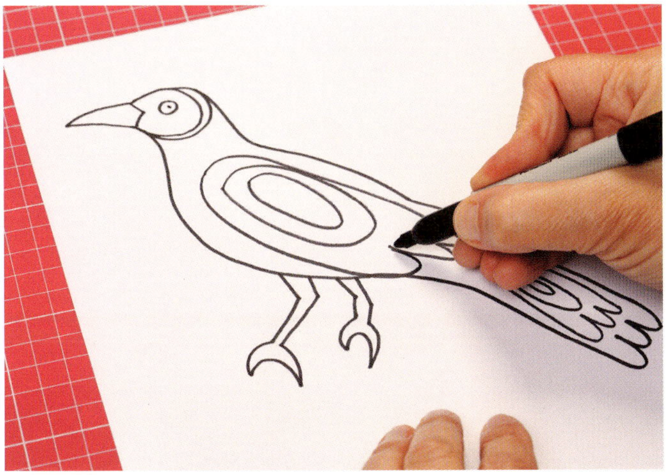

Using the easy to follow handy hint instructions, draw your bird of paradise.

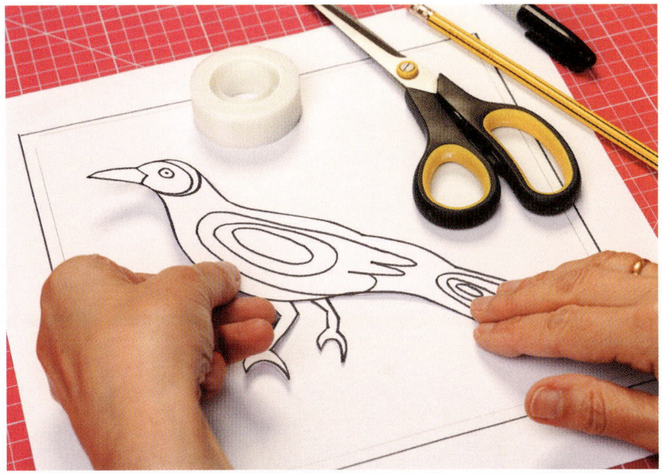

Once you are happy with the composition, stick the bird in place using sticky tape.

HANDY HINT DRAWING A BIRD

It only takes a few basic shapes to achieve the general outline of a bird, which can then be embellished to make your very own fantasy bird of paradise. On a piece of paper and using a pencil, draw an oval in a diagonal direction, which measures approximately 12 × 6cm (4¾ × 2½in) – this will be the body shape for the bird. Once this has been achieved, draw a smaller oval in the middle – this will be the bird's wing. Next, draw a circle for the head at the top of the body oval, which measures 3cm (1¼in) in diameter. Add an elongated triangle to the side of the circle, measuring 2.5cm (1in) long for the beak, and add a 6 × 2.5cm (2½ × 1in) oblong at the opposite end of the oval for the tail. Legs can be achieved by drawing two oblongs on the underside of the oval with an inverted semicircle at each end to represent the bird's feet.

Draw a line around the outside of the shapes to create the initial bird outline and draw in an eye. Adding additional lines on the head, wing and tail can give the bird further definition, which can then be translated into extra colour, pattern or texture when choosing fabrics for the appliqué. This bird image and any of the bird's components can be made either larger or smaller by simply increasing or reducing the size of the shapes.

2 ARRANGING THE COMPOSITION

Drawing and cutting out the components for the picture in paper gives you the freedom to arrange the pieces first before committing to the final composition. Firstly, try out the arrangement in a couple of scenarios and when you are happy with your created picture, stick down the pieces using sticky tape and write 'front' at the top of the picture.

This drawing will be used as the basis for your fabric appliqué picture. Turn over the drawing and place it on the light box and using the black permanent marker, trace the drawing through. When completed, write 'back' at the top of the picture. The image needs to be drawn out for reference and also put into reverse. Once the fusible fabric has been attached to the back of the fabric pieces, each piece can then be cut out and placed right side down onto the background fabric, ready to be secured in place.

HANDY HINT HOW TO USE FUSIBLE FABRIC

First, determine which side of the fusible fabric has glue on it. To do this, hold it up to the light and look for the mottled textured side – this is the glue side; the other side is the paper side, which is always the side to be ironed. To adhere the fusible fabric to your chosen fabric piece, place the fusible fabric glue side down onto the reverse side of the cotton fabric piece. Apply a hot iron to the paper side to allow the glue to melt onto the cotton fabric. When cool, the fabric is ready to be used.

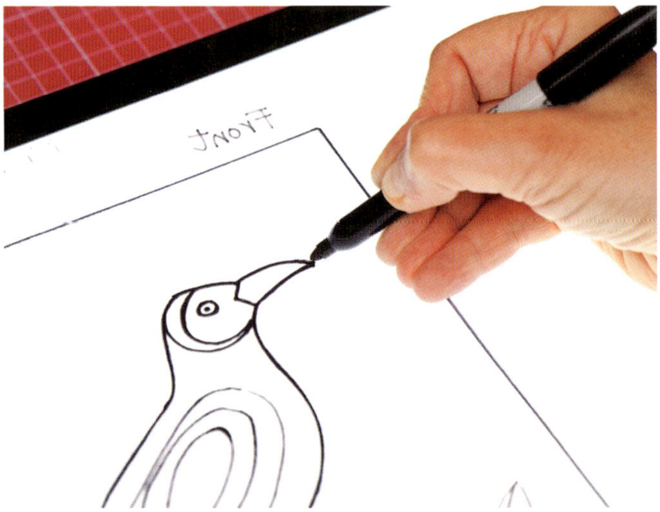

Using a light box, trace the drawing through onto the reverse side of the paper.

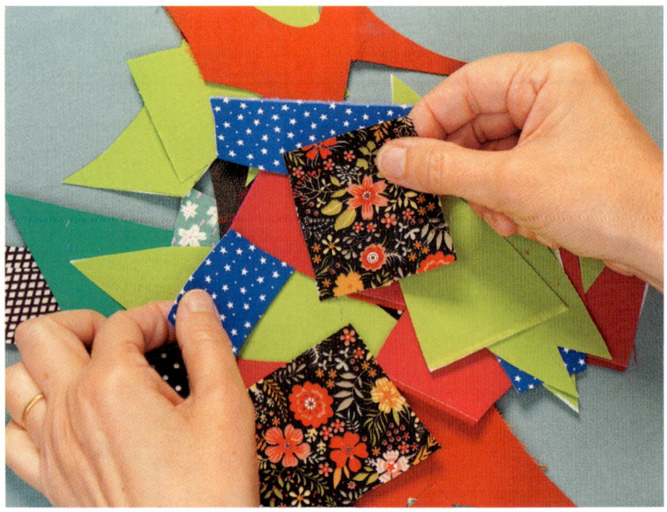

A selection of patterned and coloured fabric pieces will make your bird stand out.

3 PREPARING THE FABRICS

//

Once you have chosen the selection of patterned, coloured and plain fabric pieces that you wish to work with, press each piece of the cotton fabric to remove any creases. Turn each piece over, so that the reverse of the fabric is showing, and put to one side.

Beginning with the background fabric, cut a piece of the fusible fabric measuring 27 × 27cm (10¾ × 10¾in) and iron this onto the back of the background fabric. When it is cool, cut around the outside edge of the paper and peel it away. Iron this piece on to the middle of the piece of calico, right side up. Press thoroughly with the iron and do not worry if any fraying occurs.

When cool, lay the frame onto the middle of the fabric square and, using a piece of tailor's chalk, mark the four inside corners of the frame onto the fabric. The imagery will be placed inside this marked boxed; any imagery outside this area will not show once the piece is set within the frame.

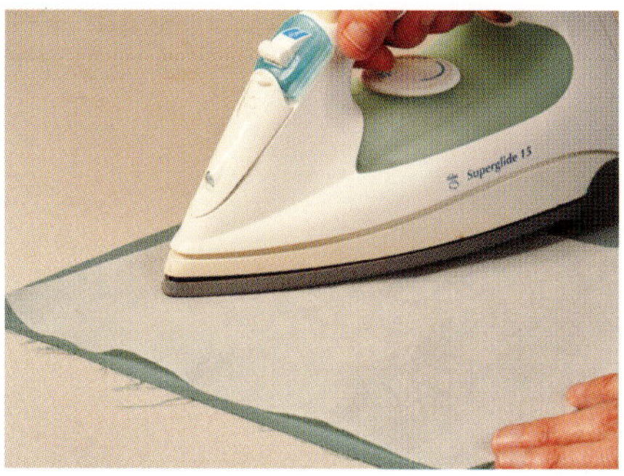

Iron the fusible fabric onto the back of the background fabric piece using a hot iron.

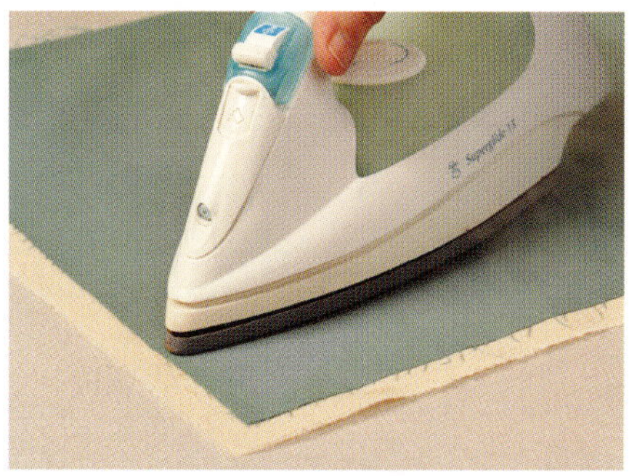

Peel away the paper and carefully iron the fusible fabric onto the lightweight calico.

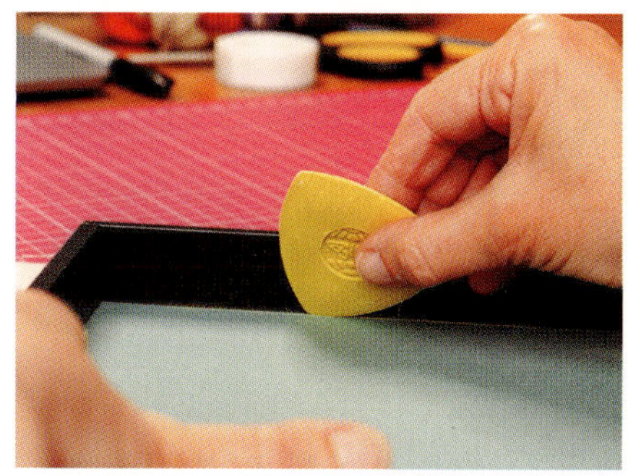

Using a brightly coloured piece of tailor's chalk helps the marked line to stand out.

4 DRAWING AND CUTTING THE FUSED FABRIC PIECES

///

Using the 'back' of your drawing as the pattern guide, and with the aid of the lightbox, lay a piece of the fusible fabric glue side down over the drawing and trace off the two branch shapes onto the paper side of the fusible fabric with the permanent black marker pen. With a pair of paper scissors, cut around these traced shapes, leaving a border of approximately 1cm (⅜in), and then iron both onto the back of the chosen branch-coloured fabric.

Wait until it has cooled and then cut them both out along the black border line. Place the pieces the right side up (fabric showing), roughly in position on the background fabric, using your drawing 'front' side up as the picture guide for placement of the branches. Turn the drawing over once more and lay another piece of the fusible fabric, again glue side down, over the 'back' of the drawing and trace off the leaf shapes. Cut out each leaf, making sure that a 1cm (⅜in) border is left around each of the shapes, and then iron onto the three different shades of green fabric. Once cool, cut along the drawn black line and place each leaf in a balanced arrangement on both branches.

Place a piece of the fusible fabric glue side down on the drawing and trace off the entire bird shape, excluding the beak and legs. Again, cut out the shape leaving a 1cm (⅜in) border and iron it onto the fabric selected for the bird's body. Then cut out the fabric shape following the black outline and place in the centre of the background fabric.

Continue tracing and cutting out the remaining fabric shapes in the same way. If you have chosen a couple of contrasting fabrics for the wing and tail feathers, trace and cut out the bigger pieces first and the smaller ones last and then place them all onto the fabric bird shape.

To complete your bird and bring it to life, the final component needed is an eye. An easy option for the eye is to use a small piece of black-and-white polka-dot fabric. First iron a small piece of the fusible fabric onto the back of a piece of

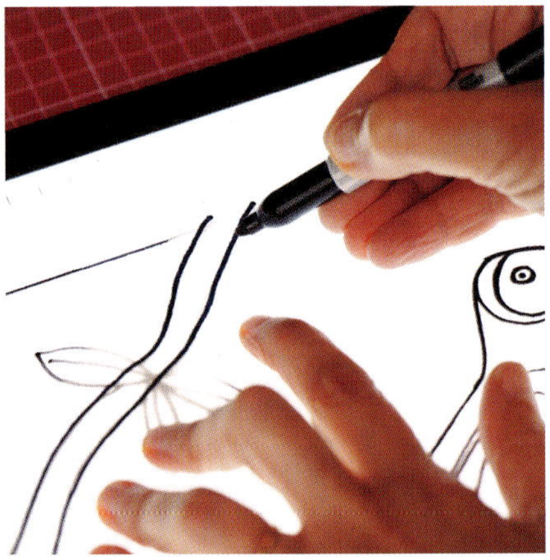

With the 'back' of the drawing facing up, trace the image onto the fusible fabric.

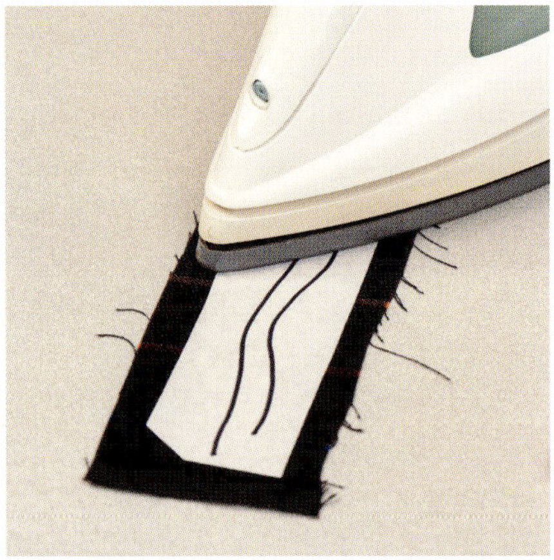

Iron a piece of the fusible fabric onto the back of a piece of the branch-coloured fabric.

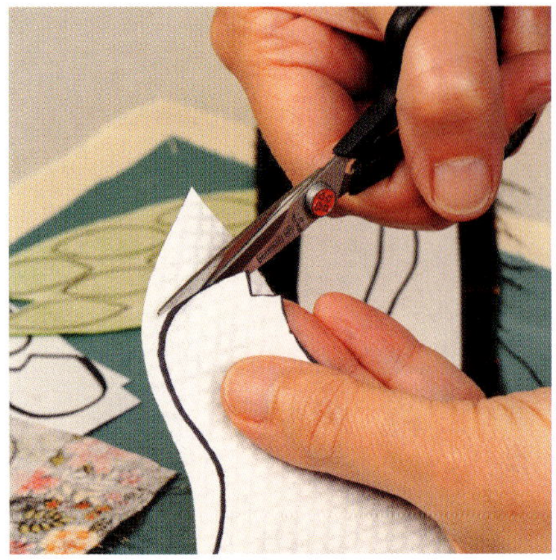

Using a sharp pair of scissors and following the marker pen lines, cut out all the shapes.

spotty fabric and, when cool, cut out a circle with a white dot in the middle. Wherever you place the eye will give your bird all the character it needs, so try the eye out in different parts of its head to see what best suits your bird. If you do not have any suitable fabric, a small bead, button or sequin can be used instead, hand sewn in place once all the machine sewing has been completed.

HANDY HINT MAXIMIZING THE FUSIBLE FABRIC AND FABRIC PIECES

To get the most out of your fusible fabric and the chosen fabric pieces that you are using, draw all the imagery close together on the fusible fabric. When desired, iron it on as near to the fabric edge as possible. This will maximize the space on both the fusible fabric and the scrap fabric pieces.

5 PLACING THE IMAGERY

It is important to consider the composition and question the arrangement of your fabric pieces before ironing them in place onto the background fabric. You must ensure that all the fabric pieces sit within the tailor's chalk marks; any picture components outside of this marked area will be hidden within the frame and backing board.

By using the 'front' of your drawing as a guide, you will see where your fabric pieces will need to be placed onto the backing fabric. If you feel your composition would benefit from any additional elements, such as more leaves or another branch, then you can add them in at this stage by following the above steps.

Alternatively, you may wish to adjust the positioning of the bird or reshape some of the fabric pieces such as the wings, tail feathers, legs or beak. If so, this is the perfect opportunity to do so. If you are in any doubt, it is best to leave the arrangement as it is and return to it a few hours later to have another look. Remember, once the picture pieces have been secured it is very difficult to change it, so if you do want to make any alterations, do take your time. Ensure you place the branches and leaves down first and then the bird and its components on top.

HANDY HINT TRYING OUT DIFFERENT COMPOSITIONS

You may find it helpful to use your phone or a similar device to take photos of your picture at different stages of the project. This allows you to place the pieces in different arrangements, while keeping a recording of each one for reference; it is then easy to reassemble the picture pieces in your preferred composition.

6 ADHERING THE PIECES

When you are happy with your composition, peel off the paper backing from the fabric shapes and place all the pieces in sequence upon the background fabric. You will find that once the paper has been removed, the cloth shapes are quite static and stick easily to the fabric background. Tuck the wide end of the beak under the bird's head to ensure there are no raw edges together and to give a neater appearance; similarly tuck the tops of the legs under the bird's body.

Using a hot iron, press the fabric picture pieces down, taking care not to dislodge them with the iron or scorch the fabric. Rather than 'ironing them down' by moving the iron across them, simply hold the iron over the pieces, pressing firmly until they are fixed in place. How the fabric responds to being used in this way will depend on the type of cotton fabrics you have used: a more loosely woven cotton is likely to fray a little, whereas a printed cotton fabric will generally refrain from unravelling. However, do not worry about this – a few little separating edges will simply add more texture to your textile picture.

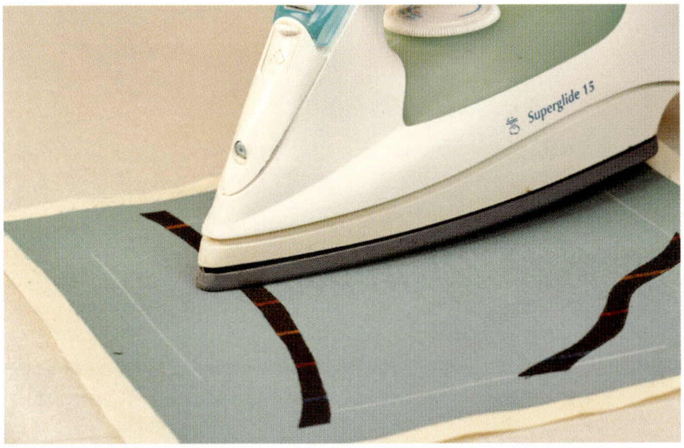

Consider the composition, ensuring all the pieces fit within the tailor's chalk markings.

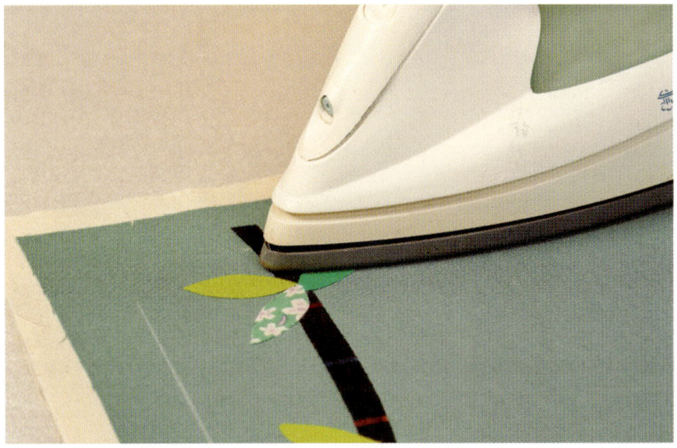

More leaves can be added to the branches before securing each one with a hot iron.

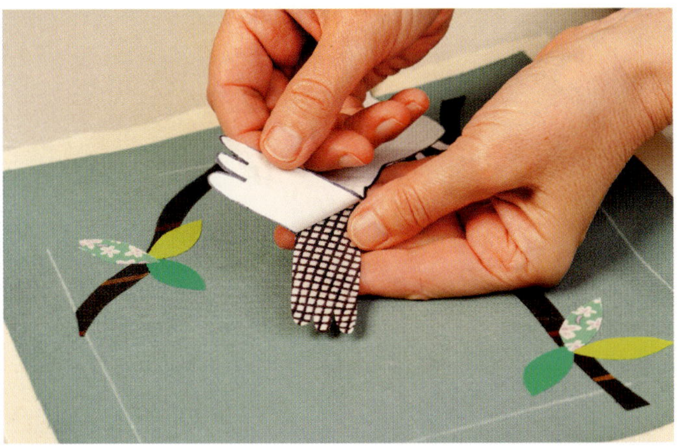

Peel away the paper backing and lay the initial bird shape onto the background fabric.

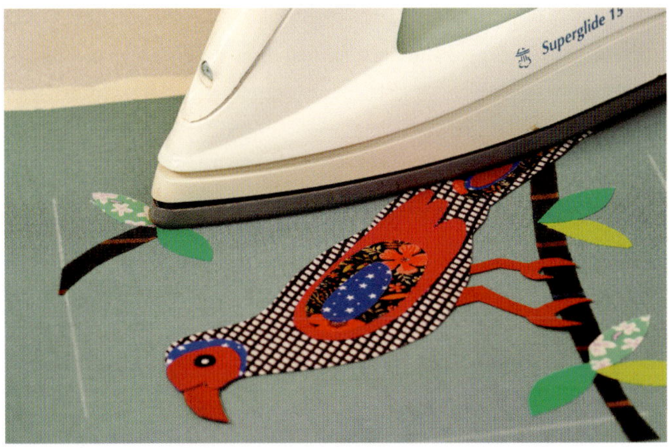

Once all the bird's components have been placed, secure them with a hot iron.

7 DRAWING WITH STITCH

Thread up your sewing machine with the black thread and place a wound bobbin with the same colour thread in the machine. Fit the free machine embroidery foot and lower the feed dog teeth, then follow the instructions in Chapter 3, Step 4. An embroidery hoop is not required for the free machine embroidery stitch, as the fabric layers will be stiff enough to be worked on without any difficulty or puckering of the fabric.

Starting in the middle of your bird image, begin drawing with the black thread in a continuous line, approximately 3mm in from the outside edge of the fabric shapes, and follow the outline of the bird. Continuing with the same stitch line, follow the shape of the wings, head, beak and then the feet. Continue stitching in the same manner on both the branches and the leaves. Do not worry if you find that your free stitch line is a little wobbly – this will simply add to the individuality of your picture.

You can always add another stitch line to give a double outline, add a few stitched feathers to embellish the bird's body, or create a stitched vein structure upon some or all of the leaves. These little added extras will make the picture your very own. When all the free machine embroidery stitching has been completed, use a small, soft, clean brush to remove the tailor's chalk marks and then press the picture with a hot steam iron.

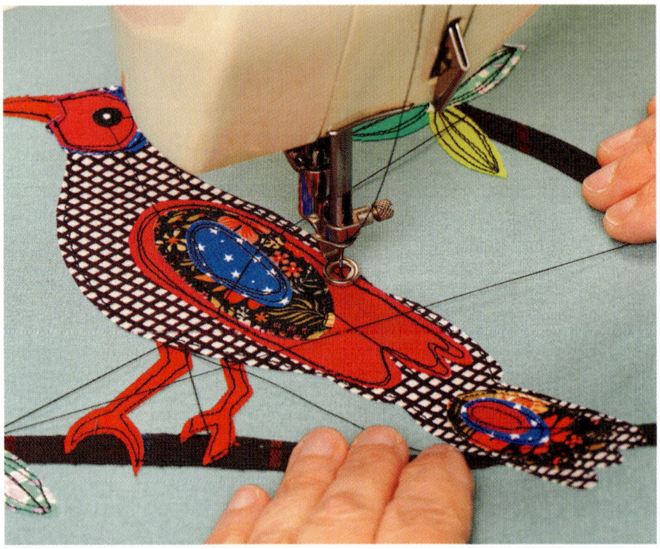

Using black thread, draw with the stitch line approximately 3mm in from the outside edge.

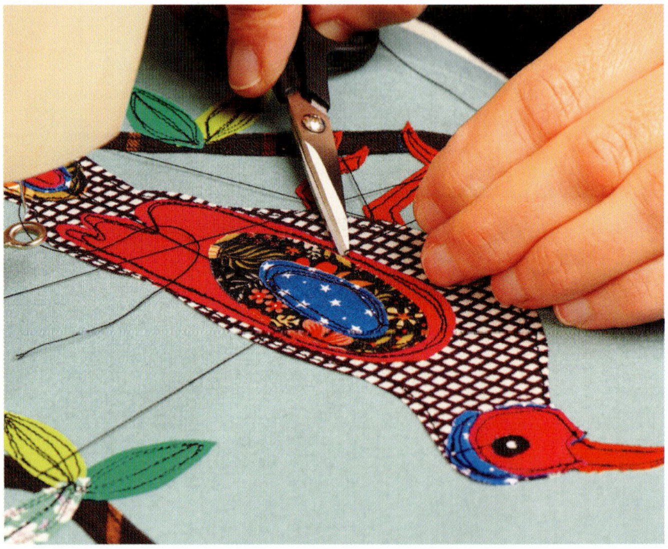

Every thread that has been carried over needs to be cut away from the fabric surface.

HANDY HINT PRACTICE MAKES PERFECT

You may find it helpful to create a sample collage of fabric appliqué, using the steps above, on which to practise your free machine embroidery stitching. You can use the scrap remains from your picture to do this and practise stitching by following near to the edge of the shapes. You will find that by working on a practice piece first, you will be more confident with the embellishing of your bird of paradise.

8 PREPARING THE PICTURE FOR MOUNTING AND FRAMING

In order to fit the frame and its backing board, the completed picture needs to measure 27 × 27cm (10¾ × 10¾in). Using the tape measure, ensuring the image is central, measure the picture and mark with the tailor's chalk. Then cut away the excess calico. Thread up your sewing machine with the pale grey sewing thread and ensure you have the bobbin to match.

Fit an ordinary sewing foot, raise the feed dog teeth and set your sewing machine to a zigzag stitch. Zigzag around the outside edge of your picture. This will reduce the fraying of the outside edge and make it easier to frame the piece. Press the picture with a hot iron once more. For presentation and framing, see Chapter 9.

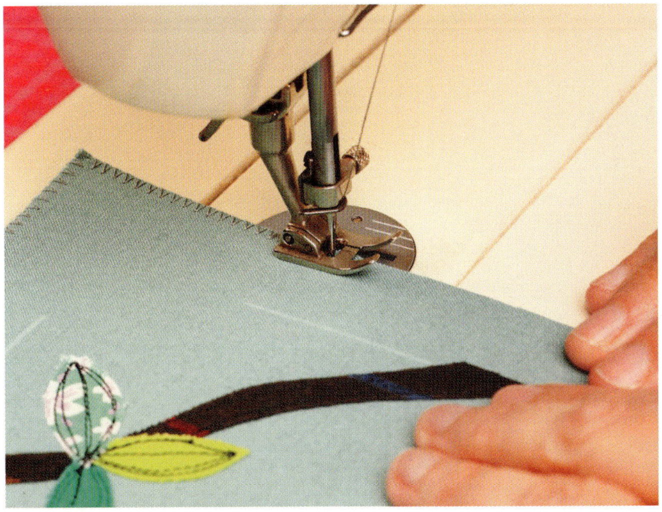

Use a grey thread and a zigzag stitch to finish off the picture's edges before framing it.

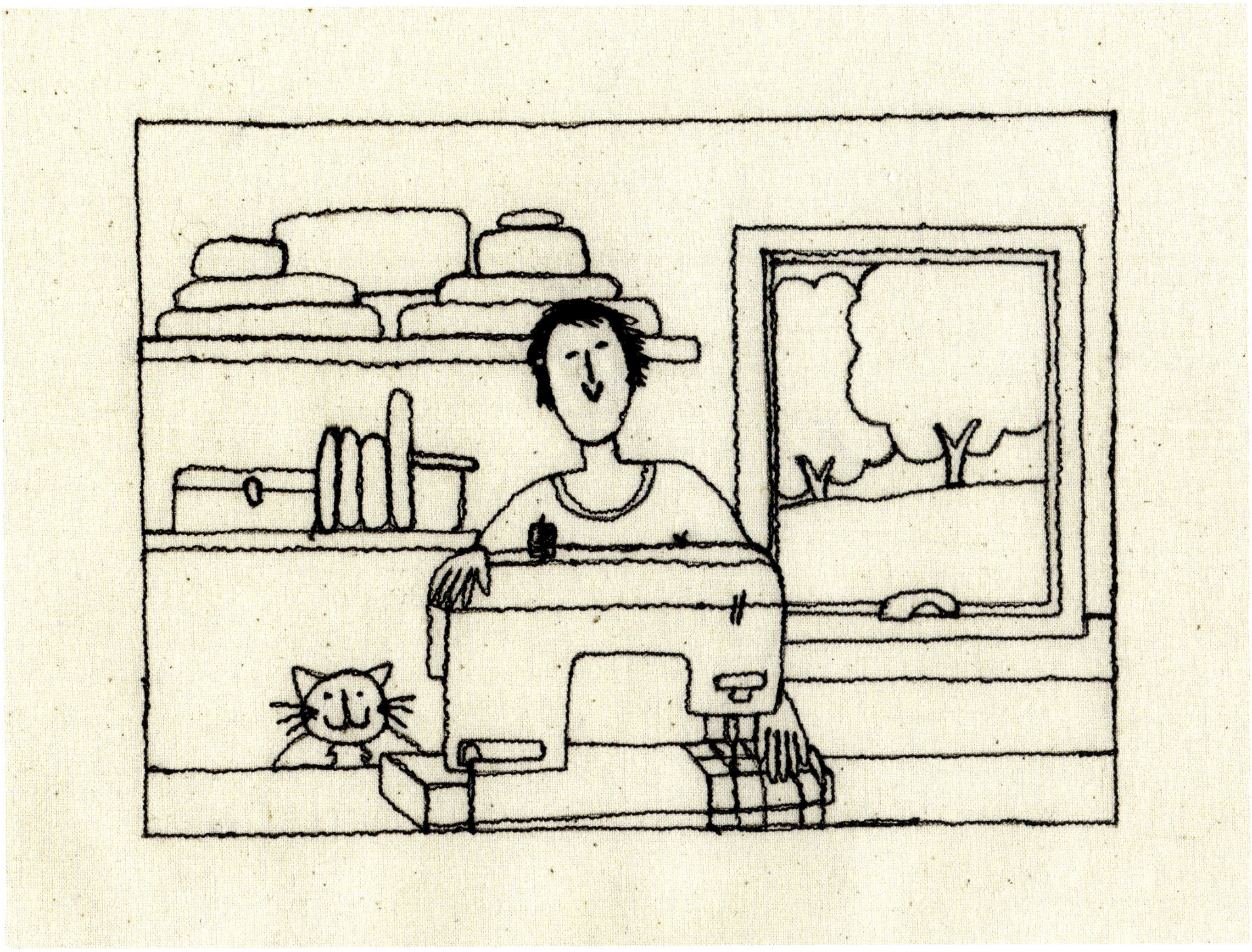

A Happy Place by Linda Miller, 12 x 17cm (5 x 6½in), free machine embroidery. (Photo: Michael Jennings)

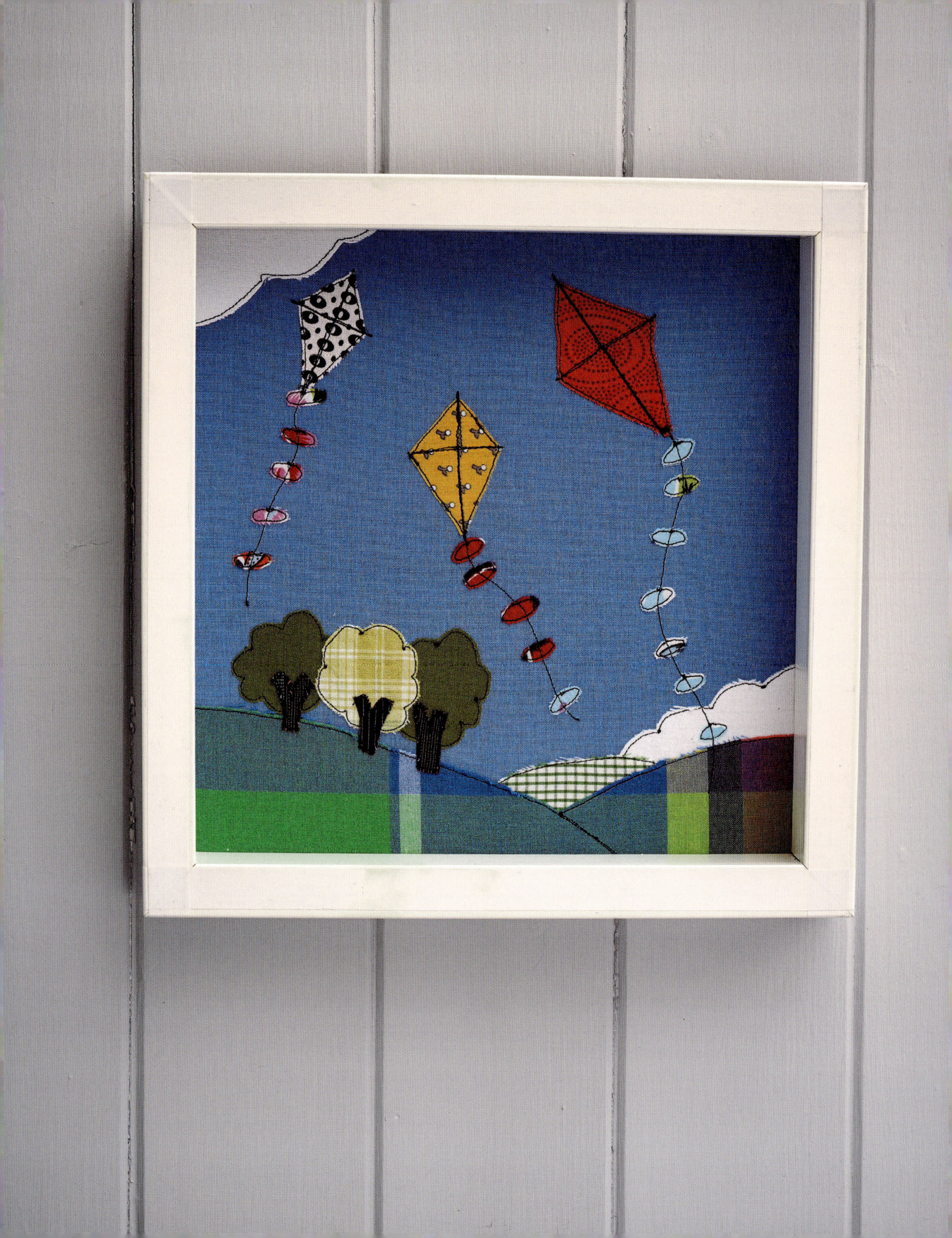

CHAPTER 7

DRAWING AND DESIGN

PICTURE PROJECT
Colourful Kites – Reverse Fabric Appliqué

We can all draw and we know this because as children we drew pictures and didn't think anything of it – we loved drawing and were proud of our work! Although as we age we may become a little shyer of expressing ourselves creatively through the medium of drawing, it is never too late to rediscover the enthusiasm of our younger selves. Drawing or sketching is a very expressive medium that we can use to explore the world around us. Use the practice for capturing inspiration and ideas that you can explore and develop in your sewn images by using your sewing machine as a drawing tool. The medium of reverse fabric appliqué provides a quick, satisfying and surprising way to realize your ideas and drawings.

Our everyday surroundings provide a wealth of things to see, study and sketch that we can use in our creative textile work. Whether you are a beginner or wish you had stronger drawing skills, keeping a sketchbook and developing a daily sketching practice will enable you to grow your confidence in creating drawings from observation. You may find it challenging at first, but you will begin to appreciate your own personal style and follow your intuition within your drawings, so be brave and stick with it!

A good starting point is a still life, which provides an excellent way of engaging with the medium of drawing. For centuries, artists have drawn from still life and continue to do so. Traditionally commonplace items such as fruit, flowers,

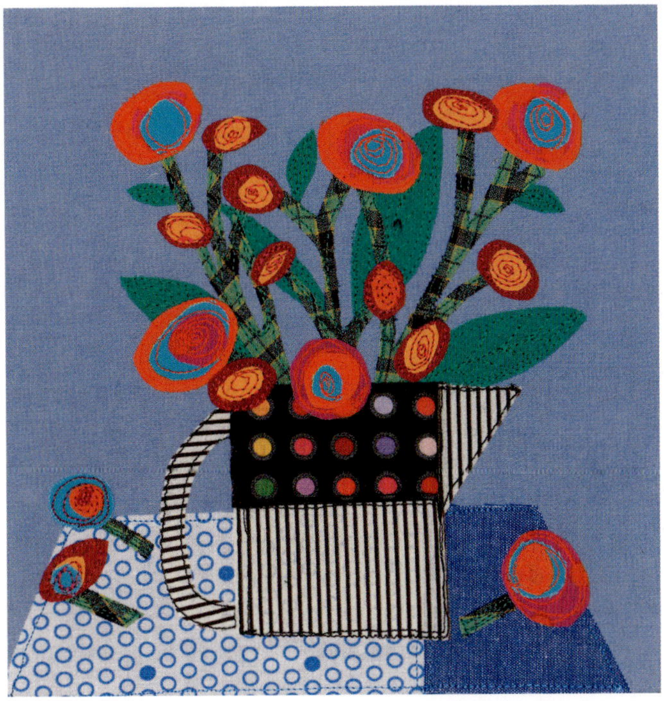

Spotty and Stripy Jug by Linda Miller, 25 × 25cm (10 × 10in), fabric appliqué and free machine embroidery.

glasses, books and patterned cloth in a variety of contrasting shapes, sizes and textures are placed in an arrangement to be studied. Looking in this way makes one consider and question the relationship between all the grouped objects. Once you have made your arrangement, start by capturing on paper with

◀ *Colourful Kites,* presented and framed in a wooden box frame.

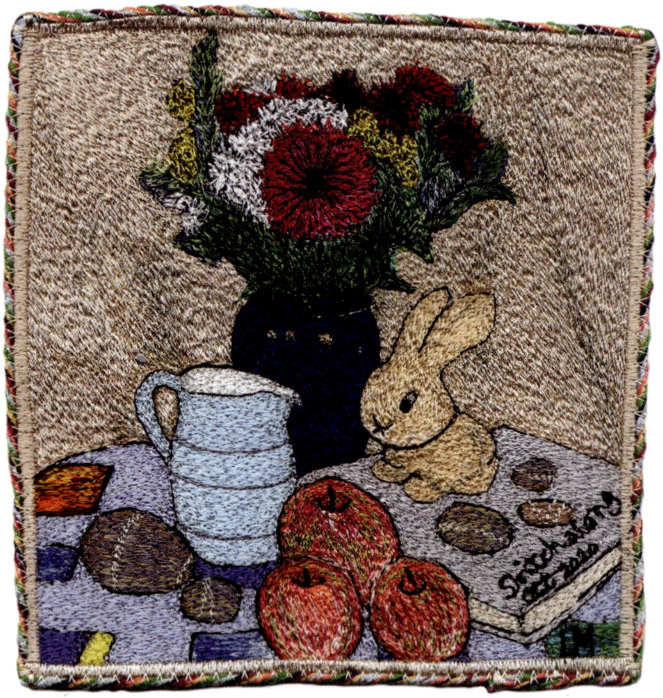

Still Life Stitch Along by Linda Miller, 15 × 15cm (6 × 6in), free machine embroidery. (Photo: Michael Jennings)

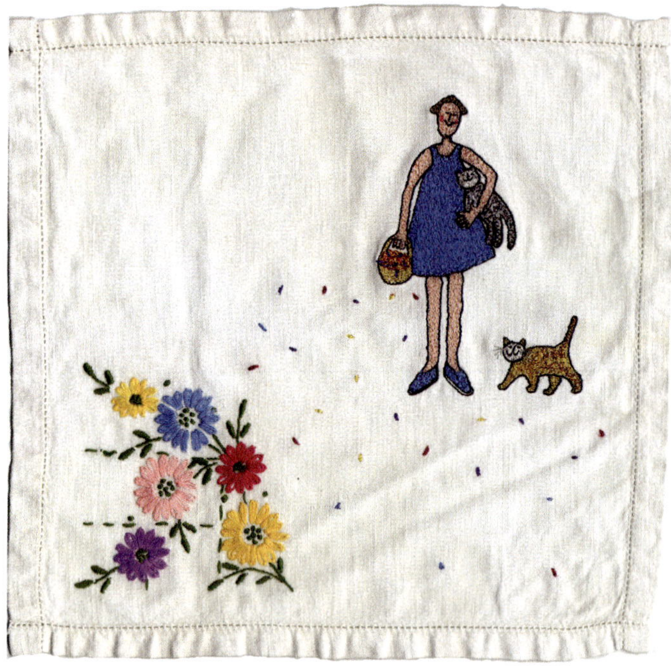

Flower Basket by Linda Miller, 30 × 30cm (12 × 12in), free machine embroidery and hand embroidery on linen cloth. (Photo: Michael Jennings)

a pencil the correct perspective of the grouping. To realize this perspective, simplify the objects into a series of shapes, taking into consideration their height, width, depth and position in relation to one another. It may be challenging at first, but with practice comes confidence and a better understanding of what you are looking at and how to record it. You will be surprised by how quickly you become absorbed by the still life itself and your drawing. If you feel daunted at the prospect of attempting to capture a still life arrangement, why not start with an apple? Make a quick sketch of it, do not worry about the outcome and enjoy the freedom of mark making.

The vista from our windows can also make an excellent subject to study all year round, as the seasons change and provide a different view of the same scene. Whether a rural aspect or a more urban cityscape, our familiar surroundings provide us with a wealth of subject matter to observe and record, and may even provide inspiration for a fabric picture. You will notice how the light changes at different times of the day and year and in doing so creates atmosphere for us to capture in our drawings. As with still life, you need to be looking at the relationship of the object that you are observing, such as a tree or lamp post, with what it stands next to. Looking through your sketchbook, you will notice how with each drawing your practice has naturally developed and improved.

Observing a friend or partner watching television or reading is the perfect opportunity to practise capturing the human form. Again, you need to focus on the detail of what you are looking at: the shape of their head, the length of their arms and how they are sitting. Practice will undoubtedly reveal a greater understanding of the complexities of drawing people and, again, this subject matter should get easier with each undertaking. The same can be said for drawing pets too (preferably when they are asleep!)

Taking a sketchbook with you wherever you go will allow you to record any inspiration you find while out and about. For example, you may come across an everyday object that captures your interest, such as an unusual art deco jug, or see a rural vista that you want to sketch as you feel it may lend itself to being developed into a fabric picture. It is easy to quickly sketch the object or view in question and make a few notes about any interesting features such as colouring, patterning and how the light falls upon it. You will find a wide selection of

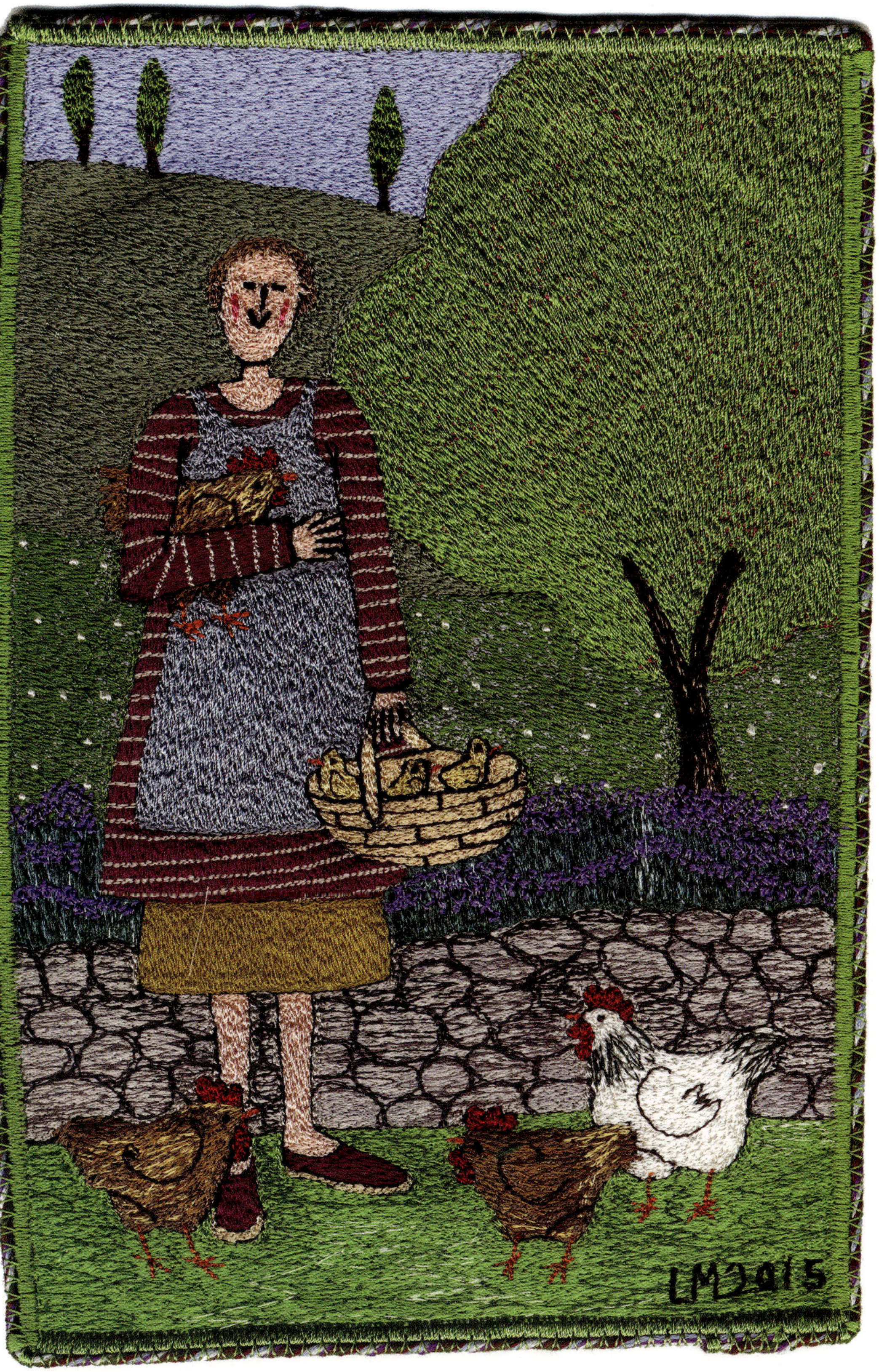

A Basket Full of Chicks by Linda Miller, 23 × 17cm (9 × 6¾in), free machine embroidery. (Photo: Michael Jennings)

sketchbooks and portable drawing materials readily available in your local stationers or art supply shop. For simplicity and ease, why not start with a couple of standard graphite drawing pencils and a small selection of coloured pencils, together with a small sketchbook? These are all you need to capture those inspirations.

Although not as portable as a sketchbook and pencil, your sewing machine can be used just as effectively as a drawing tool. When incorporating different fabrics and coloured threads into your creative textile work, you can achieve a painterly approach. A sketch can easily be transferred onto fabric by redrawing the image using an air-soluble pen before embellishing with stitch. Drawing directly onto fabric with machine stitch requires concentration and good hand-to-eye coordination, and using a continuous stitched line is a valuable exercise for us to improve the skill of looking and recording.

Whatever materials we choose and whatever techniques we put into practice, it is our own individual style and approach that will ultimately give us a unique body of creative work. In Chapter 6, the use of fabric appliqué in the picture project was relatively controlled: the fabric pieces were cut out, adhered to the background with a fusible fabric and then enhanced with a drawn stitch line. In the *Colourful Kites* project, the technique of fabric appliqué is used once more but with a more intuitive approach. The method used here is called reverse fabric appliqué, and although as before it is a layered approach, this time the layers are unseen while they are being stitched into. Assorted fabric pieces are placed on the front of the base fabric and are attached by a free machine stitched line. This stitching follows an initial drawing that has been first applied to the reverse side of the base fabric to create the illustration. Once the fabric shapes have been stitched on, any waste material is trimmed away to reveal the picture imagery. This technique provides a spontaneous result, as while stitching you are not necessarily aware of the colour and pattern outcome in your picture. Spontaneity can provide us with an exciting, freeing experience of image-making and sometimes gives surprising results, which in turn can naturally change the direction that we take our work in.

As in the previous chapter, using fabric appliqué is a very satisfying way to use up leftover pieces of fabric in a variety of sizes and shapes that we may otherwise struggle to use. For best results, always use 100 per cent cotton fabric pieces that can withstand a hot iron, making the picture easier to press as it is assembled. This picture project begins with making a fused fabric background before adding layers of unbonded fabric pieces. The layering makes the perfect surface on which to draw with free machine stitch on both sides of the fabric, without the need for an embroidery hoop.

The reverse fabric appliqué technique allows the freedom to work intuitively. Using a selection of patterned and plain coloured fabrics together with drawing in stitch onto the reverse of the work results in a surprising but deceptively simple landscape scene in which colourful kites dance in a gentle summer breeze. Simply framed, this project will make a beautiful work of art.

The finished picture will fit a frame that measures 25 × 25cm (10 × 10in).

With this project, you will be sewing on both the back and front.

You can opt to use similar colours, as in this example, or, of course, choose your own. Patterned and plain cotton fabrics in a selection of colours will suit this picture project.

The measurements for the *Colourful Kites* drawing are an approximate guide size. You may choose to make your imagery slightly bigger or smaller; whatever you decide, make sure that your imagery finishes at least 3cm (1¼in) from each side of the background fabric edge to allow the picture to sit comfortably without the frame cutting into the imagery.

If you choose to alter the size of your fabric appliqué picture, you will require a different size frame than the instructions for this picture project recommend.

It is important that all drawn lines on the fabric do not smudge or bleed – to ensure this doesn't happen, use a permanent marker pen and not a pencil or biro.

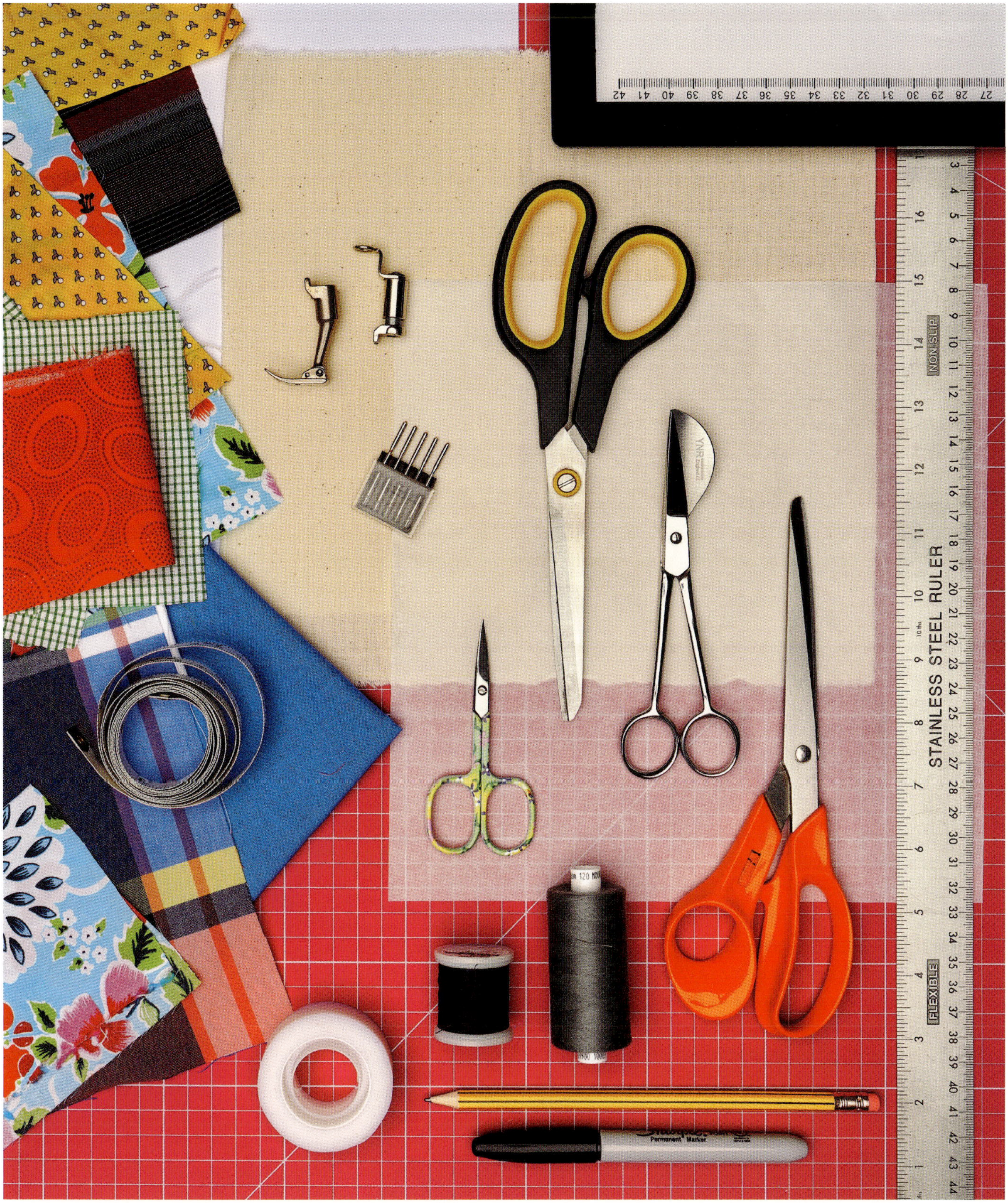

A selection of materials needed to make the picture project, *Colourful Kites*.

PICTURE PROJECT: *COLOURFUL KITES*

The Landscape Simplified

This picture project makes effective use of perspective. Positioning the countryside at the bottom of the picture allows for a big sky to be portrayed above it – perfect for the three brightly coloured kites to fly in. The scenery consists of three rolling hills that have been created using two pieces of different fabric: one striped piece in the foreground, which has been made into two by using a dividing stitch line, and a third hill in a contrasting fabric behind.

The picture is balanced by two clouds that are positioned diagonally across from each other: one in the top left and the other in the bottom right. To give a greater feeling of depth, the lower cloud is half hidden by the rolling hills. A group of three trees sits on the left hill with the same coloured trunks and with canopies in two complementary coloured materials. Each shape within this group is very easy to draw, and like all the picture projects in this book, once the shapes have been realized it is your selection of fabric that will make the picture complete, unique and personal to you.

YOU WILL NEED

Items from the basic tool kit, as listed in Chapter 1 Tools and Equipment, and the following materials:

- Piece of fusible fabric measuring 27 × 27cm (10¾ × 10¾in)
- Piece of lightweight calico measuring 30 × 30cm (12 × 12in)
- Eleven pieces of fabric in a selection of sizes and colours for the clouds, trees, hills and kites, either in your own choice of colours or as a suggestion:
  - Sky background: mid blue measuring 27 × 27cm (10¾ × 10¾in)
  - Clouds: white
  - Tree canopies: two different greens in a mixture of patterned and plain
  - Tree trunks: one shade of dark brown, either patterned or plain
  - Hills: two shades, one plain one stripy
  - Kites: three different colours with small printed patterned fabric
  - Kite tails: one multicoloured large printed patterned fabric
- Spool of black machine embroidery/machine sewing thread
- Spool of mid grey sewing thread
- Piece of good-quality mount board in a neutral colour, cut to the size of the frame's recess
- Unglazed box frame measuring 25 × 25cm (10 × 10in)

1 GETTING STARTED

On a sheet of paper and using a pencil, draw out a square box that measures 24 × 24cm (9½ × 9½in). Take your chosen frame apart and carefully lay the front of the frame onto the drawn square so that the square is central.

Using the pencil, mark the inside of the frame recess onto the paper. Any imagery drawn outside of this box will be hidden by the frame, but to avoid the abrupt end of the picture within the frame, allow a little of the background imagery to bleed outside of this box. Draw the hills, clouds, trees and kites, following the instructions given in the Handy Hints.

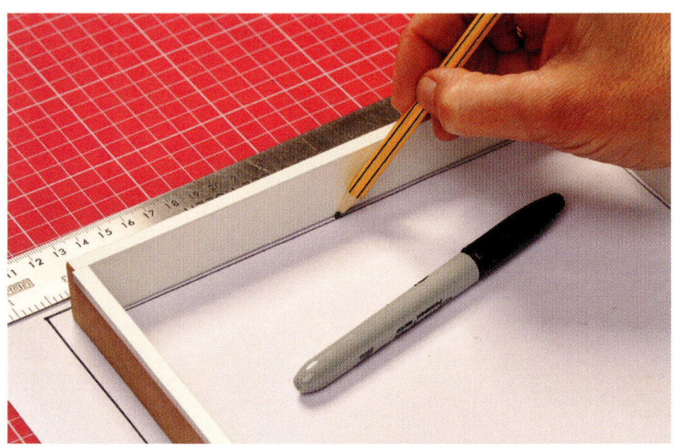

Centrally place the frame's recess in a box measuring 24 × 24cm (9½ × 9½in) and mark with a pencil.

HANDY HINT DRAWING THE HILLS

Begin by drawing the hills, which will be situated at the bottom of the picture. One hill will measure approximately 6 × 17cm (2½ × 6¾in) and the other 5 × 12cm (2 × 4¾in). Using a ruler, measure 6cm (2½in) vertically from the bottom left-hand side of the outside box (that is the 24cm/9½in square drawn box) and mark with a pencil. Then measure 5cm (2in) vertically from the bottom right-hand side and make another mark. Once these marks have been made, from the left-hand edge measure along the bottom outside line and mark off 12cm (4¾in) and then 17cm (6¾in).

Place your pencil on the 6cm (2½in) vertical mark on the left-hand edge and, going from left to right, draw a semicircle, ending up at the bottom pencil mark at 17cm (6¾in). Next place your pencil on the right-hand vertical mark and draw another semicircle from right to left, finishing up at the bottom 12cm (4¾in) mark. You now have two hills. Where they meet, you will create a third hill in the distance. To create this hill, draw another semicircle measuring approximately 2cm (¾in) in height from the dip and 7cm (2¾in) from one hill to the other. There are now three hills.

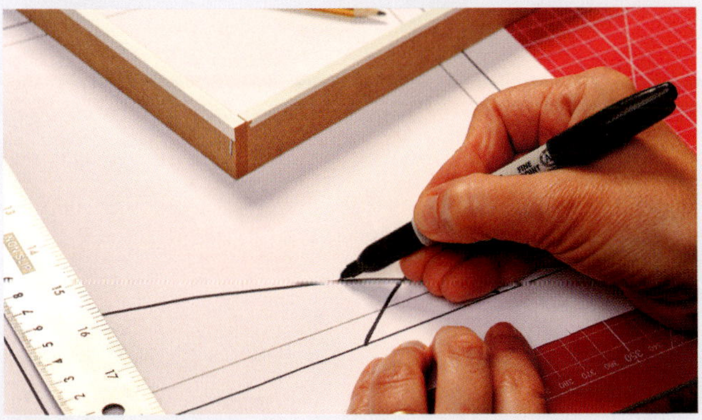

Draw out three hills before going over the pencil lines using a permanent marker pen.

HANDY HINT DRAWING THE CLOUDS

Next draw two fluffy clouds. Concentrating on the bottom cloud first, from the bottom right-hand corner make an 8cm (3¼in) vertical mark. Then, placing your pencil on the distant hill, draw four little semicircles, ending up at the 8cm (3¼in) mark. This will create the first cloud.

In the top left-hand corner measure down 4cm (1½in) and make a mark, and then make a horizontal mark from the left-hand side of 8cm (3¼in). Using three little semicircle shapes, join up these two measurements to create the second cloud.

HANDY HINT DRAWING THE TREES

To complete the landscape, draw a row of three trees on the left-hand hill. Draw three circles that overlap each other, approximately 3cm (1¼in) away from the left-hand side and 1cm (⅜in) away from the top of the hill. Each circle needs to measure approximately 4cm (1½in).

To create the tree shape, draw a series of small semicircles over each of the circles and then erase the circles, leaving the tree shape behind. Each tree canopy will be attached to the hillside by a Y shape, representing the tree's trunk.

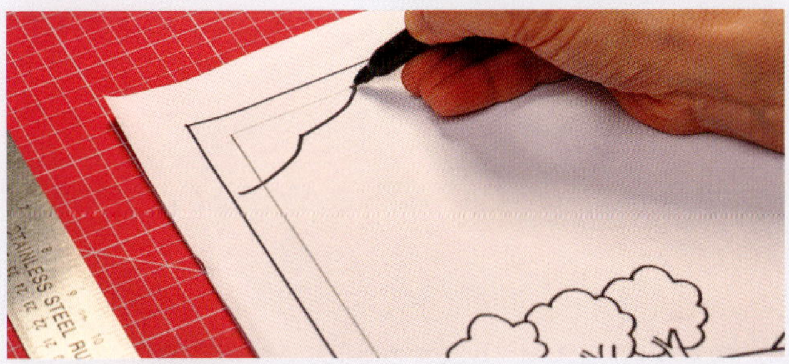

Two fluffy clouds and three trees are needed to make the landscape complete.

HANDY HINT DRAWING THE KITES

The last components needed to complete the picture are the kites. On a separate piece of paper, draw out three kites in varying sizes with long swirling tails.

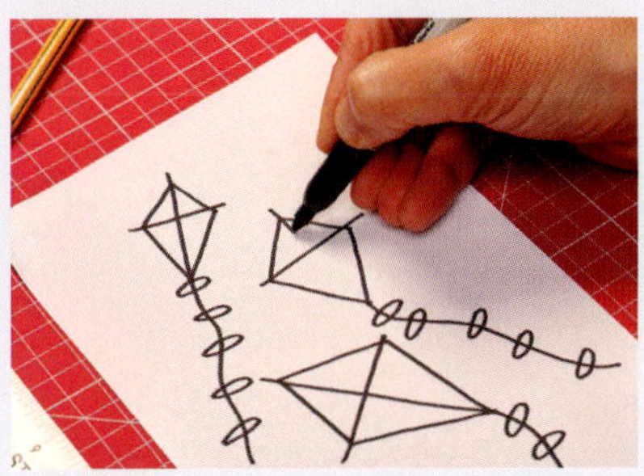

On a separate piece of paper, draw out three kites and their tails, which all vary in size.

2 ADDING THE KITES TO THE COMPOSITION

Once you are happy with your kites, cut them out and place each one onto your drawing. Move them around until you are content with their placement within the composition and then stick each one down using sticky tape. Use black permanent marker pen to trace over the entire pencil drawing, including the inside and outside boxes, then write 'front' at the top of this image. Turn the drawing over and place it on the lightbox and again trace over the entire drawing and box, writing 'back' at the top. Put the drawing to one side.

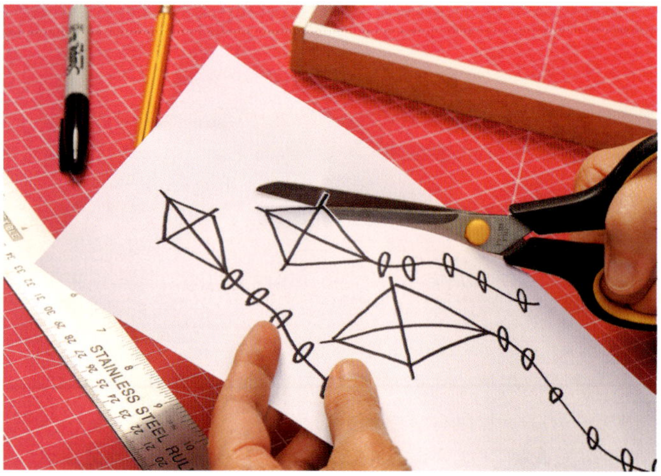

Carefully cut around the drawn outline of each kite using sharp paper scissors.

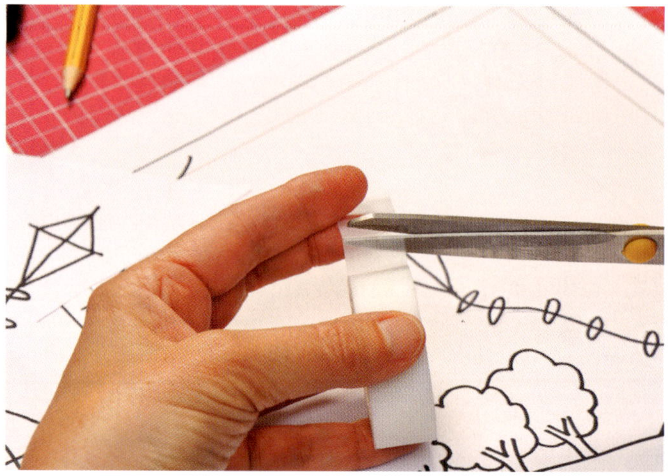

Lay the three kites in place and, when happy with the arrangement, stick them down.

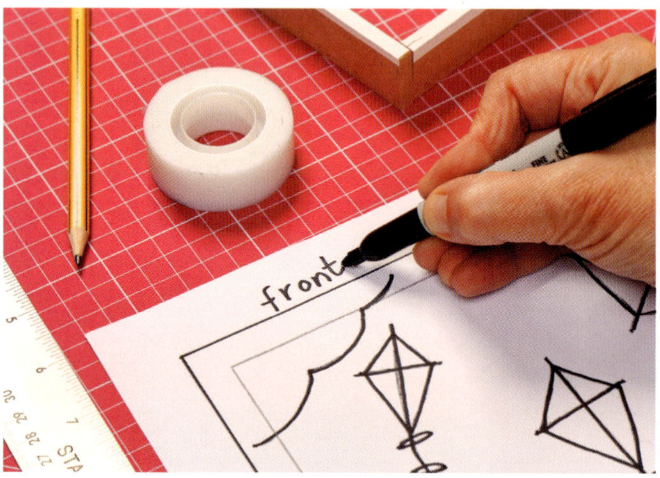

Trace over the drawing with a black marker pen and write 'front' at the top.

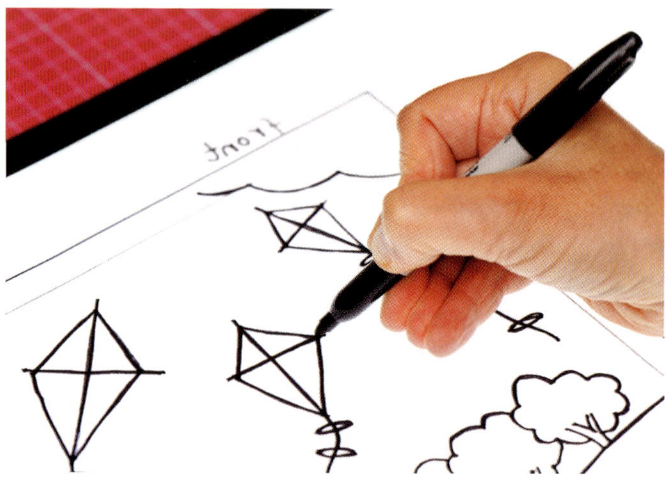

With the 'front' side down, trace the image through and write 'back' at the top.

3 CHOOSING YOUR COLOURS

From your fabric stash, pull out a selection of cotton materials in a variety of colours and patterns. Eleven different fabrics will be needed in total; these will be for the sky, clouds, hills, trees, kites and the kites' tails. The principal colour will be for the sky, so you will need a larger piece of fabric for this measuring 27 × 27cm (10¾ × 10¾in). For inspiration on choosing fabric and colours refer to Chapter 6 Handy Hint: Choosing a palette of colourful fabric scraps to work with. When the selected fabrics have been chosen, press them, along with the piece of calico for the backing, to remove any creases.

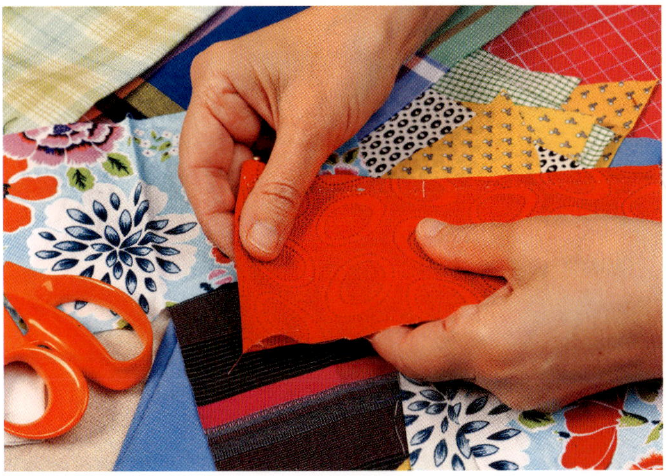

Eleven fabrics in contrasting colours and patterns are needed for the composition.

HANDY HINT BEING INTUITIVE WITH YOUR PALETTE OF COLOURFUL FABRIC SCRAPS

Our instinctive colour choice when making our fabric selection, alongside an element of chance, plays a part in this reverse fabric appliqué technique, and the two together will determine the uniqueness of the resulting colourful picture. The main colour is the sky, and this fabric will set the mood for the illustration. Select a shade that you are most attracted to and that you feel will best complement the other colours within the picture. Note: the sky does not have to be blue, but could be a light grey or orange for a sunset.

For the smaller imagery components, such as the hills, trees and kites, use a selection of printed, patterned and tightly woven fabrics in a variety of both bright and muted shades. As you look at the fabric, turn it to see how the pattern looks upside down or diagonally. Fabric with a subtle mottled effect is great for a large expanse of sky or a collection of clouds. Stripes are good to use for hills, as the direction of the stripe can be an indication of the slope. Small checks and spots make the perfect tree canopy and can give the suggestion of fruit or blossom. Selecting a fabric with a larger print will increase the chance element of any section of the pattern image piece being used and so may give a serendipitous outcome.

HANDY HINT USING FABRIC SCRAPS OF VARYING SIZES

If you feel that any fabric scrap is too big to work with then cut it down to a more manageable size. Alternatively, if you have a couple of pieces of favourite fabric scraps that are too small to work with, you can sew them together. Once sewn, press out the seam to ensure that it lays flat upon the surface of your background fabric, ready to be stitched into place.

4 DRAWING ONTO THE CALICO

Next, place the drawing right side down on the lightbox and lay the calico on the 'back' of the drawing, centring it as you do so. Use a permanent black marker pen to trace off both the drawing and the two marked inside and outside boxes. When completed, remove the calico from the drawing and turn the paper over to reveal the 'front' of the drawing.

The marker pen line on your calico is the line that you will be following with stitch. Although you will be stitching and working on the 'back' of your calico, it is the front where the picture will be made, so keep your paper drawing for reference and put it to one side or pin it up on your mood board where you can see it clearly. With the drawing on the calico face down and using the tailor's chalk, trace the outside edge line through so that the 'front' of the calico piece has a box drawn upon it in tailor's chalk.

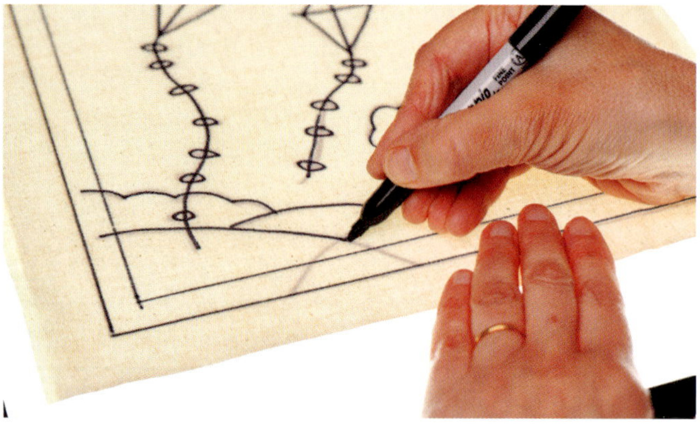

Lay the drawing right side down on the lightbox and trace it through onto the calico.

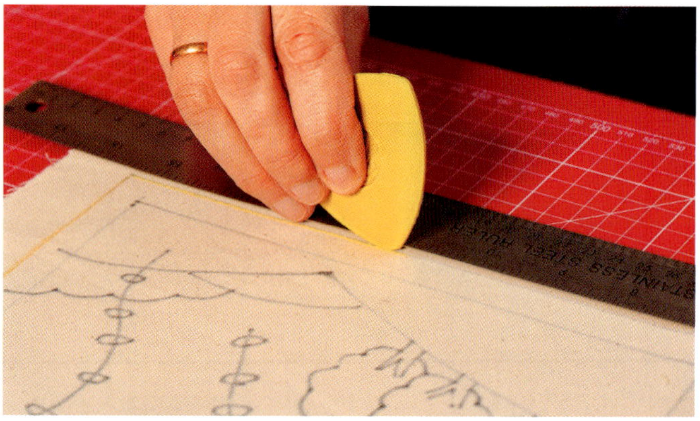

A piece of tailor's chalk is used to mark the outside edge on the front of the calico.

5 PREPARING THE BACKGROUND FABRIC

For instructions on how to use the fusible fabric, refer to Chapter 6, Handy Hint: How to use fusible fabric. Iron the piece of fusible fabric onto the back of the sky-coloured fabric. When it has cooled, cut around the outside edge and peel away the paper. Place the fabric onto the middle of the piece of calico, adhesive side down, using the tailor's chalk markings as reference – when centrally placed, the fabric will fit 1.5cm (¾in) over the markings. This layered and bonded fabric is the base of your picture. The line drawing is on the 'back' and the sky-coloured fabric is already on the 'front'.

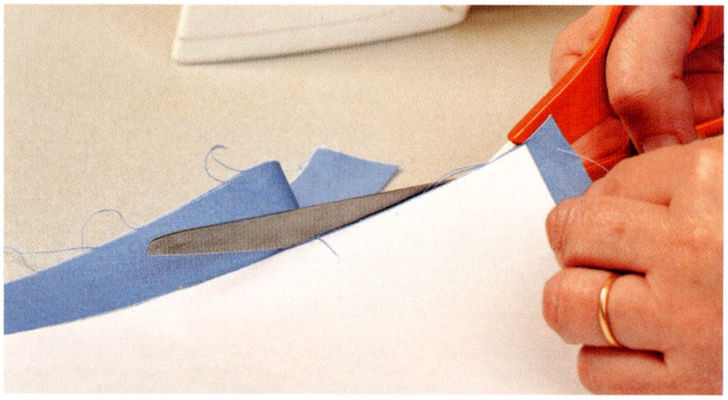

Once the fusible fabric has cooled, cut around the outside edge of the paper.

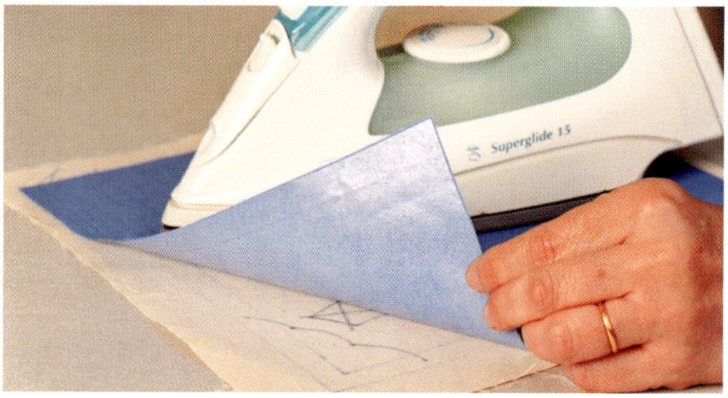

Iron down the fusible sky-coloured fabric, using the tailor's chalk markings as reference.

HANDY HINT **LAYERING THE FABRICS AND STITCHING INTO PLACE**

Building a picture in fabric appliqué requires each piece to be laid down and stitched into place in strict sequence. For instance, in this picture, when looking at the landscape you can see that the object we have drawn furthest in the distance is the cloud on the horizon. This fabric piece is the first piece to be laid down on top of the sky-coloured fabric base. Any objects that are in the foreground are applied last, such as the kites and their tails.

When working with reverse fabric appliqué, any picture component that has another piece of fabric overlapping it – for instance where the two hills meet – requires the first piece of applied fabric to be made a little bigger, along with a slightly extended stitch line to secure the piece in place. This means the first fabric piece is partially hidden underneath the next piece of applied fabric, which is placed on top of it. Utilizing this process will create a neater fabric edge and means only a single line of stitch is visible, together giving the overall picture depth and a greater sense of perspective.

6 STARTING TO STITCH THE FABRIC SCRAPS IN PLACE

Thread up your sewing machine with the black thread and place a wound bobbin of the same colour into the machine. Fit the free machine embroidery foot and lower the feed dog teeth, then follow the instructions in Chapter 3, Step 4. An embroidery hoop is not required for the free machine embroidery stitch in this project, as the fabric layers are stiff enough to be worked on without any difficulty or puckering of the fabric.

Starting with the cloud image at the bottom of your drawing, place the chosen fabric scrap right side up over this area on the front of the sky-coloured fabric, aiming to line it up with the drawn image on the 'back'. This fabric scrap needs to sit in the middle of the cloud shape, with about 1–2cm ($\frac{3}{8}$–$\frac{3}{4}$in) of excess fabric around the outside edge of the cloud shape. Once positioned, press with a hot iron – this action will not adhere it to the base fabric but will cause a little static, which will help to keep it in place.

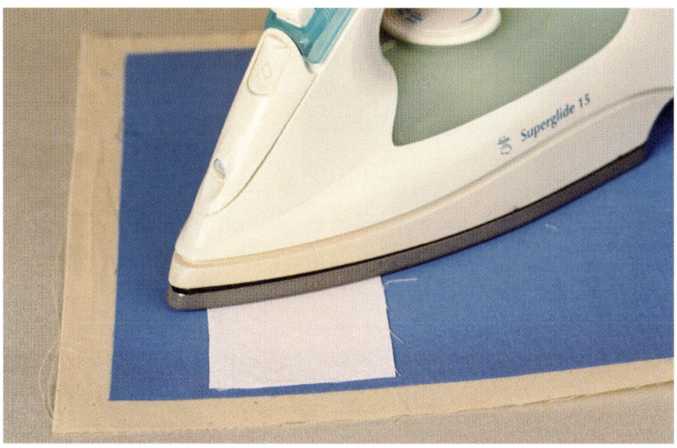

Place the white cloud on the background fabric and iron it to make the fabrics static.

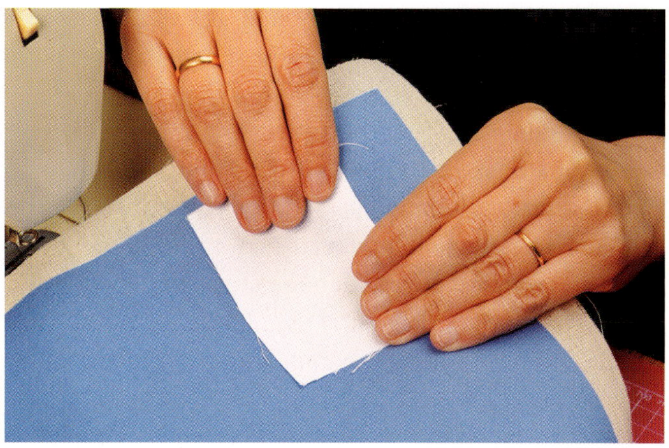

Hold the fabric in place before turning it over, so the back of the fabric is facing you.

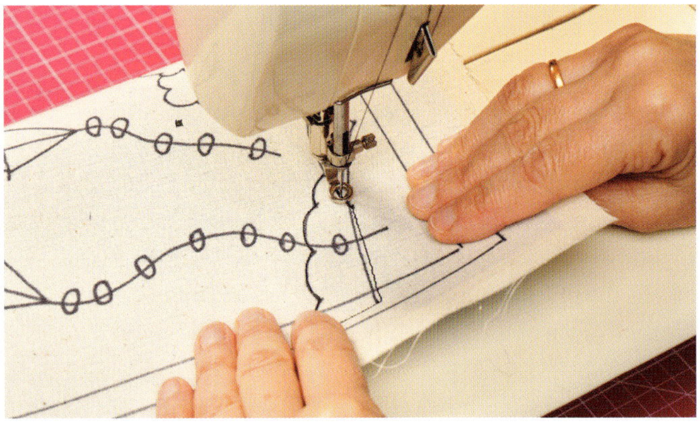

Using black thread and a free machine embroidery stitch, follow the marker pen line.

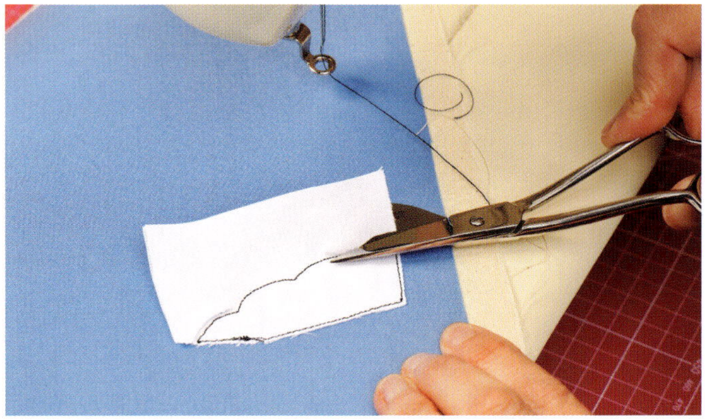

Carefully cut away the outside of the cloud shape with the paddle scissors.

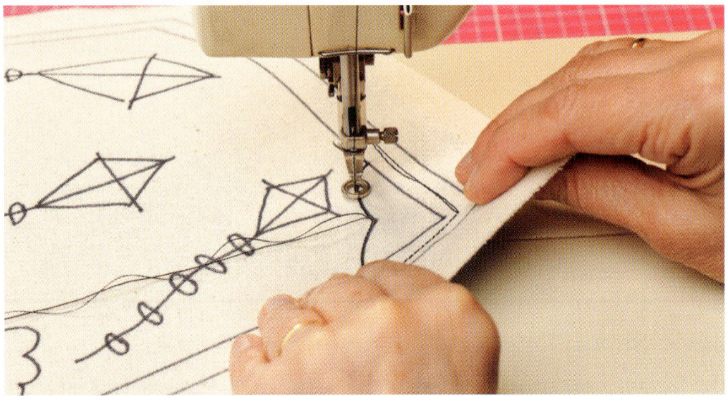

With the second piece of white fabric in place, follow the outline of the cloud shape.

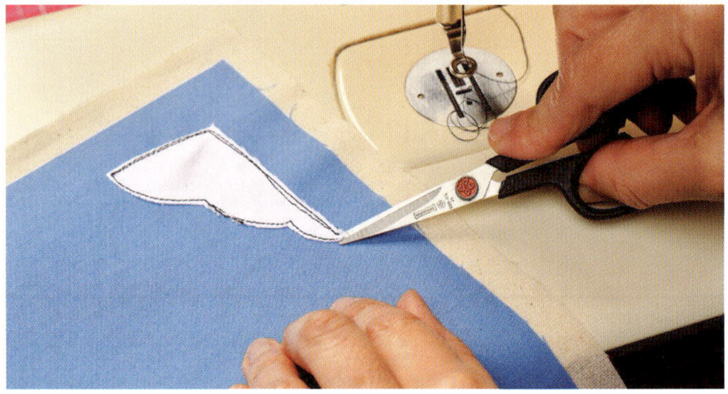

Any small, sharp scissors can be used as an alternative to paddle scissors.

Carefully place the layered fabrics face down under the sewing machine foot, with the 'back' of the fabric facing you. Using a free machine embroidery stitch, follow the black marker line that goes around the cloud, as well as the corner of the outside box. You can choose to stitch over these lines once or twice.

When completed, cut away both the top and bottom threads and turn over the base fabric. You will see that the stitch line on the fabric appliqué resembles the drawn line on your paper drawing. Press this shape with the hot iron and then, using paddle scissors, carefully cut away the excess fabric from around the outside edge of the cloud.

Be sure to leave a wider border along the bottom of the cloud, as explained above in Handy Hint: Layering the fabrics and stitching into place. Pay attention not to cut into the actual picture. Do not be concerned if the fabric frays a little after the excess has been cut away – this doesn't matter as it is a natural feature of cotton fabric and will add a little extra charm to your finished picture. Press again thoroughly, and repeat the process with the fabric for the second cloud, which is situated at the top of the picture.

HANDY HINT THE COLOUR OF THE DRAWING THREAD

As you will be drawing with stitch on the back of your picture, following the black pen lines, it is the bobbin thread that will show on the front of your picture, along with the fabric appliquéd pieces. Therefore, it is important that your sewing machine is threaded up with black thread, both on the top and in the bobbin, giving a solid line of one colour.

To finish off the stitch drawing you will be briefly drawing with stitch on the front of your picture. To ensure continuity throughout, check that your machine is threaded with the same colour at all times during this reverse fabric appliqué picture project.

7 CREATING THE ROLLING HILLS OF THE LANDSCAPE

The next scraps of fabric to be placed and stitched down are the hills. There are three hills in total: one in the distance and two in the foreground. These comprise two pieces of fabric: one small and one large. The larger piece of fabric has a dividing line sewn through it, making one hill into two.

The hill in the middle distance needs to be placed first. Select the chosen piece of fabric for this hill and iron it in place on the sky-coloured background. Then, using the free machine embroidery stitch, carefully sew along the pen outline on the reverse, which will attach the fabric piece to the base fabric. Be mindful once more to sew slightly over where the cloud meets the landscape, as described in Handy Hint: Layering the fabrics and stitching into place.

Once stitched, cut the waste threads and press the fabric, then carefully cut away the excess fabric from this shape, being cautious to leave a wider border at the bottom of this hill. Iron and place the larger piece of fabric for the two hills in place. If using a patterned fabric, you may want to consider how the direction of the pattern, for instance a gingham fabric placed on the bias, will give a diamond effect, whereas laying horizontally will give a check.

When you are happy with the fabric arrangement, be mindful to sew along the outside box, as well as a few millimetres over the pen line of the drawing where this hill meets the previous one, and along the bottom of the cloud. This will create a neater single line of stitch beneath the cloud and previous hill, creating the effect of a distant landscape setting. Once stitched in place, continue the stitch line from one of the hills to the bottom of the picture; this will create the dividing line of the hills. Press, cutting away the excess fabric, and press once more.

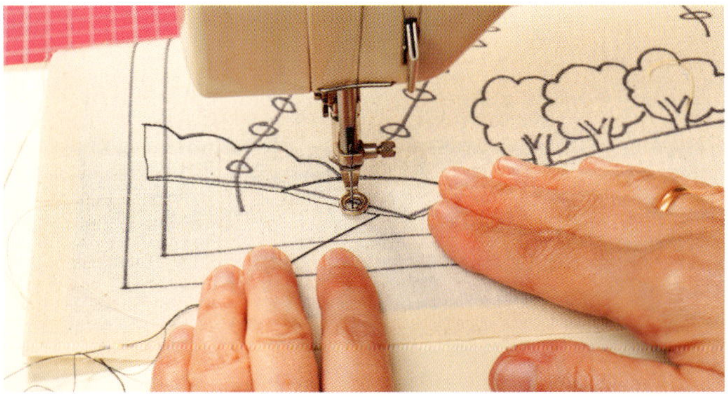

Stitch the side and bottom of the first hill a little bigger when following the drawn line.

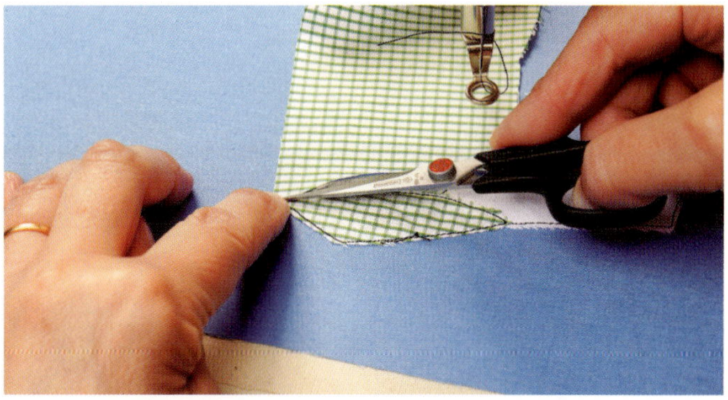

When trimming away the outside of the hill fabric, be mindful not to cut into the cloud.

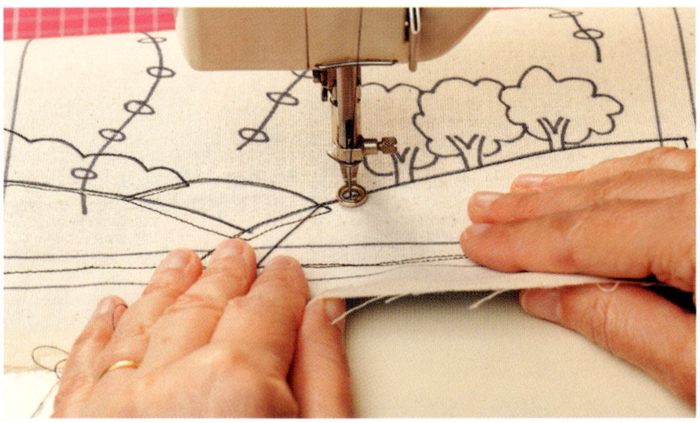

Consider the direction of the fabric pattern before stitching the remaining hills in place.

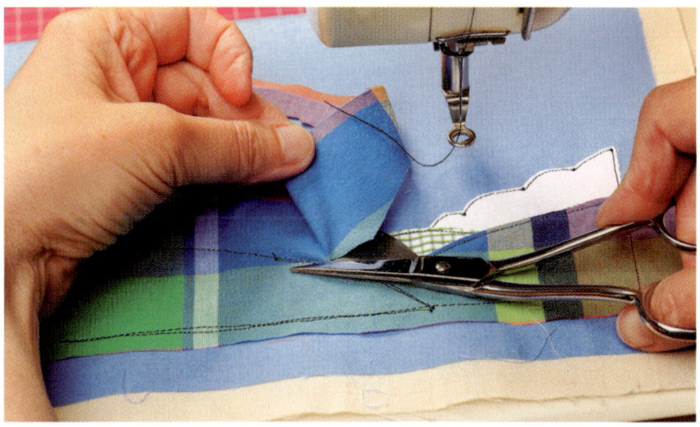

Stitching a dividing line will create two hills out of one, before cutting the fabric away.

8 ADDING THE TREES AND KITES

The fabric scraps used for the trees can be patterned or plain. Again, rotate the fabric pieces to determine the best direction of patterning for the tree canopies. Using the same fabric colour for the two outside trees gives continuity to the little spinney. As before, follow the pen outline to secure the fabric scraps in place with stitch, then cut away the excess fabric and press in readiness for the third tree to be applied. Select your fabric piece for the trunks and repeat the whole process once more.

Do the same for the kites, using three different contrasting colours. For the kite bows, take one piece of your multi-coloured large printed patterned fabric and lay it on the sky. Press it down to adhere a little, then turn the picture over and follow in stitch the line of all the little oval-shaped kite bows. Once completed, cut away the top and bottom threads and turn over. Cut away all the waste fabric, leaving the kite bows in place. Press the work.

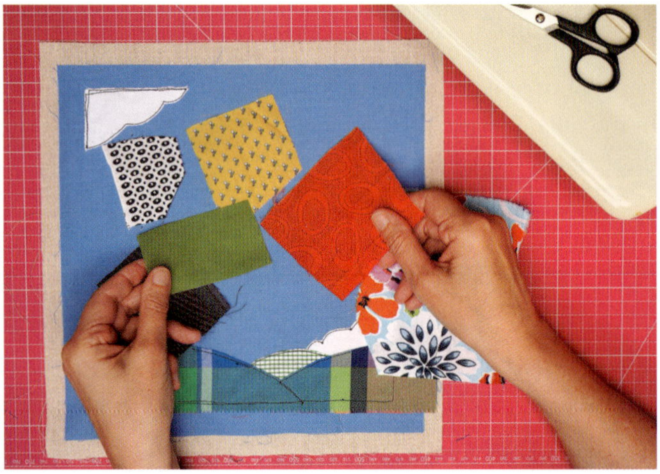

Small prints in bold colours work well together when selecting fabrics for the kites.

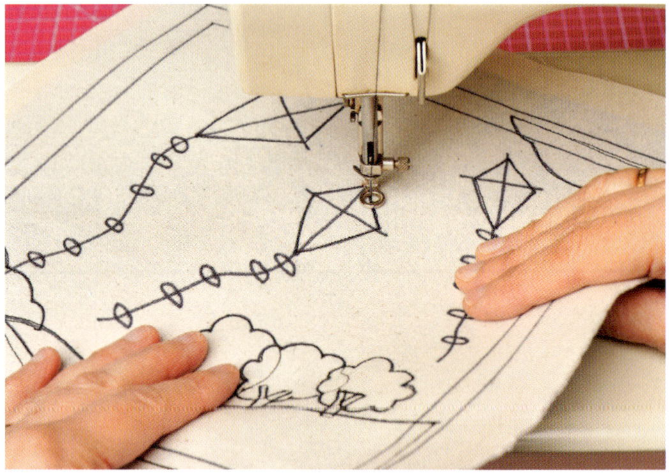

Place the kite-coloured fabric on the 'front' and stitch along the marker pen lines.

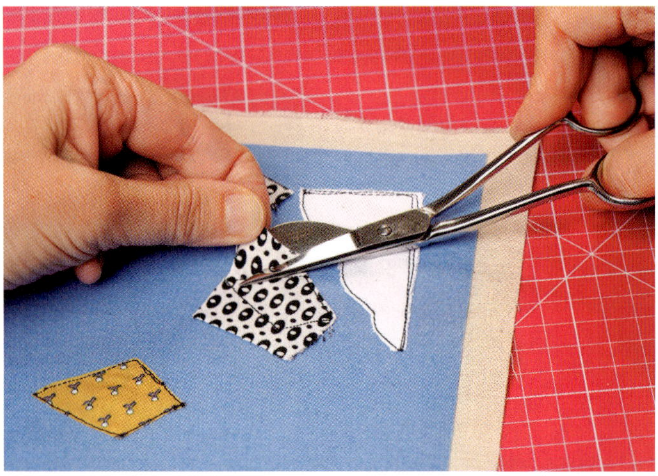

Cutting away the excess fabric reveals the three shapes of the brightly coloured kites.

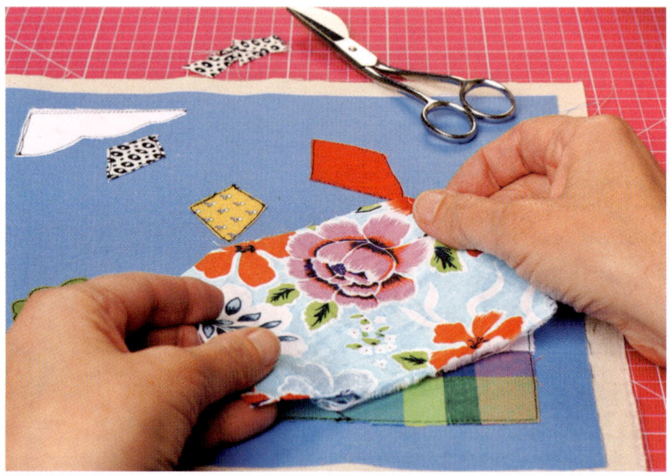

By selecting a large printed colourful fabric, each kite tail can be different in colour.

9 EMBELLISHING WITH STITCH ON THE FRONT OF THE APPLIQUÉ

To enhance and complete the appliqué picture, each colourful kite needs to be embellished with top stitch to denote the kite's structure and complete the kite tails. To achieve this, you will be working on the 'front' of your fabric appliqué picture. To keep continuity throughout the work, continue using black thread top and bottom, as indicated above.

Beginning with the kite on the left, draw with stitch around the kite to suggest its framework before taking the stitch line down through each one of the bows to create the tail. Once all the stitching has been completed, press, and cut away any waste threads. Remember, any fraying is part of the technique and should be celebrated rather than tidied!

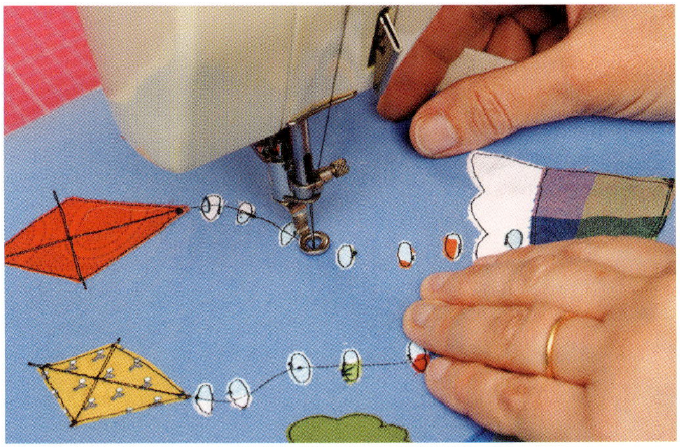

To finish off, top stitch the kite's framework, and then the tail again, using black thread.

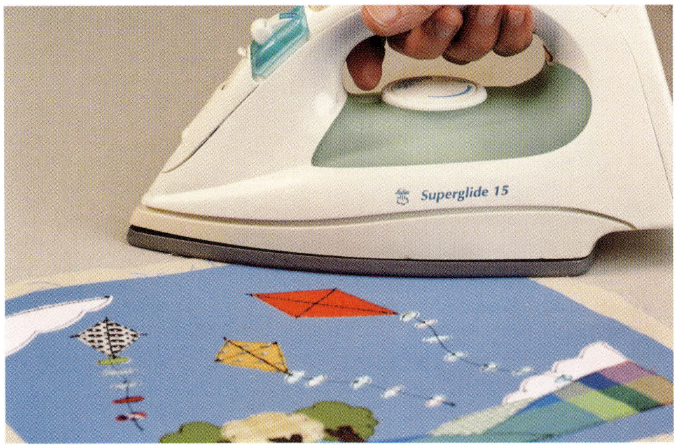

Press, before trimming away any excess fabric, then edge with a zigzag stitch.

10 PREPARING THE PICTURE FOR MOUNTING AND FRAMING

In order to fit the frame and its backing board, the completed picture needs to measure 27 × 27cm (10¾ × 10¾in). Using the tape measure and ensuring the image is central, measure the picture and mark with the tailor's chalk. Then cut away the excess calico.

Thread up your sewing machine with the pale grey sewing thread and ensure you have the bobbin to match. Fit a zigzag sewing foot, raise the feed dog teeth and set your sewing machine to a zigzag stitch. Zigzag around the outside edge of your picture. This will reduce the fraying of the outside edge and make it easier to frame the piece. Press the picture with a hot iron once more. For presentation and framing, see Chapter 9.

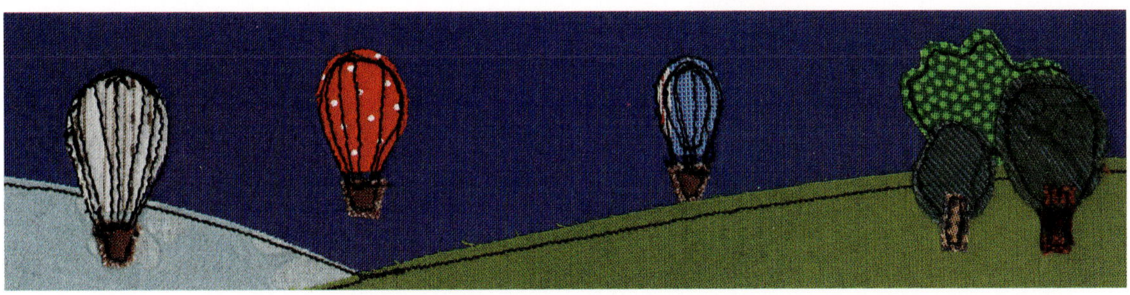

Hot Air Balloons by Linda Miller, 5 × 20cm (2 × 8in), fabric appliqué and free machine embroidery. (Photo: Michael Jennings)

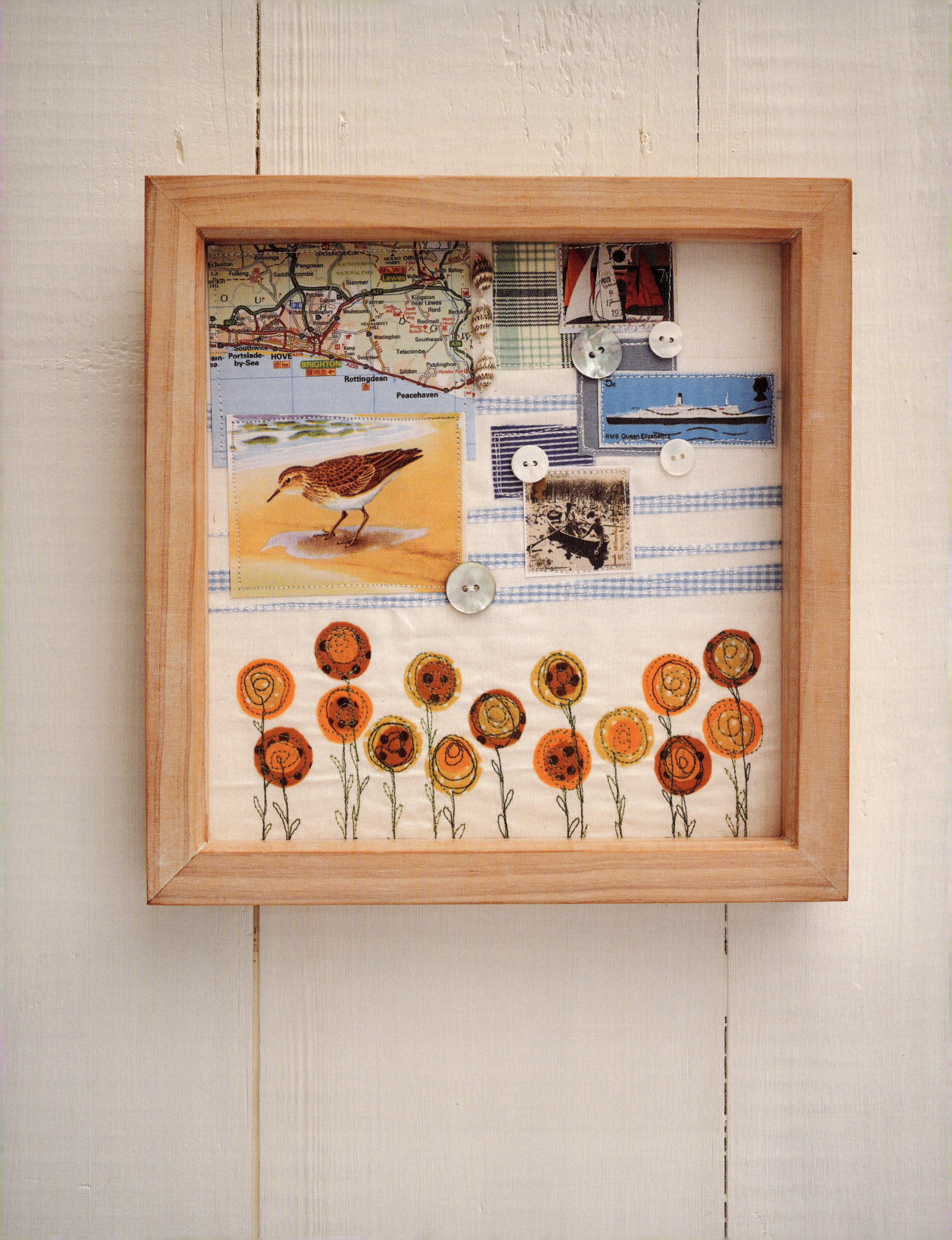
Stanmer
Lewes
Kingston near Lewes
Southwick
Portslade-by-Sea
HOVE
BRIGHTON
Rottingdean
Telscombe
Peacehaven
RMS Queen Elizabeth 2

CHAPTER 8

STYLE, INSPIRATION AND PLACING IMAGERY

PICTURE PROJECT
Seaside Story – Mixed Media, Found Objects and Stitch

We can each celebrate our own creative style, which comes from our individuality. As we increase in confidence in our making skills, this uniqueness develops and becomes more recognizable in our work. As makers, we are naturally influenced by a combination of outside factors, such as the natural world, textiles, art and design. These inspirations, intermingled with our personality and exploration of themes or ideas, create our own unique body of work. As we progress, we can look back on earlier work and see for ourselves how our practice has developed and how it is naturally driven forward by these influences.

Sometimes we need to widen our source of inspiration, for example if we have been asked to make something on a specific theme or colourway for a friend that may sit outside our familiar way of working. The Bloomsbury Group, an artistic movement that formed in the first half of the twentieth century, consisted of artists such as Vanessa Bell, as well as makers, writers and intellectuals who broke away from traditional Victorian and Edwardian values to create a bohemian lifestyle that they explored in their artistic work and writing, including textile design and surface pattern. The group's work is still popular today and its influences can be seen in textiles and homewares that evoke the interwar period. The Bloomsbury Group's retreat was at Charleston Farmhouse, situated in the Sussex Downs. Like many artists, writers and makers, their house and gardens are often open to the public. If you are seeking inspiration, why not take a day out and explore one such property, which can be full of creative resources and can lead to new ideas for your projects? Don't forget to take your sketchbook!

◀ *Seaside Story*, presented and framed in a wooden box frame.

Inspiration can be taken by using a single element from a piece of artwork, such as mood, style, colour, surface pattern or composition, which we can then translate into our own making. However, while we can legitimately take inspiration from existing makers' work, we must always take care that we do not copy. Directly copying the work of others causes the evaporation of individuality. We can remain true to our own style by being mindful of the amount of influence we are using in our work. By acknowledging the source of our inspiration, we keep our work unique and our own.

We never know when inspiration will strike, and keeping a notebook to hand enables us to instantly record any ideas and thoughts that come to us. Whether we are pottering around at home or out and about, it is important to record these considerations before we lose them. Use words to describe something that you see before you can add an element of depth to a description of the visual reference that you wish to capture. The effect of sunlight on water, snippets of an overheard conversation, thoughts on our ongoing work and projects – all these references can be jotted down, ready to be used within our work when the time is right. As mentioned in earlier chapters, using a camera is invaluable. Nowadays our smartphones are inbuilt with excellent-quality cameras that have an array of filters such as 'monochrome' or 'warm', which you can use to manipulate an image to provide different effects. Capturing images in this way can provide inspirations to explore in your work.

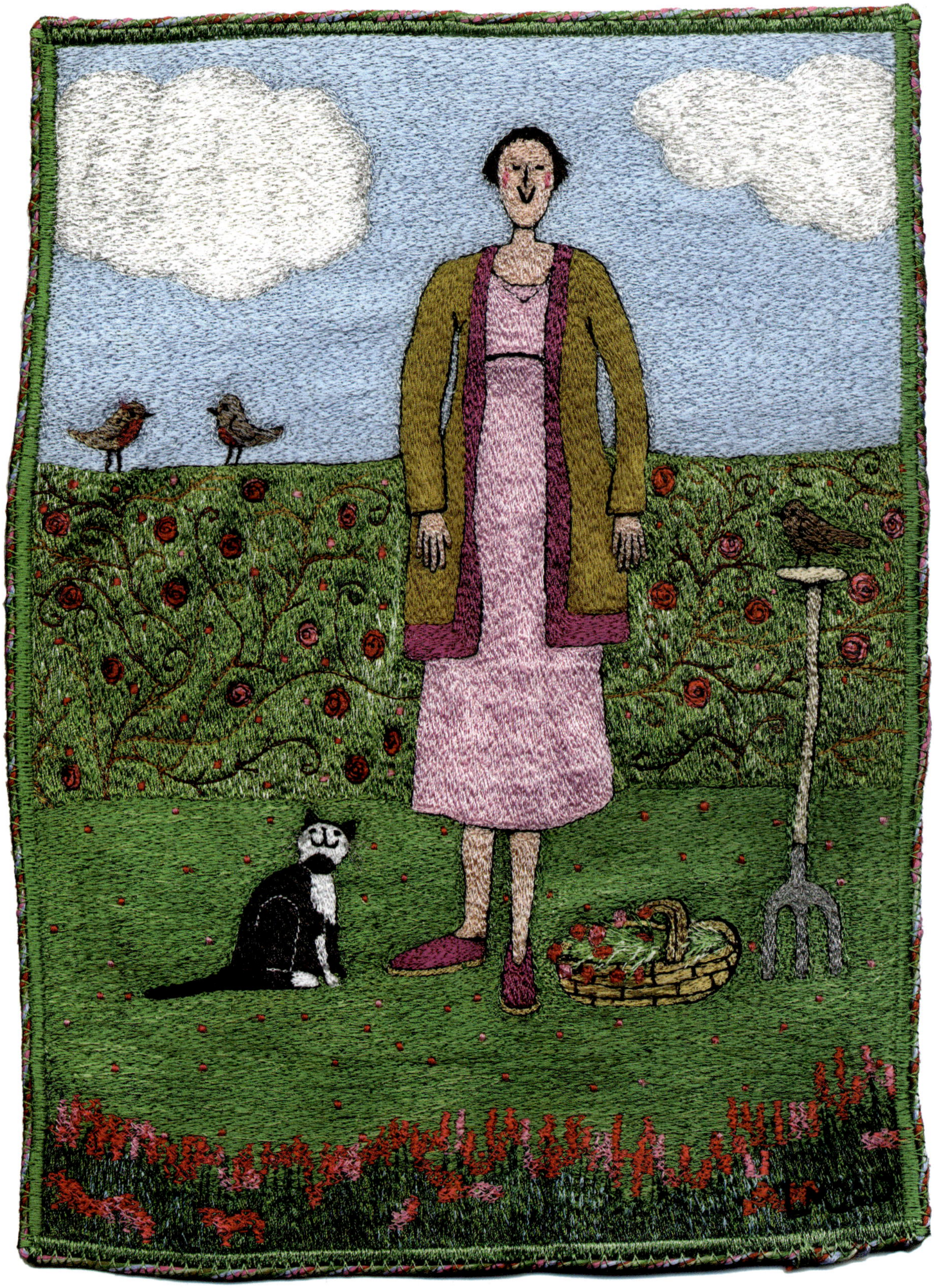

Every Cloud by Linda Miller, 21 × 27cm (8¼ × 10¾in), free machine embroidery. (Photo: Michael Jennings)

However we choose to record visual inspirations for future use, it is important that we do so, as it is the starting point from which we begin to express ourselves through our making. Keeping a mood board near to our work desk with collaged inspirations such as photographs, colour charts, magazine cuttings, patterned fabric swatches – or indeed anything that we are drawn to visually – means we have an instant and easy reference source to help shape our thinking. By referring to the initial ideas contained within your notebook, on your mood board and in your sketches, you can start to develop your concept for a particular creative textile project. Preliminary sketches can be made and developed into a finished drawing for a project prior to commencing fabric and stitch work.When planning any picture project that uses a variety of component pieces, such as the example given in this chapter, *Seaside Story*, it is crucial to ensure that the composition is balanced. With careful placement and arrangement of the disparate elements we have chosen, we form a composition in readiness for the overall illustration. This can be a time-consuming process, but it is a vital stage that must not be hurried. Rely on your gut instinct to tell you when the arrangement is perfect. However, sometimes finding the ideal picture composition can prove very difficult. At times like these, it is best to walk away and come back to it later, and no doubt with fresh eyes you will find the best arrangement.

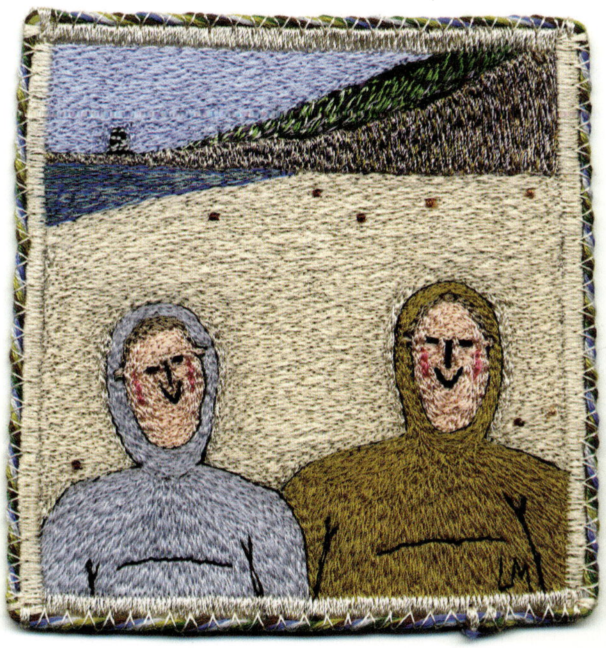

Blowy Beach by Linda Miller, 9 × 9cm (3½ × 3½in), free machine embroidery. (Photo: Michael Jennings)

Remember, a picture with too much in it can look cluttered and complicated. When constructing a picture, consider that less is more. You are taking the viewer through your picture, allowing their eye to wander as they explore all the different facets of the image. View the blank space around the imagery as a positive area and not as negative space that needs to be filled. Whether you are creating a piece for yourself or for someone else, rely on your intuition and be true to yourself; after all, it is *your* work and that is what makes it unique and desirable.

To create a textile picture, you do not necessarily have to use traditional textile materials such as fabric, thread or yarn. You can utilize paper, card, wood and all sorts of found objects within a textiles piece. Materials such as twisted paper thread, vegetable fibre or even wire can be used to secure the work. It is the overall construction that makes the piece, whether it is sewn, bound, woven or wrapped.

Whichever orientation – landscape, portrait or square – you choose for your project will change the overall mood, feeling and meaning of the picture. Try out your composition in these three shapes to see which one your work suits best. You may find an arrangement that works so successfully you want to repeat it; if this is the case, remember to make a couple of changes to keep the pictures as fresh and unique as possible. Changing the colourway and one core element to alter the look of an artwork will take it in a slightly different direction, while allowing the composition to have a similar feel to the original picture, and may even lead to the creation of a series of works.

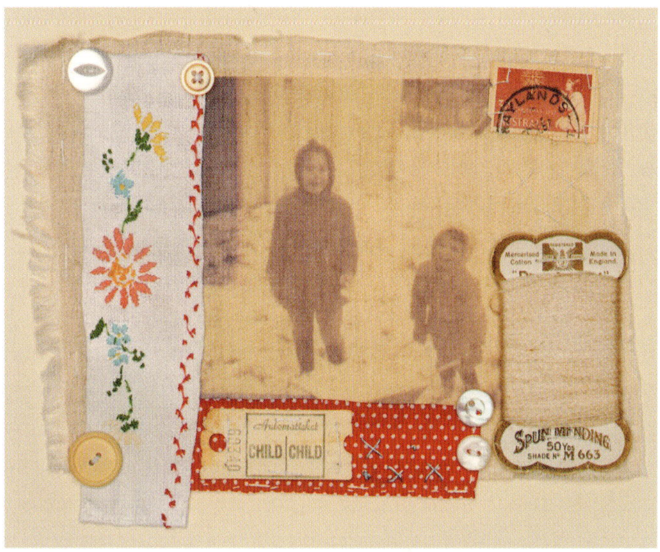

Laughing in the Snow, 18 × 22cm (7 × 8½in), mixed media collage and free machine stitch.

PICTURE PROJECT: *SEASIDE STORY*

Printed Paper, Fabric and Found Objects – What to Use

The starting point for this picture is a collection of printed images alongside found objects and a selection of old and new fabrics. Vintage pocket guides, such as those used to identify birds, shells, wild flowers and fungi, are ideal to use as source material. If you do not already have any of this type of book, they are easily found in your local second-hand bookshop and charity shops. These kinds of guides are full of beautiful little illustrations accompanied by text in classic typefaces, making them ideal for instant inspiration. If you are able to find one that has signs of natural wear and tear, or even has handwritten notes from a previous reader jotted in the margin, this will make the chosen image unique and give your picture a tangible suggestion of memory.

Old printed materials that have a soft, worn quality and come in muted tones like greens, pinks and creams can evoke recollections of times gone by. The precious memories that these items hold make the quality of them more desirable and ideal for this type of mixed media project. Almost any kind of printed ephemera such as bus tickets, stamps, family recipes, shopping lists or vintage postcards will work – you just need to decide on your theme and select accordingly.

Fabric that is textured or has remnants of stitch, like hems or seams, is suitable to use as background in this picture project. Alternatively, sew a selection of new and old fabric pieces together, in neutral tones, which will complement your collection of ephemera.

Found objects, such as pressed flowers, feathers, seeds, bottle tops and washers, are unusual, hold curiosity value and have their own stories to tell. Your selection of found objects will make the picture even more personal and unique.

Choosing items that are similar in colour and theme will give continuity throughout the composition.

The theme I have chosen for this picture is a memory image from my childhood. Every summer, my family visited the seaside and on the promenade was a somewhat garishly planted municipal flower garden, which has rather stuck in my mind! The juxtaposition of the brightly coloured planting, the golden sand and the sparkling sea conjures up happy, carefree summertime days. I have assembled a treasured collection of both found objects and paper imagery to illustrate this memory within the composition.

Assembling contrasting media, such as fabric, paper and found objects, together with stitch allows the discovery of new creative terrain that can be explored visually. Mixing up textures enables us to tell a story while creating a journey through the placed and stitched imagery.

Finished picture will fit a frame that measures 25 × 25cm (10 × 10in).

With this project you will be sewing on the front.

HANDY HINT HOW TO AGE PAPER AND COTTON FABRIC FOR A VINTAGE FEEL

Leave a couple of teabags to steep in hot water. When the liquid is cold it can be applied with a soft cotton rag onto any new paper and left to dry. This will give the paper surface an aged appearance.

The same technique can be used for cotton or linen fabric. Wash the fabric piece first in a laundry liquid to remove any fabric dressing and to allow for shrinkage, then soak the fabric piece in the tea liquid. When the required colour has been achieved, gently squeeze out the excess liquid and hang the piece to dry. The tea-stain solution can be made lighter or darker with the number of tea bags that are used – the more bags used, the darker the fabric will become.

The measurements for the *Seaside Story* drawing are an approximate guide size. You may choose to make your imagery slightly bigger or smaller. Whatever you decide, make sure that your imagery finishes just outside of the tailor's chalk marks on the background fabric to allow the picture to sit comfortably without the frame cutting into the imagery.

This project will fit a frame that measures 25 × 25cm (10 × 10in).

If you choose to alter the size of your picture, you will require a different size frame than the instructions for this picture project recommend.

You can either use your own memories, ideas and collection of visual materials within your mixed media picture or follow the theme in this project.

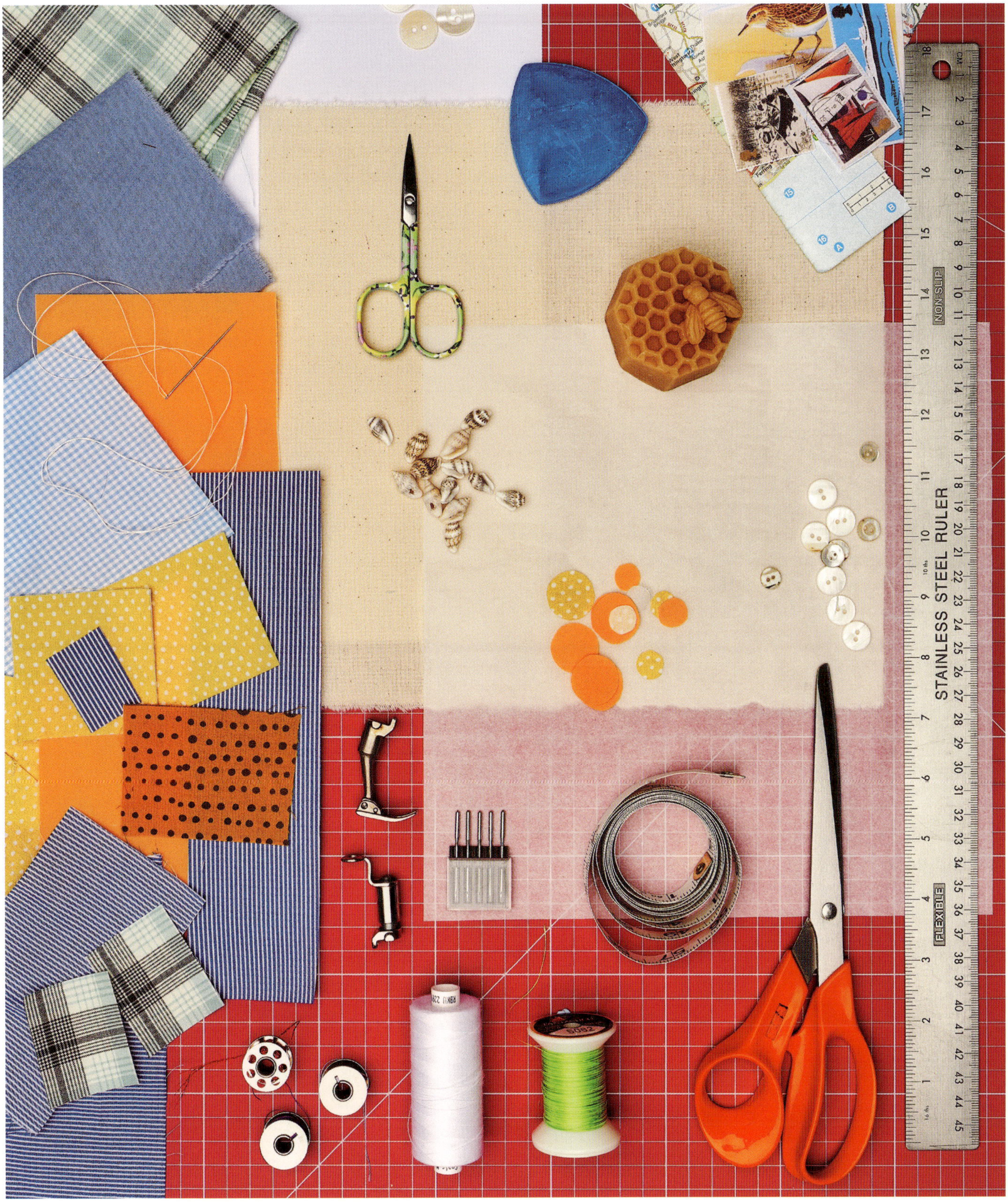

A selection of materials needed to make the picture project, *Seaside Story*.

YOU WILL NEED

Items from the basic tool kit, as listed in Chapter 1 Tools and Equipment, and the following materials:

- Piece of lightweight calico measuring 30 × 30cm (12 × 12in)
- Selection of both vintage and new cotton fabric pieces, either in your own choice of colours or as a suggestion:
  - Piece of cotton fabric in a neutral colour measuring 25 × 25cm (10 × 10in)
  - Flowers: three pieces of yellow fabric in three varying shades, each measuring 15 × 10cm (6 × 4in)
  - Waves 1: Piece of blue gingham fabric measuring 5 × 25cm (2 × 10in)
  - Waves 2: Piece of blue and white striped fabric measuring 3 × 4cm (1¼ × 1½in)
  - Waves 3: Piece of mid blue/grey fabric measuring 5 × 5cm (2 × 2in)
  - Distant shore: Piece of checked fabric in colours of teal, brown and white measuring 6 × 5cm (2½ × 2in)
- Packet of fusible fabric measuring 1.2 × 1.75m (1¼ × 2yd)
- Spool of multicoloured green machine embroidery thread
- Spool of white machine sewing thread
- Selection of vintage printed pictures on paper or thin card, either in your own choice of subjects or as a suggestion:
  - Piece of a map measuring 7.5 × 9cm (3 × 3½in)
  - Picture of a sea bird measuring 6 × 8.5cm (2½ × 3½in)
- Three stamps, either in your own choice of subjects or as a suggestion:
  - Picture of a ship
  - Picture of yachts
  - Picture of a rowing boat
- A selection of bought natural materials:
  - Three small shells
  - Five mother-of-pearl buttons in various sizes
- Piece of good-quality mount board in a neutral colour, cut to the size of the frame's recess
- Unglazed box frame measuring 25 × 25cm (10 × 10in)

1 GETTING STARTED: CREATING THE BACKGROUND

Cut a piece of the fusible fabric measuring 25 × 25cm (10 × 10in) and iron it onto the reverse side of the background fabric using a hot iron and an ironing board. When cool, carefully cut around the fusible fabric and peel away the paper.

Next, lay the background fabric right side up. Place it centrally onto the lightweight piece of calico and iron it in place. Lay the frame's recess in this square and, using the tailor's chalk, mark the outside of the recess. Any imagery placed outside this box will be hidden by the frame, but to avoid the abrupt end of the picture allow a little of the background imagery to continue outside of this box.

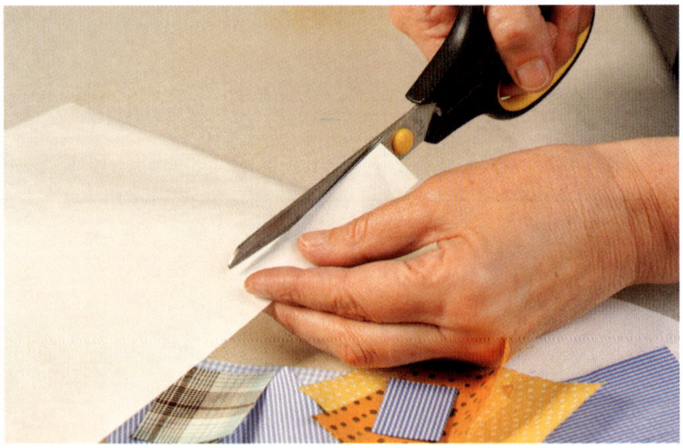

Cut the fusible fabric in readiness to be ironed onto the chosen pieces of fabric.

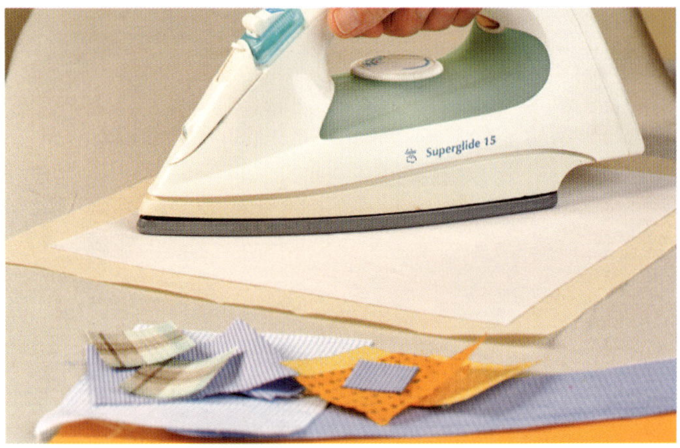

After peeling away the protective paper, iron the background fabric onto the calico.

2 CUTTING AND ARRANGING THE YELLOW FLOWER HEADS

Each yellow flower head is made from two different sized circles that are cut from contrasting yellow fabrics, with a smaller circle sitting on top of a larger circle. To make the flower heads, cut three pieces of the fusible fabric, each measuring approximately 15 × 10cm (6 × 4in).

Iron each piece onto the reverse side of the three pieces of yellow cotton fabric. Once cool, using your scissors, free cut out ten circles of varying sizes from each piece of yellow fabric – aim to have the circles ranging from 1cm (⅜in) to 2cm (¾in) in diameter. There will be thirty circles in total of differing sizes made from the three different fabrics. These differing dimensions allow for some freedom in creating flowers in different sizes and contrasting pattern and colour combinations.

Once all the flower circles have been cut, they should be laid in place within the two sides marked by the tailor's chalk, and no higher than 8cm (3¼in) from the bottom edge of the tailor's chalk mark. Once you are happy with the arrangement, remove the paper backing and iron in place onto the background fabric.

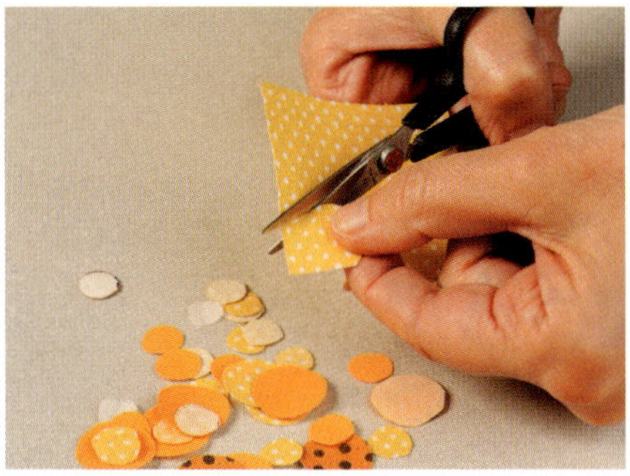

Free cut thirty flower head circles from the three chosen cotton yellow fabrics.

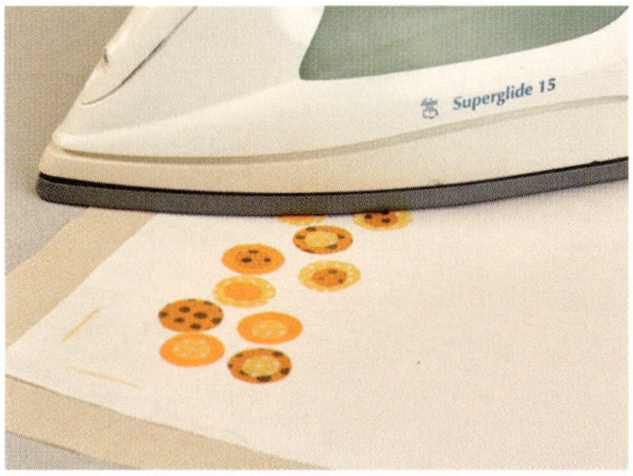

Use a hot iron to secure the flower heads in place upon the background fabric.

HANDY HINT PLACING AND ARRANGING THE FLOWER HEADS

Place a piece of white A4 copier paper by the side of you as you cut out the flower heads. The cut circles can be placed in pairs and arranged in your desired sequence onto the paper. As the arranged flower border is created, it will be easy to transfer the flower pairs from the paper onto the background fabric in your chosen configuration.

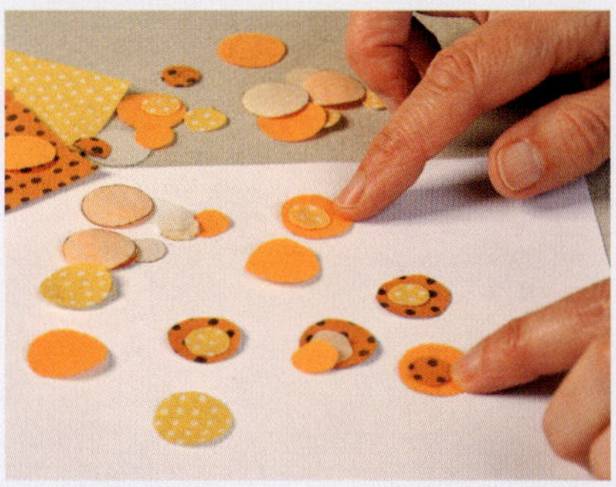

Take your time in arranging the flower heads in sequence upon a piece of white paper.

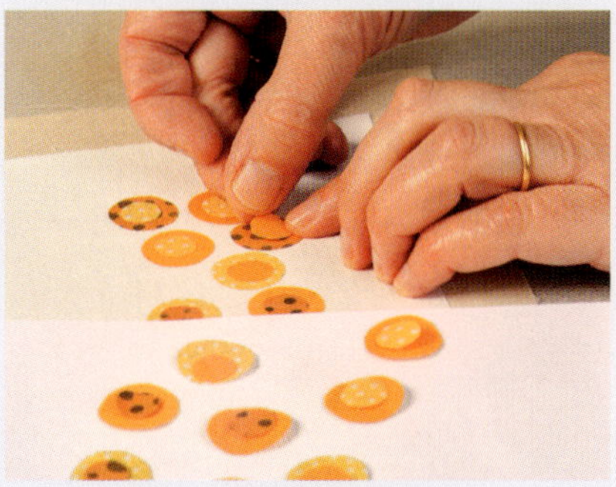

It is easy to transfer the flowerheads from the paper onto the background fabric.

HANDY HINT FREE CUTTING THE FABRIC

Free cutting the fabric pieces without the use of paper templates allows an element of chance while constructing the pieces for the composition. Working without an initial drawing allows the maker spontaneity and freedom in the construction of the picture. Although this technique is not appropriate for all methods of picture making, it does suit working with found objects. The various shapes can be moved about the composition until the desired balance is achieved and then the pieces can be fixed in place.

3 EMBELLISHING THE FLOWER HEADS WITH FREE MACHINE EMBROIDERY STITCH

Thread up the sewing machine with the multicoloured green machine embroidery thread and place a wound bobbin of the same colour in the machine. Fit the free machine embroidery foot, lower the feed dog teeth and then follow the instructions in Chapter 3, Step 4. The bonded background fabric is stiff enough to be worked on with ease, so an embroidery hoop is not required.

Starting on the left-hand side of the background fabric, place the needle of the sewing machine just under the tailor's chalk mark on the bottom edge and bring up the bobbin thread. Lower the presser foot, make a couple of small stitches to secure your work, and then cut away the two waste threads close to the fabric surface. Begin slowly to draw with your needle in a horizontal line in the green multicoloured thread until the needle is below the first flower head. Stop with the needle in the fabric.

Next, take the stitch line in a vertical direction to meet the flower head – this will create the flower's stem. When the flower head is reached, draw in stitch a spiral over both of the yellow circles and then follow the vertical stitch line back towards the bottom of the fabric. As you sew over this stem line, make little oval leaf motifs on either side until the bottom of this line is reached. Aim to have between three and five leaf shapes on each stem. Continue along the bottom line until your stitch line is below the next yellow circle. Then take the stitch in a vertical direction to meet the flower head and repeat the spiral stitching and the sewing of the small leaf motifs. Continue in this fashion until all of the flower heads and stems have been drawn in stitch.

If any of the flower heads are situated behind or on top of one another, simply sew over the flowers in the foreground to reach the flowers in the background. This action will create depth within the flower border.

Don't worry if any of the stems, flower spirals or leaves have a wobble or are slightly off-centre. This will merely add to the charm of your flowerbed.

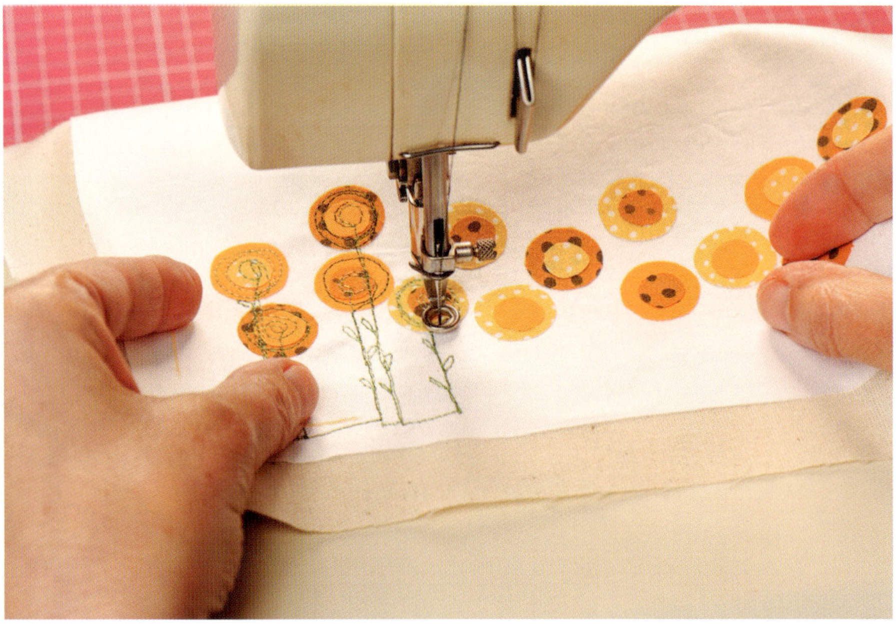

Free machine embroider over the flower heads using the multicoloured green thread.

4 MAKING WAVES

Select the fabrics for the waves. Cut to fit the fusible fabric for each wave piece and iron it onto the reverse side with a hot iron. Place to one side to cool.

Beginning with the blue gingham fabric, free cut it into four long, thin, wedge-shaped pieces. The widest edge should measure approximately 1cm (⅜in) and should taper to the opposite end, which finishes in a point. Lay these four pieces above the yellow flower border in the sequence of: wide end, tapered end, wide end, tapered end. Space the gingham pieces by focusing on the middle of the picture: the first wave should be 5mm away from the top of the tallest yellow flower head; the second wave should be approximately 5mm away from the first; the third wave 1cm (⅜in) away from the second; and the fourth wave should be approximately 3cm (1¼in) away from the third. Once you are happy with the position, remove the backing paper from each of the fabric pieces and iron the wave shapes into place.

Next, cut the blue and white striped fabric to a size of 2.5 × 3.5cm (1 × 1½in) and place between the third and fourth wave so that the right-hand edge of this shape is 7cm (2¾in) away from the right-hand side of the tailor's chalk mark. Once placed, remove the paper backing and iron on.

The final shape of wave-themed fabric in the colours of mid blue/grey should be cut to an approximate size of 4 × 3.5cm (1½ × 1⅜in). Lay this so that the bottom left-hand corner is approximately 1cm (⅜in) over the top right-hand corner of the blue and white striped fabric and that the right-hand side is approximately 4cm (1½in) away from the outside edge of the tailor's chalk mark. Peel away the backing paper and iron into place.

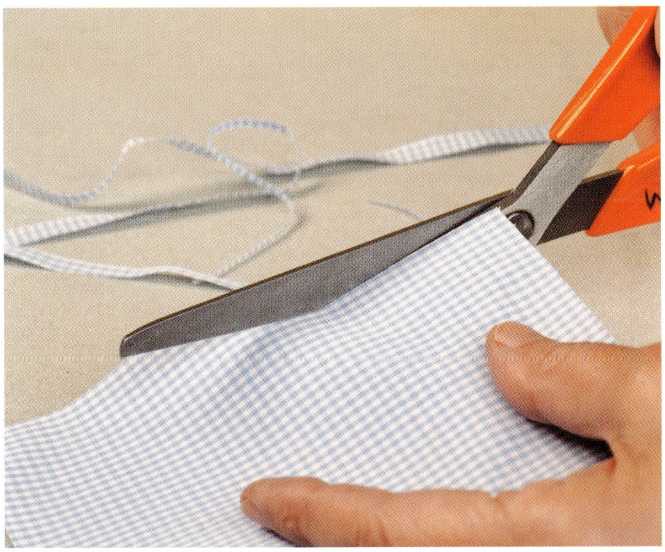

Using sharp dressmaking scissors, cut the blue gingham fabric into long thin ribbons.

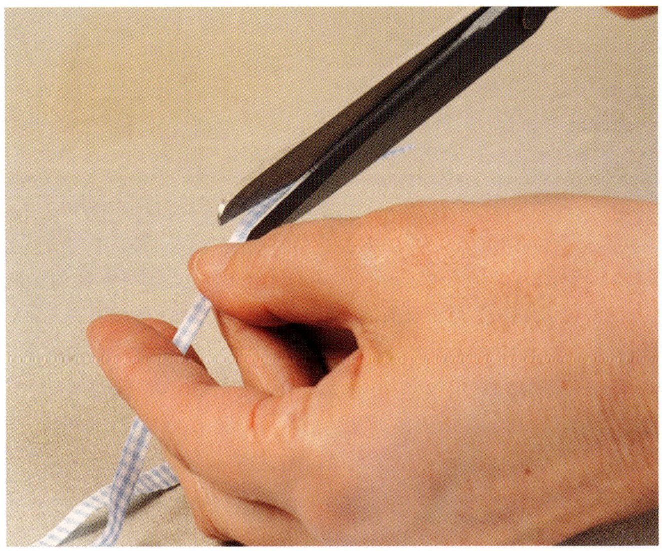

Trim up each strip of blue gingham to make all the wave shapes needed for the picture.

5 A DISTANT SHORE

The last piece to be applied to the background fabric is the rectangular-shaped checked material in the colours of teal, brown and white. Cut a piece of fusible fabric to fit and iron it on to the reverse side of the checked material; leave to cool. Then cut the piece to 5 × 4cm (2 × 1½in) in size. Lay this piece at the top of the background fabric, approximately 7cm (2¾in) in from the right-hand side chalk mark. It should also cover 1.5cm (¾in) over the left-hand top corner of the mid blue/grey material. Peel off the backing paper and iron in place.

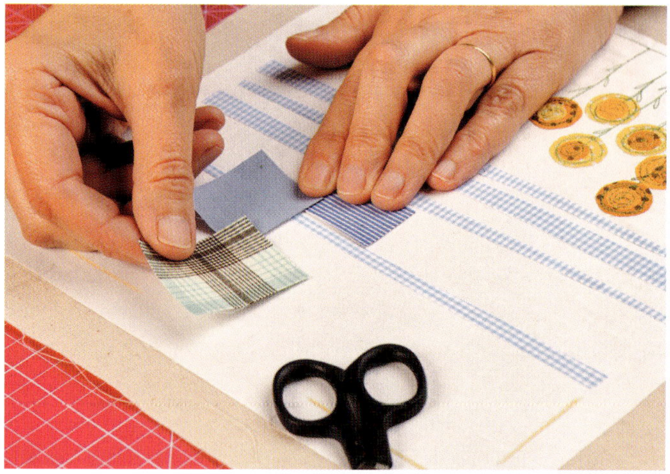

Arrange each piece of the wave-themed fabric before ironing them all in place.

6 ADDING STITCH TO THE ADHERED PIECES

Raise the feed dog teeth and fit the general-purpose sewing foot to stitch around the outside edge of the adhered fabric pieces. Thread up the sewing machine with the white sewing thread and fit a bobbin in the machine of the same colour.

Place your needle at one end of the first blue gingham wave and make a couple of small stitches to secure your work. Cut away the waste thread, close to the fabric surface. Continue to sew around the edge of each adhered fabric piece. You will need to sew over some of the adhered pieces to reach all the fabric edges – this does not matter.

When the last piece has been edged, lift the needle out of the work and cut away the waste threads, close to the fabric surface, on both the top and the reverse side. When decorating with stitch you can choose to go around the edge of the fabric pieces just once or a couple of times.

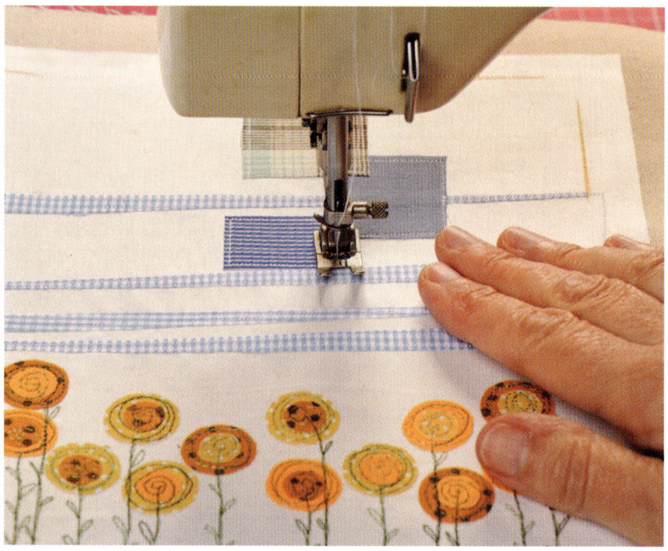

Sew around each of the applied fabric pieces using a running stitch and white thread.

7 PLACING THE PAPER IMAGES

Place the piece of the map onto the background fabric so it sits towards the top left-hand corner of the background fabric. Check that it is approximately 1cm (⅜in) in from the tailor's chalk mark before sewing it in place around the outside edge.

Once completed, cut off the top and bottom thread and then lay the picture of the sea bird just below the map image. Stitch in place, as before.

The last printed images to be sited are the three stamps. Place one stamp on each piece of the three rectangles of fabric, aiming to have each one slightly off-centre. Move them about until you are happy with the placement and stitch in place, again around the edge of each image. In order to protect the delicate printed paper material, ensure you gently press on the back of the picture with an iron.

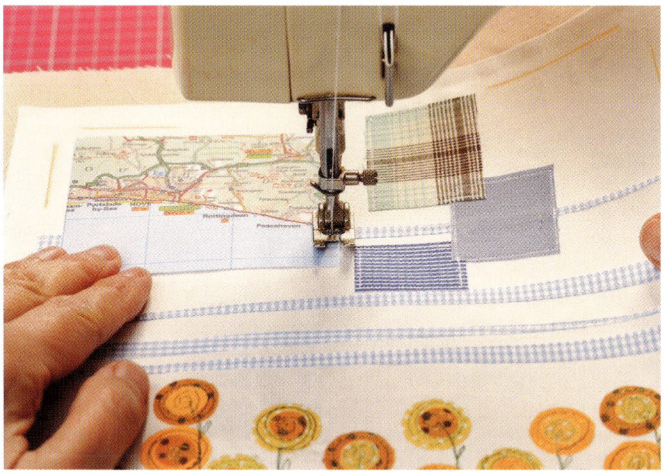

Lay the map in place and sew around the edge, ensuring the paper does not move.

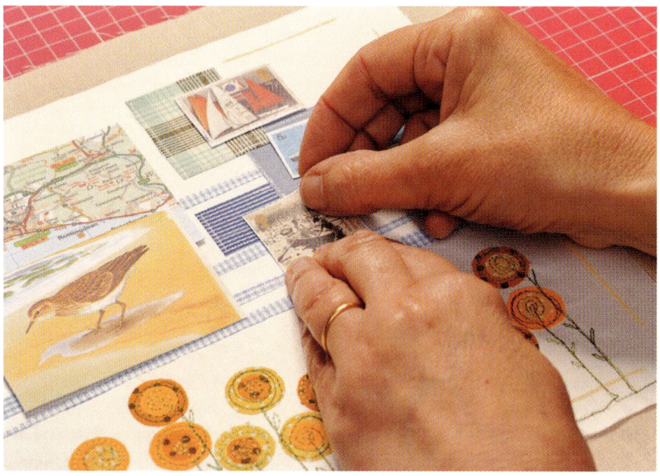

The last paper images to be arranged on the background fabric are the three stamps.

HANDY HINT TEXTURED PAPER EDGES

The technique of tearing the paper gives a visual softening to the outside edge of any piece of paper or printed picture, and also can give a vintage look. To create this effect, place a metal ruler on the paper and hold down securely. Pull the side of the unsecured paper towards you to create a torn edge. Repeat on the remaining sides of the item. Tearing to fit is a very effective way to reduce the size of a desired picture that would otherwise be too large for the composition.

HANDY HINT STRENGTHENING THE PAPER IMAGE

If the paper imagery you have chosen is a little fragile and you do not think it will withstand stitching, cut a piece of iron-on light interfacing to size and carefully iron it onto the back of the chosen paper. Remember to use the iron without water, as any steam may damage the picture or any handwritten text.

8 SHELLS AND BUTTONS

The last items to be attached to complete the picture are three shells and five buttons. Place and arrange the three shells in between the map piece and the distant shoreline fabric. Remember that all these elements need to be placed 1.5cm (¾in) in from all of the tailor's chalk marks and will need to be sewn down by hand.

Thread up a hand sewing needle with the white sewing thread and run it through the beeswax – this will help the thread to run smoothly through the layers of fabric. Sew the shells in place using an overstitch – you can utilize any existing small holes to secure.

Arrange the buttons in an irregular pattern on a couple of the corners of the printed pictures until you are happy with their placement. Using the hand sewing needle and white thread, sew each one in place through the buttonholes. Take your time with the placement of these little objects and enjoy the hand sewing. When all the stitching has been completed, use a soft brush and gently brush away the tailor's chalk marks.

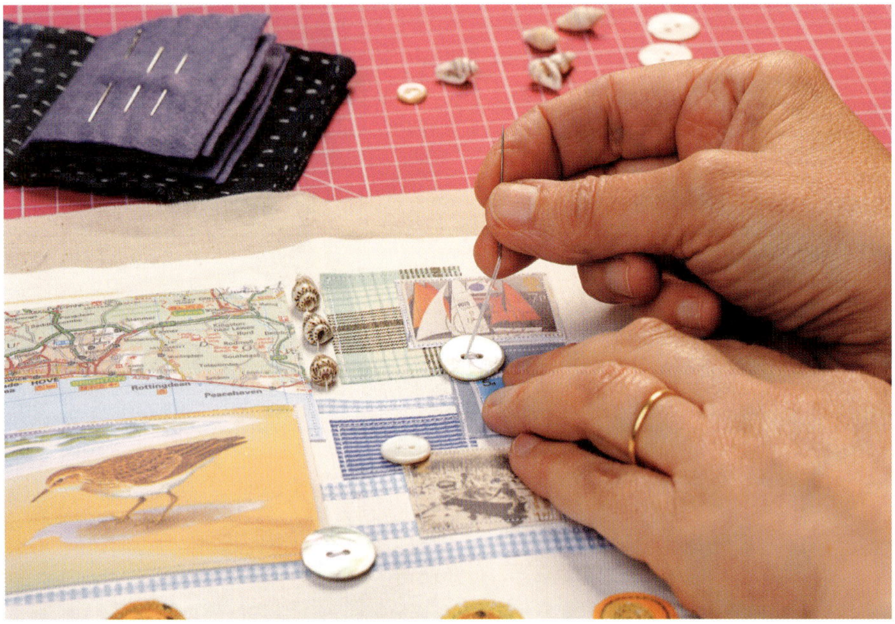

Hand sewing mother-of-pearl buttons and small shells in place finishes off the picture.

9 PREPARING THE PICTURE FOR MOUNTING AND FRAMING

In order to fit the frame and its backing board, the completed picture needs to measure 25 × 25cm (10 × 10in). Cut away the waste calico and, once trimmed to the required size, fit a zigzag foot. Set the sewing machine to a zigzag stitch and using the white sewing thread zigzag around the outside edge. This will reduce the fraying of the outside edge and make it easier to frame. Gently press the outside edge on the reverse side, making sure not to crush any of the shells or buttons.

Turn your picture over and congratulate yourself on all your hard work! This inspiring collage is just one of your collection of handmade stitched pictures. Well done – be proud of what you have achieved. For presentation and framing, see Chapter 9.

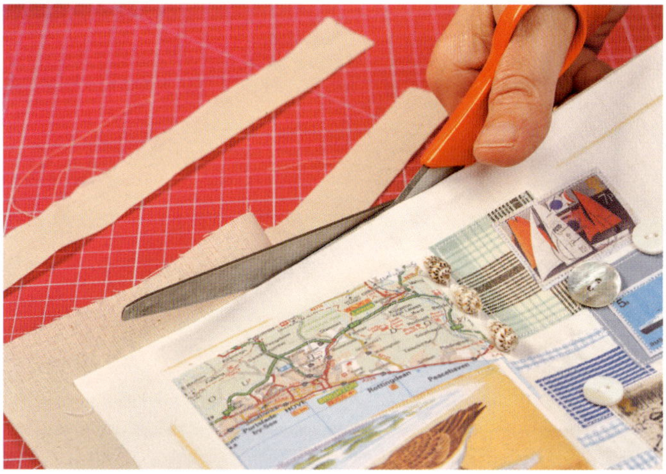

When all the machine and hand sewing has been achieved, trim up the waste fabric.

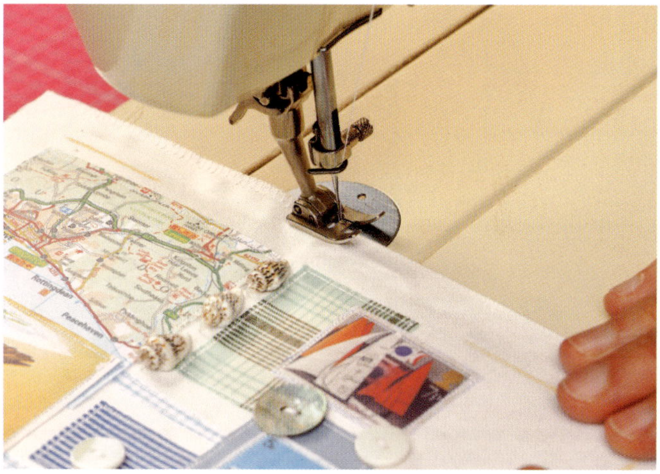

Fit a zigzag foot to the sewing machine and zigzag around the outside edge.

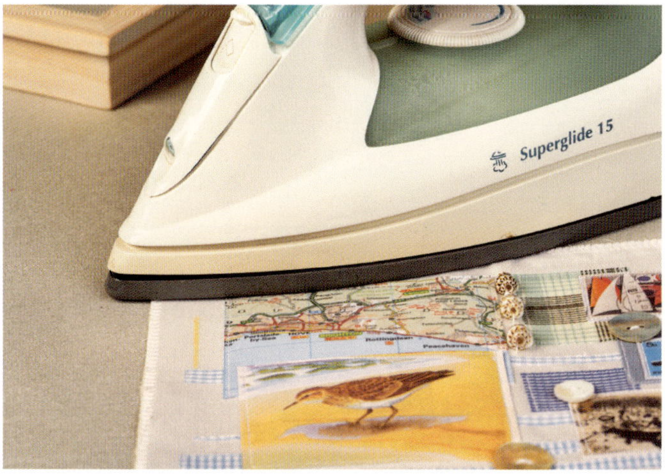

Gently press the outside of the picture, being mindful not to crush the shells or buttons.

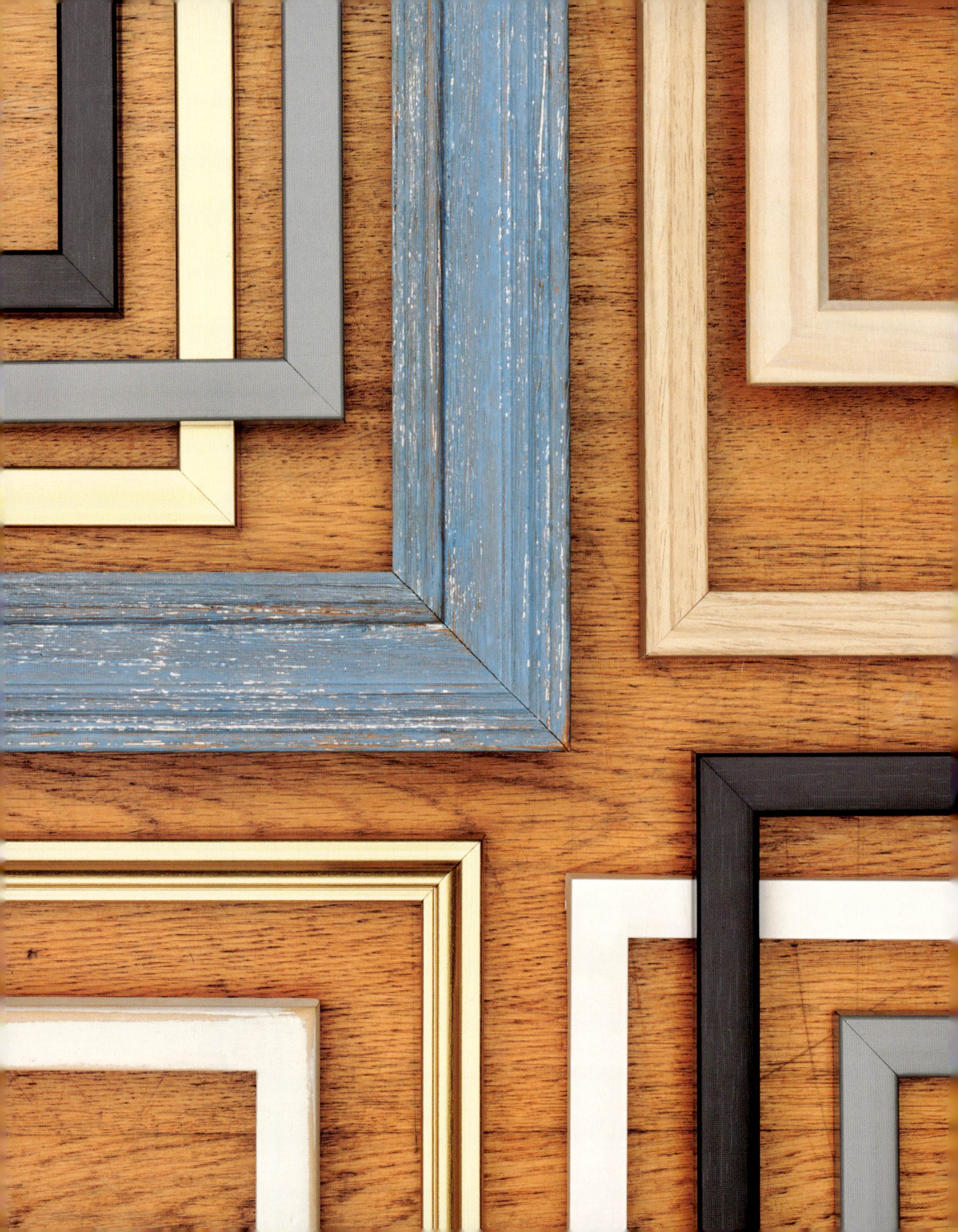

CHAPTER 9

PRESENTATION AND FRAMING

How to Present and Frame the Picture Projects

After enjoying many hours and much energy, concentration and skill in making your stitched pictures, you will now need to turn your attention to considering how best to present and frame your pieces of work. As you will have discovered during the making of the picture projects in this book, there are many stages involved in the process of constructing a work of textile art, including drawing, colour consideration, fabric choices, placement, free machine embroidery and hand stitch. Similarly, there are a few steps to be considered when presenting and framing the finished textile picture. A little time must be given to deliberating on how to display your work to exploit its full and deserved potential.

There are numerous ways in which to present the stitched pictures; from placing them in a glazed frame to suspending them from a simple pole upon a wall, finding the best one to suit the piece of work is particularly important. Not every framing solution will necessarily suit a particular piece of work. For example, with a smaller piece it is best to present it in a frame – if placed directly on a wall it may get lost; however, a larger piece of work can hold its own and may suit free mounting, that is being suspended directly on the wall.

As enthusiasts, we may have visited exhibitions and galleries where we have admired beautiful textile works and observed how they are framed. How a textile picture has been presented will determine how it is perceived by the viewer and how its integral worth is valued. If we are to take our textile art seriously, we must take the presentation seriously too. A professionally presented textile piece can have a greater physical presence and the viewer can immediately understand it

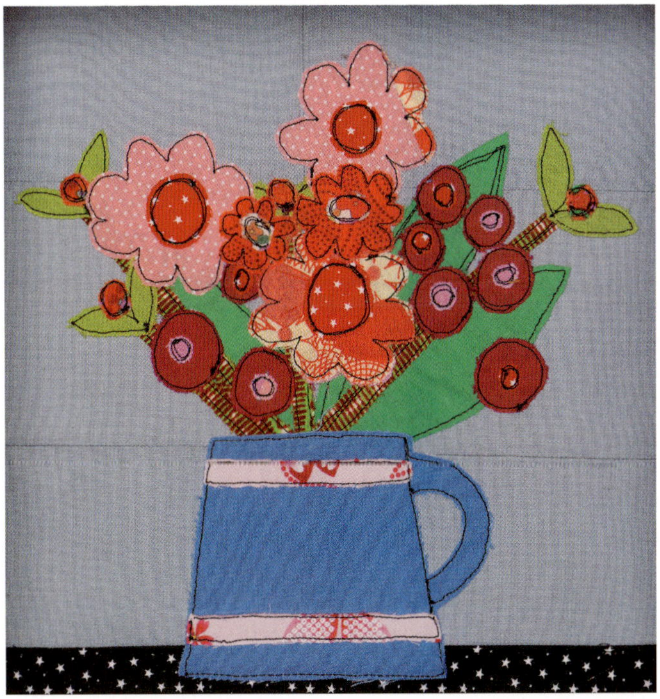

The Blue Jug by Linda Miller, 25 × 25cm (10 × 10in), reverse fabric appliqué and free machine embroidery.

◀ Ready-made frames come in all sizes and colours and are easily found in the high street or on the internet.

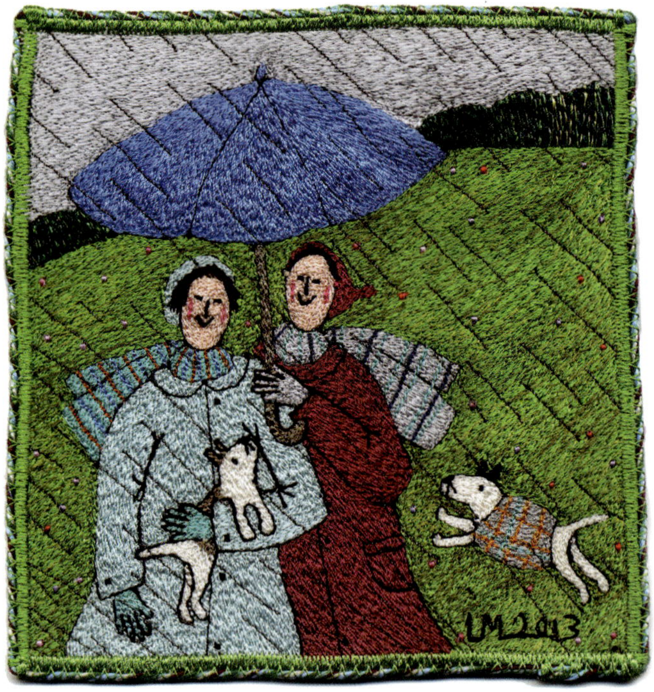

Rain by Linda Miller, 15 × 14cm (6 × 5½in), free machine embroidery. (Photo: Michael Jennings)

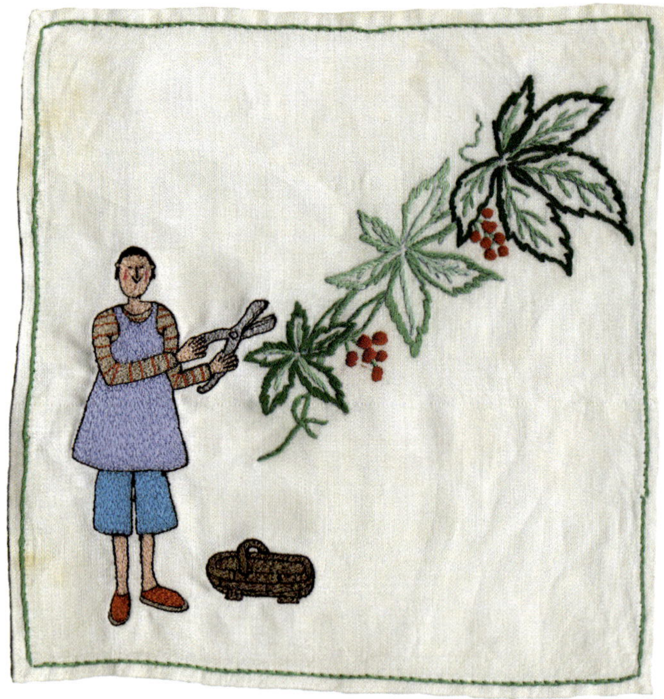

Gardening by Linda Miller, 30 × 30cm (12 × 12in), free machine embroidery and hand embroidery on linen cloth. (Photo: Michael Jennings)

as a piece of art. Effective presentation elevates not only the medium of textiles but the textile maker too, and gives them both the deserved recognition that is automatically given to any serious painter or fine artist working in their chosen field.

Whether you are making a piece as a gift for family or friends or making for yourself, it is always easier to hang a piece of work if it has been framed or presented proficiently. It is certainly more straightforward for the recipient to receive a piece of work that is easy to display. You may wish to use a specialist framer; if so, then ensure whoever you choose to undertake the framing has an understanding and previous experience of framing textiles. Do not be afraid to ask them for examples of other textile commissions they have undertaken so that you can be assured of their capability and sympathy with the medium. However, be aware that that while professional framing should provide excellent results, it can be expensive!

An alternative to using a specialist framer is to undertake the task yourself, and off-the-shelf frames are a good substitute. Ready-made frames can be found easily in homeware and DIY stores, and even supermarkets. They come in a range of sizes, styles and finishes such as wood, metallic or gloss. Be warned, they also vary in quality, so remember the old adage: 'buy cheap, buy twice'. Of course, second-hand frames can be given a new lease of life by upcycling, which presents an opportunity to create something unique to house your work. A very straightforward option is to choose natural wood or a neutral or sympathetic colour. However, if you choose a colourful, patterned or ornate frame, ensure that it does not overwhelm the fabric picture but provides synergy to the whole composition of work and frame. Take time to consider what type and style of frame will suit your work the best; you want the frame to complement your piece of work and not to distract or compromise what is being presented so that your work is shown to its full and deserved potential. Like so many factors, this is a very personal choice.

Once you have chosen your good-quality frame, there are a few simple guidelines and practical considerations that need to be thought through. Firstly, it is imperative that you refrain from using glue, tape, staples or nails to hold your textile picture in place. Using such fixings may cause damage and stain your precious work, which you should avoid at all costs. You will have noticed for each of the picture projects in this book, an unglazed box frame is recommended to be used for framing. A box frame has a recess inside that is deep enough to house a complex, multi-layered piece of textile work. Using an unglazed box frame allows a clear view of all the features of the textile picture, and having the work set back in a deep frame gives the picture both weight and depth. Of course, you may choose to use a glazed frame and, if you do so, it is important that the frame is deep enough that the artwork does not touch the glass, which may attract moisture and cause mildew.

For the projects in this book, frame sizes are recommended that are relevant to the size of the finished work. In some of the projects, the frame will sit over the picture so there is no space around the image; for others, there is a clear space around the whole piece so that the work does not appear to be hemmed in. One of the works, *Spring Greens* (see Chapter 4), does not require a traditional frame and is instead suspended from a small pole directly on the wall. This inexpensive hanging method is particularly suited for themed pictures such as gardens, flora and fauna, or the seaside, as the dowel from which it is suspended can be a garden twig or a piece of driftwood, presenting the piece in question neatly in its subject matter.

As your textile journey progresses you may wish to experiment with other presentation techniques; always consider the size of your piece of work and how you wish to present it. Some pieces of contemporary textile art are displayed hanging free-form or suspended from a ceiling; the soft draping, translucent materials move in the gentle breeze of the viewer passing by, to create further movement and ambiance.

As with all artworks, the textile picture should ideally be displayed in a relatively humid-free environment and away from direct sunlight. If the unglazed or free-standing textile picture or piece becomes dusty, it is simple to clean by using a soft, clean brush to gently brush the surface of the picture.

In this chapter, simple projects for mounting and framing the textile pictures from the picture projects in this book are explained. Using tools that you will have in your toolbox and materials that are easily found, simply follow the step-by-step instructions on how to mount, frame and present your work. Each picture project has its own specific framing solution and, by following the instructions, you will present and frame your work in a stylish way that complements your free machine stitched pictures.

HAND SEWING A TEXTILE PICTURE ONTO A PIECE OF MOUNT BOARD, READY FOR FRAMING IN A BOX FRAME

This easy-to-achieve presentation and framing method requires the machine embroidery to be hand sewn onto a mount board. Choosing both a neutral mount board and simple wooden frame will show off your work so the eye is focused on the stitched picture. This simple mounting and framing technique will suit the picture project in Chapter 3, *Strawberry Delight*.

YOU WILL NEED

Items from the basic tool kit, as listed in Chapter 1 Tools and Equipment, and the following materials:

- Unglazed wooden box picture frame measuring 12 × 12cm (4¾ × 4¾in)
- Piece of good-quality mount board in a neutral colour (you will cut to fit your frame)
- Folded blanket or bath towel
- A hand sewing needle and strong thread, such as bookbinders' thread or hand sewing buttonhole thread
- Bradawl with a thin shaft for making small holes
- Adhesive frame tape

HANDY HINT MOUNT BOARD COLOURS AND FRAME SIZES

If a textile picture is to be mounted onto a mount board and then housed within a frame, the picture needs to be situated in the middle of the piece of board with an equal distance all around it. Choose a good-quality mount board that is neutral pH (non-acidic) in a soft pale cream colour, which will emphasize the textile picture. *Strawberry Delight* is a petite picture project that will look attractive in a small frame.

HANDY HINT CUTTING MAT

A cutting mat is essential for this framing project technique to protect your table or work surface.

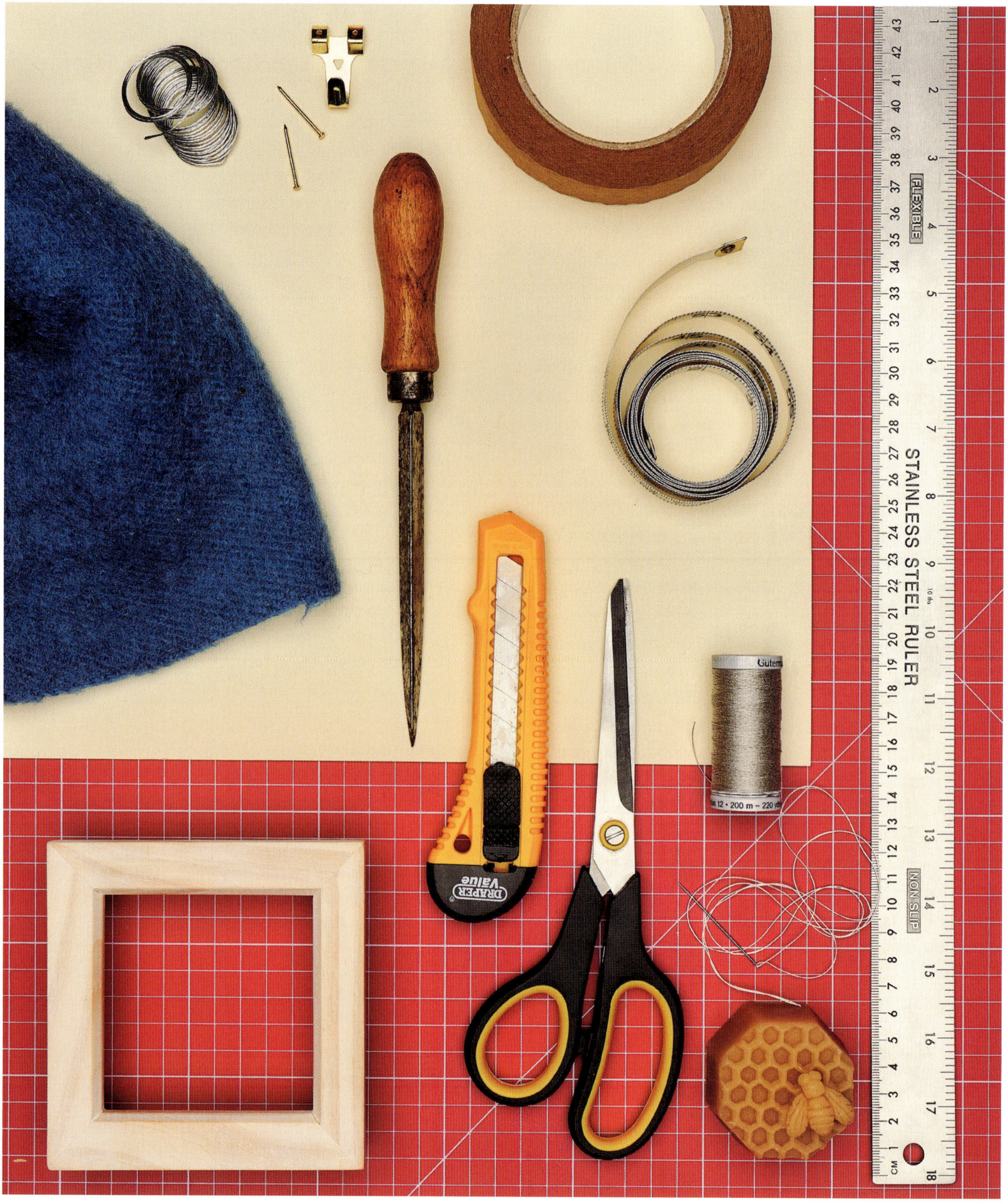

A selection of tools needed for framing *Strawberry Delight*.

1.1 GETTING STARTED: PREPARING THE FRAME AND CUTTING THE MOUNT BOARD

Start by carefully taking your frame apart. Leave any frame findings, such as turnover buttons or point driver staples, in place by gently bending them back – they will be needed when the frame is reassembled.

Place the piece of mount board on the cutting mat. Measure the frame's recess and, using a pencil, mark the measurements lightly onto the mount board. Then, using a ruler and a sharp art and craft utility knife, cut the mount board to the required size and put it to one side.

Next, fold the blanket and place it on the cutting mat. Taking the mount board, place it right side up on top of the blanket and then centrally place the textile picture with the right side showing on top of this. The area around the picture should measure about the same; ideally the two sides and top of the mount board need to measure the same distance, with the bottom measurement being a little bigger to provide the optimum balance for the eye.

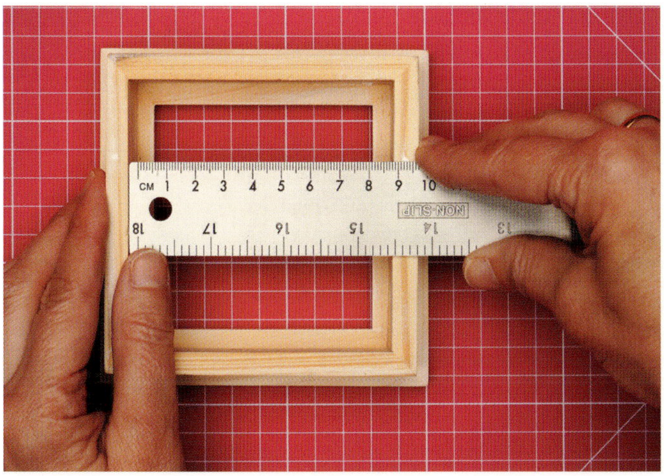

Measure the frame's recess to ensure that the mount board is cut to the same size.

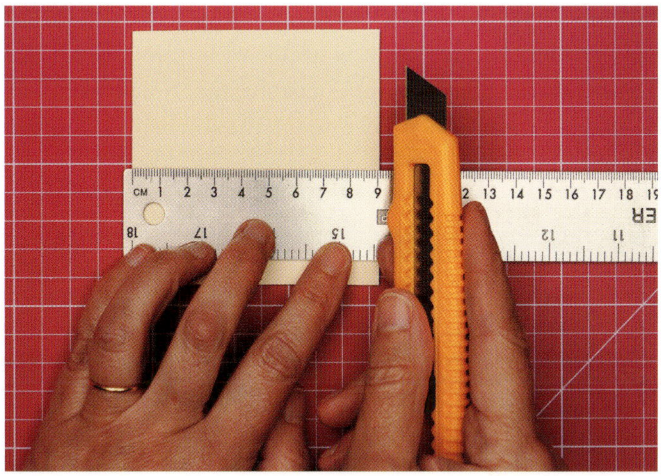

When cutting the mount board, use a cutting mat, sharp craft knife and metal ruler.

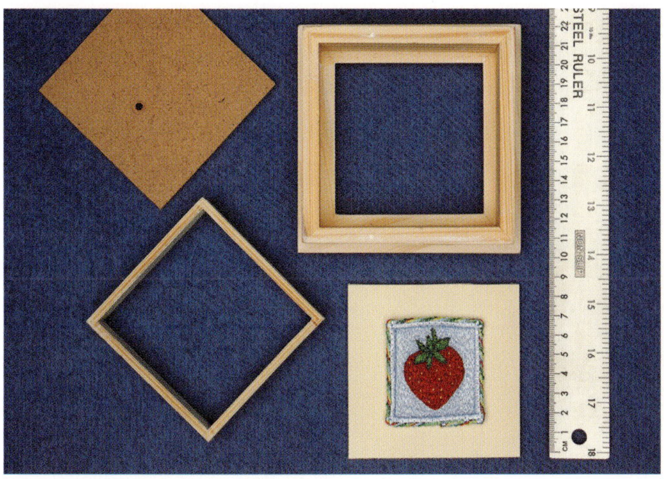

Measure the distance around the picture to ensure it is positioned in the middle.

1.2 USING THE BRADAWL AND SEWING THE PICTURE ONTO THE MOUNT BOARD

Next, take the bradawl and carefully push it through the top right-hand corner of the picture and through the mount board, approximately 5mm in from the outside edges of the picture. Then, leaving a gap of 2cm (¾in), make another small incision through both the textile picture and the board, again 5mm in from the top edge. You will now have two small holes along the top, near to the right-hand side. Push the bradawl once more through the textile picture and board, approximately 4cm (1½in) away from the second hole, again along the top edge. Continue in this fashion until there is a row of evenly spaced holes along the top of the picture.

Thread up the hand sewing needle with strong thread and run it through the beeswax – coating the thread with wax will help it to run smoothly through the stitched picture and mount board.

Starting on the right-hand side, and in the first hole, push the needle from the back of the mount board through to the front and into the back of the stitched border, just skimming the outside surface of the picture with the needle. Pick up approximately 1cm (⅜in) of the picture and push the needle back into the mount board through the second hole. While holding the end of the thread, pull the remaining thread taut so that the picture is attached to the mount board, and secure with a reef knot on the back of the mount board. Push the needle through the third hole and skim the back of the picture once more, before pushing the needle through the fourth hole.

Continue in this manner until the end of the row of holes has been reached and the top of the picture is secured to the board. Finish off the row by making another reef knot before cutting the thread. The picture will move as you sew, so it is important when a row of sewing has been completed to measure and realign the picture before continuing.

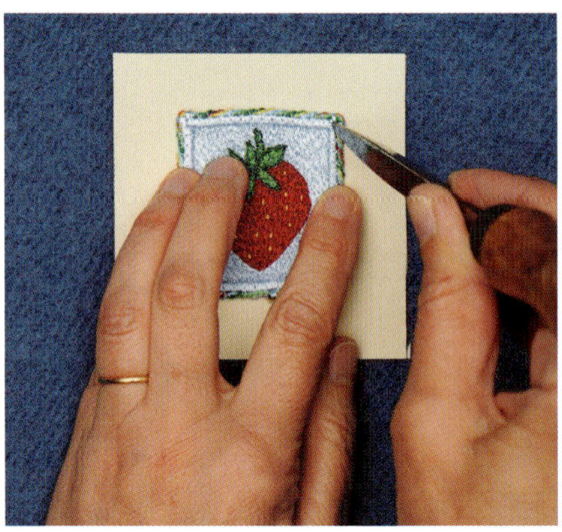

Use a bradawl to make a row of evenly spaced holes in the mount board.

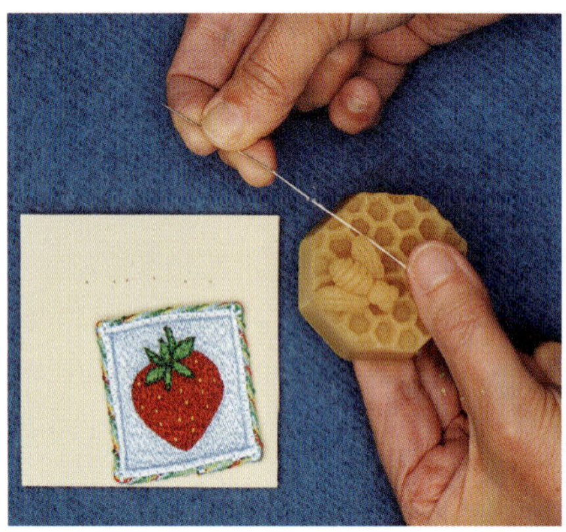

Run a length of strong thread through a piece of beeswax before using it.

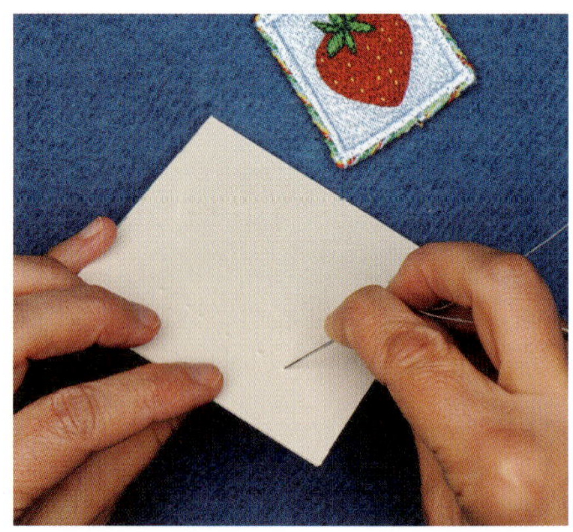

Starting on the right-hand side, push the needle through the first hole.

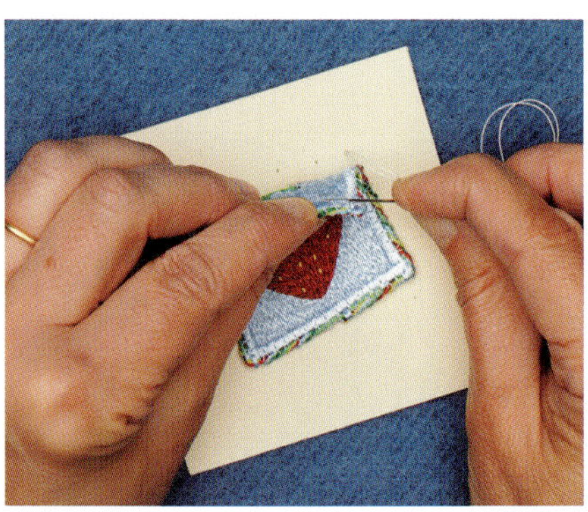

Catch the back of the embroidery with the needle and thread.

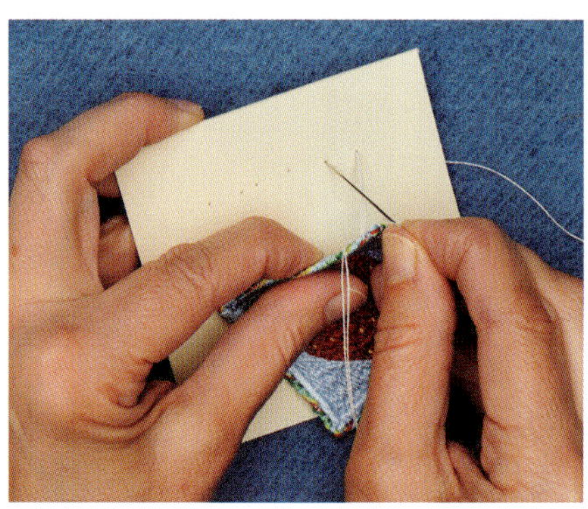

Push the needle and thread through the second hole.

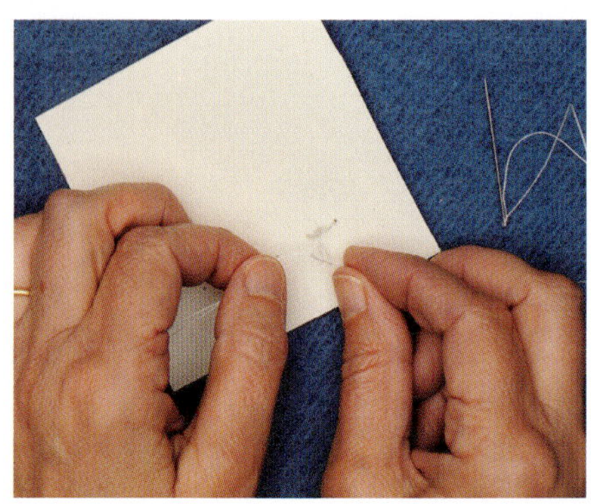

Secure the strong hand sewing thread with a knot.

Next, continue to make a row of evenly spaced holes down the left-hand side. Repeat the hand sewing technique to secure the left-hand side of the picture to the mount board; then continue in the same manner down the right-hand side and lastly along the bottom edge. Once the picture has been sewn down, it will be very secure on the mount board and ready to put into the frame. You may wish to sign the mount board with the name of the picture, your name and the date.

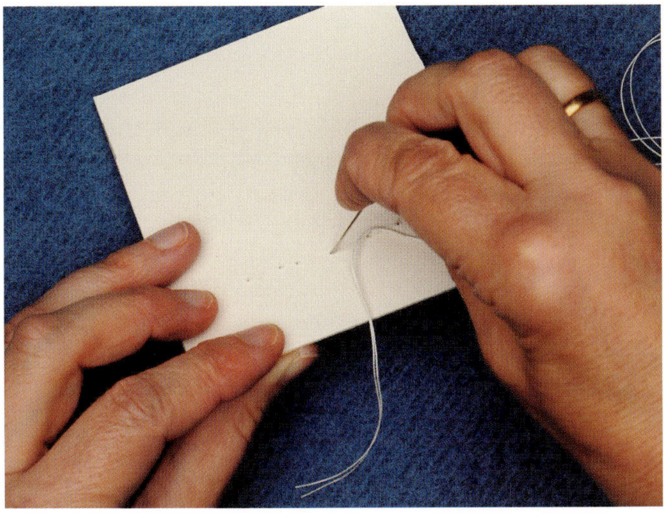

Continue stitching the embroidery to the mount board.

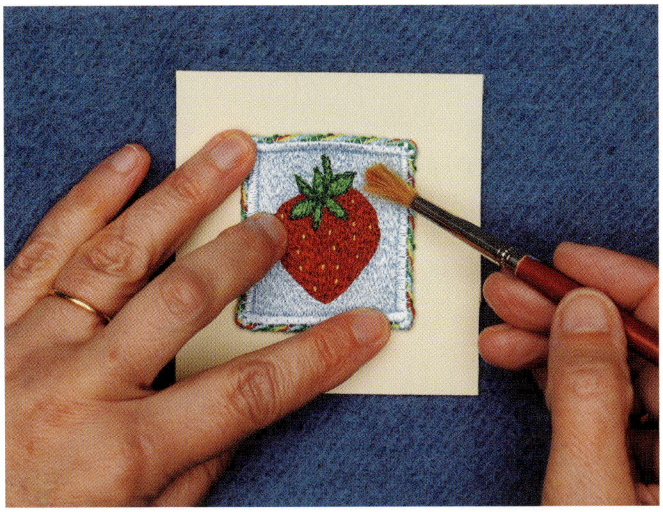

When all the sewing has been completed, gently clean the picture with a soft brush.

1.3 FINISHING OFF

Reassemble the frame and place the mount board with the picture attached onto the recess, making sure that it is the right way up for the frame. Put the backing board in place and secure the turnover buttons or point driver staples. Reattach any framing findings and, using the adhesive frame tape, cut and stick a piece of tape over each side where the backing board meets the edge of the frame, ensuring the tape is not visible from the front. The frame is now ready to hang. Congratulations stand back and admire all your hard work!

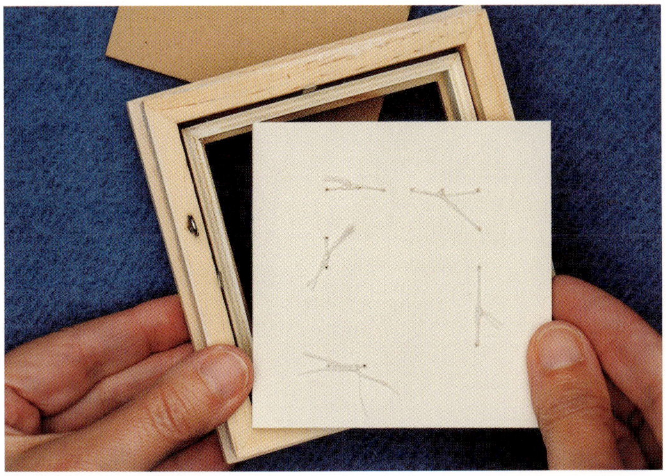

Put the finished mounted and presented picture into the frame.

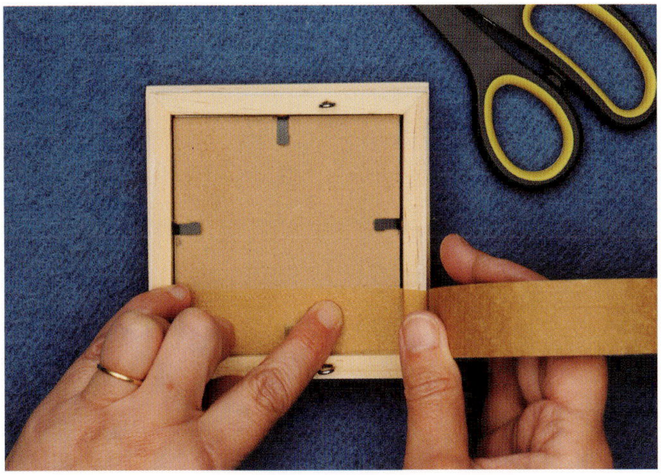

Reassemble the frame and use frame tape to neaten off the back.

SLEEVE MOUNTING, DISPLAYING A FREE-HANGING TEXTILE PIECE

Sleeve mounting is a simple technique to display any free-hanging textile piece. This mounting and framing technique will suit the textile picture from Chapter 4, *Spring Greens*.

The measurements given in the instructions below are for the *Spring Greens* picture only. When making a sleeve for any other sized textile work, be sure to accommodate the size of picture, sleeve and hanging pole for that particular project.

YOU WILL NEED

Items from the basic tool kit, as listed in Chapter 1 Tools and Equipment, and the following materials:

- Piece of plain coloured cotton fabric measuring 6 × 22cm (2½ × 8¾in) for the sleeve for the back of the finished picture
- Dry twig or small stick measuring 24cm (9½in)
- Machine sewing thread in a similar colour to the backing fabric
- Picture hanging fixings
- Length of gardener's twine (optional)

HANDY HINT BACKING FABRIC AND SLEEVE FABRIC COLOURS

To make the backing fabric and the sleeve blend in with the picture itself, choose a fabric that is similar in colour or tone to the actual picture.

HANDY HINT MAKING A DOUBLE FOLD HEM

The double fold hem is a basic standard hem. To create this, with the wrong side of the material facing you, fold the fabric over twice so the raw edge is neatly hidden inside the fold. The edge is secured with a running stitch and pressed in place.

HANDY HINT WHIP STITCH

Whip stitch is a simple hand stitch in which a sewing needle is passed in and out of the two pieces of fabric being sewn together to make a series of small stitches that loop the edge of the fabric.

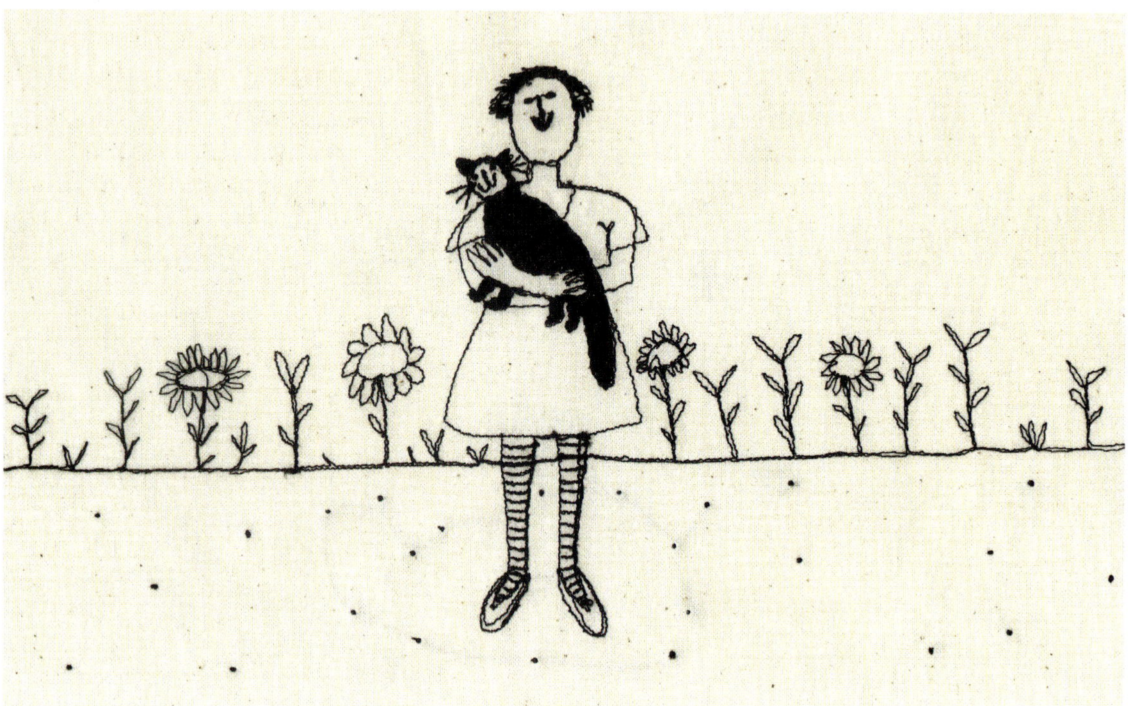

Flower Garden, by Linda Miller, 17 × 24cm (6½ × 9½in), free machine embroidery. (Photo: Michael Jennings)

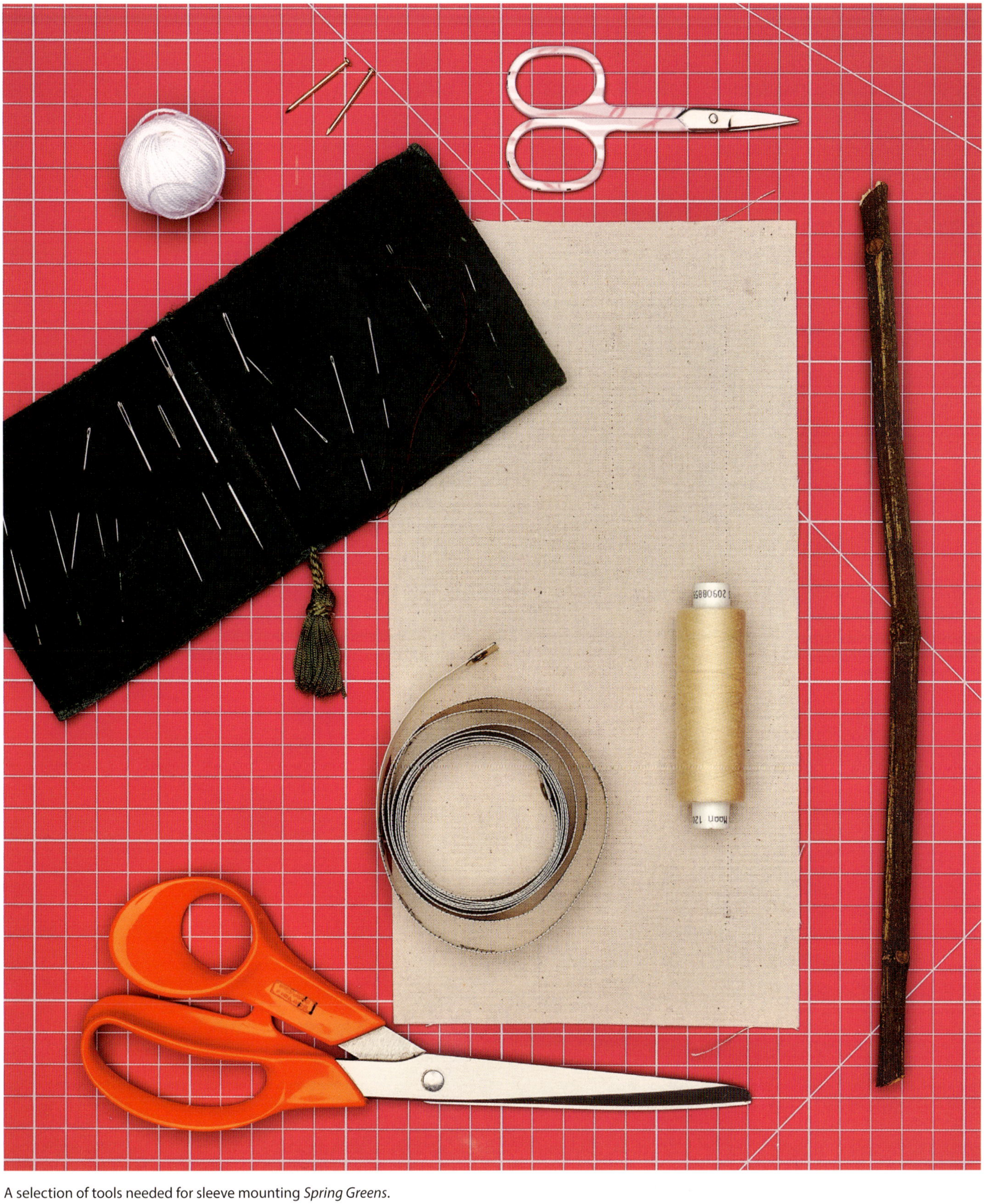

A selection of tools needed for sleeve mounting *Spring Greens*.

2.1 GETTING STARTED: SEWING THE SLEEVE CASING

Place your piece of cotton fabric right side down and using a 2cm (¾in) fold allowance, fold over both short ends of the fabric. Pin to secure before pressing. Place a bobbin in the sewing machine and thread up in the same colour. Using a seam allowance of approximately 6mm, sew both ends of the sleeve, removing the pins or clips as you do so. Press once more.

Using a fold allowance of 1cm (⅜in), fold over each long side once only (a double fold hem is not needed). Pin to secure and press. Using a seam allowance of 3mm, sew in place. Cut off any waste threads and press to secure the folded seams. The sleeve will now measure approximately 4 × 18cm (1½ × 7in).

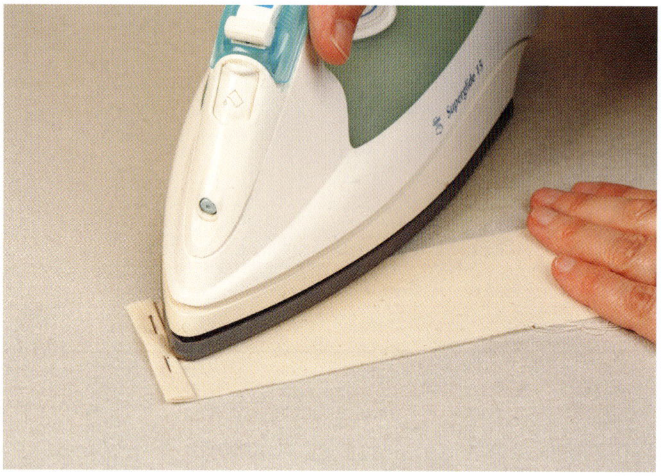

Make a double hem, using a fold allowance of 2cm (¾in) each end of the fabric strip, and press.

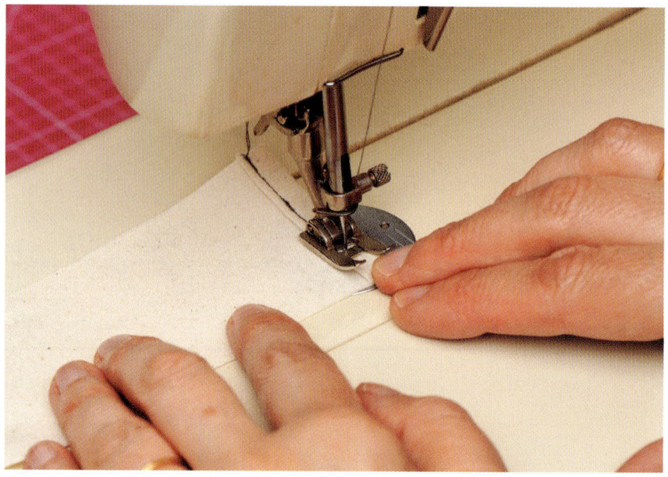

Carefully machine stitch the double hem at each end of the fabric strip.

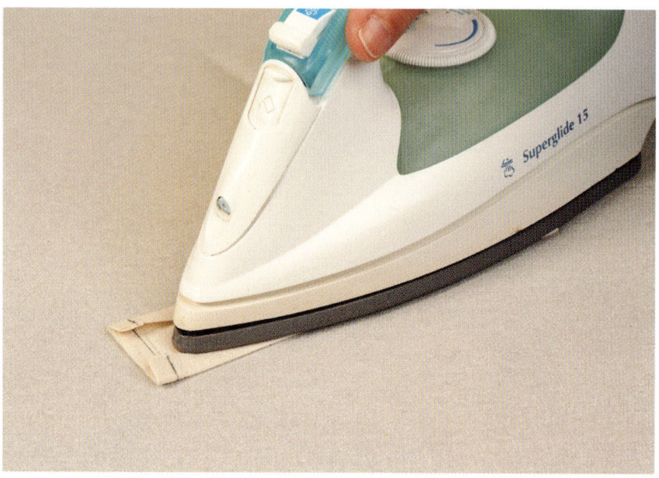

Use a fold allowance of 1cm (⅜in) to create a single fold on both sides of the fabric strip.

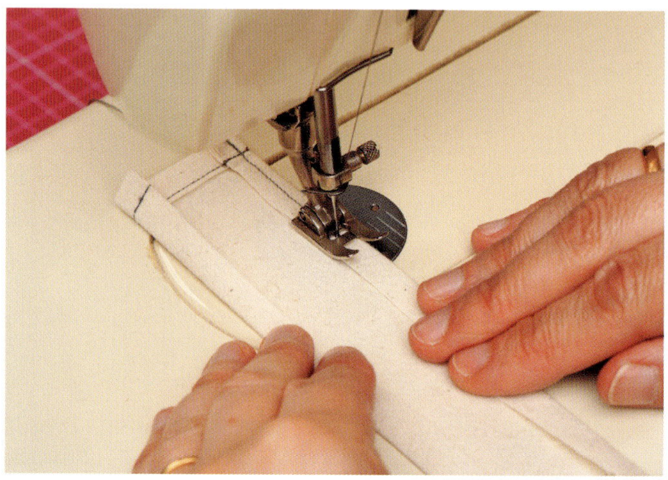

Sew the single fold in place on both sides of the fabric strip to create the sleeve.

2.2 SEWING THE SLEEVE IN PLACE

Place the sleeve on the back of the picture, positioning on the backing fabric approximately 2cm (¾in) from the top and 3cm (1¼in)[LINDA TO CHECK AGAINST CAPTION, PLEASE] from each side. Pin in place and, using a thread that is similar in colour to the sleeve and backing fabric, hand sew using a small whip stitch. Sew along the top and bottom of the sleeve, being careful not to take the stitches onto the front of the picture. Ensure you leave both ends of the opening free, remove the pins and gently press.

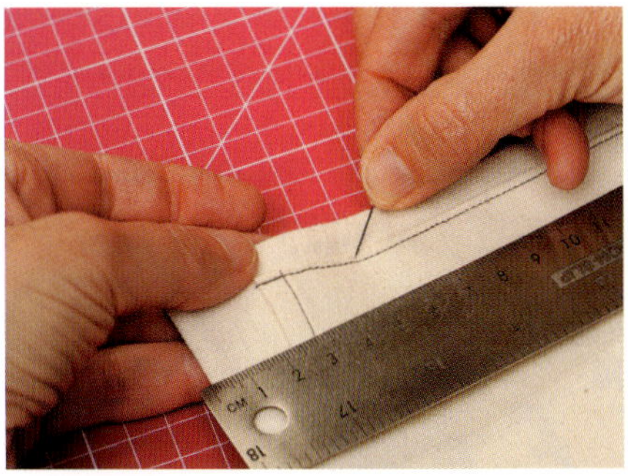

Pin the sleeve in place, approximately 2cm (¾in) from the top and 3cm (1¼in) from each side.

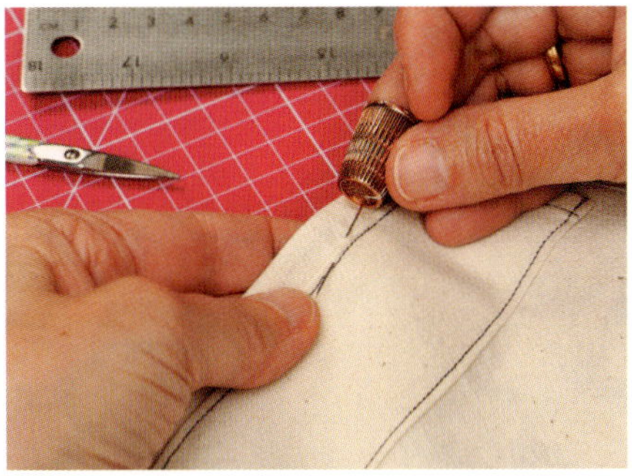

Attach using a whip stitch, being careful not to have any stitches showing on the front.

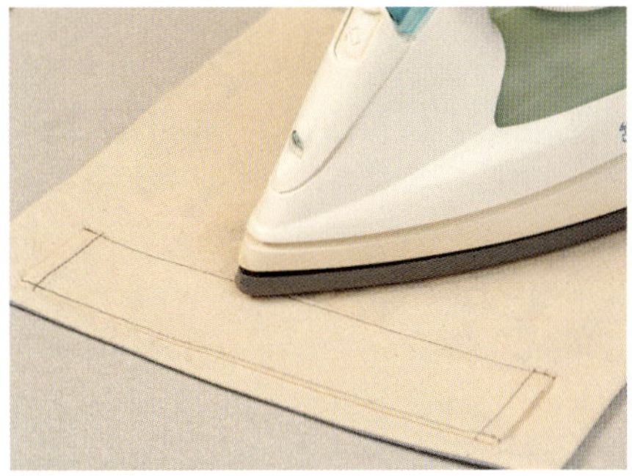

After all the hand stitching has been completed, press carefully with a hot steam iron.

2.3 FINISHING OFF

Push the twig or small stick through the sleeve. You have two options for hanging: either hang from two small nails in the wall (situated approximately 1cm, or ⅜in, from each end of the sleeve), or why not continue the garden theme and use a length of gardeners' twine by tying it to each end of the twig and hanging from a single nail?

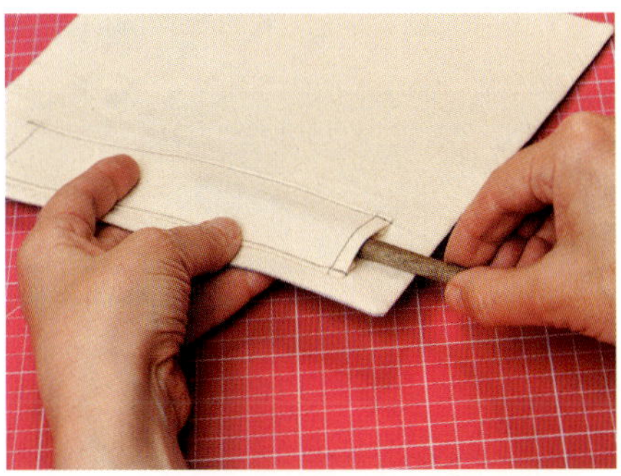

Gently bend the picture to allow the sleeve to open, ready for inserting the twig.

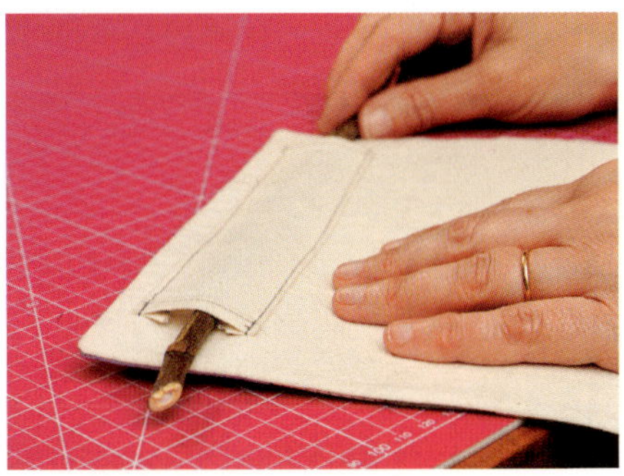

Push the twig through the sleeve, ensuring it does not catch on the backing fabric.

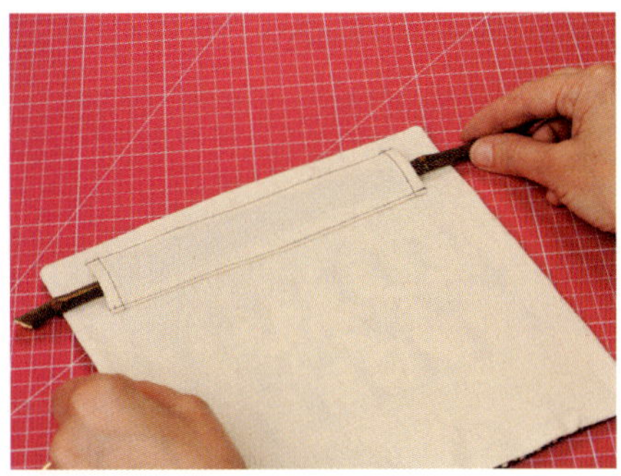

Check that the twig is centrally placed before hanging the picture on the wall.

SEMI FREE MOUNTING, DISPLAYING A FREE-HANGING PIECE IN A FRAME

As with the sleeve mounting technique, this alternative free-hanging solution gives the textile picture the appearance of gently floating within the frame. This mounting and framing technique will suit the textile picture from Chapter 5, *Embellishing a Vintage Cloth*.

3.1 GETTING STARTED: STITCHING THE LOOP TAPE TO THE COTTON TAPE

Start by carefully taking your frame apart. Leave any frame findings, such as turnover buttons or point driver staples, in place by gently bending them back. They will be needed when the frame is reassembled.

YOU WILL NEED

Items from the basic tool kit, as listed in Chapter 1 Tools and Equipment, and the following materials:

- Wooden unglazed box picture frame measuring 44 × 44cm (17½ × 17½in)
- Length of cotton tape measuring 2.5 × 32cm (1 × 12½in) in a similar colour to the backing fabric
- Adhesive frame tape
- Piece of good-quality mount board in a neutral colour (you will cut to fit your frame)
- Piece of sew-on and stick-on hook and loop tape measuring 2 × 28cm (¾ × 11in)
- Hand sewing needle
- Sewing thread in a similar colour to the tape

HANDY HINT **SEWING THE HOOK AND LOOP TAPE ONTO THE COTTON TAPE**

Hook and loop tape is used as a fastening for fabric. It consists of two pieces: one has soft loops and the other has stiff hooks. When both pieces are placed together, the tape is secure and difficult to pull apart. Therefore, by nature, it is a very strong tape and consequently can be quite stiff to sew. It can split if sewn near the edge with a machine running stitch, so to avoid this, sew it onto the cotton tape with a zigzag stitch instead. Cotton tape is pleasing to work with; being a natural product, it responds well to both machine and hand stitch.

Flower Garden, by Linda Miller, 17 × 24cm (6½ × 9½in), free machine embroidery. (Photo: Michael Jennings)

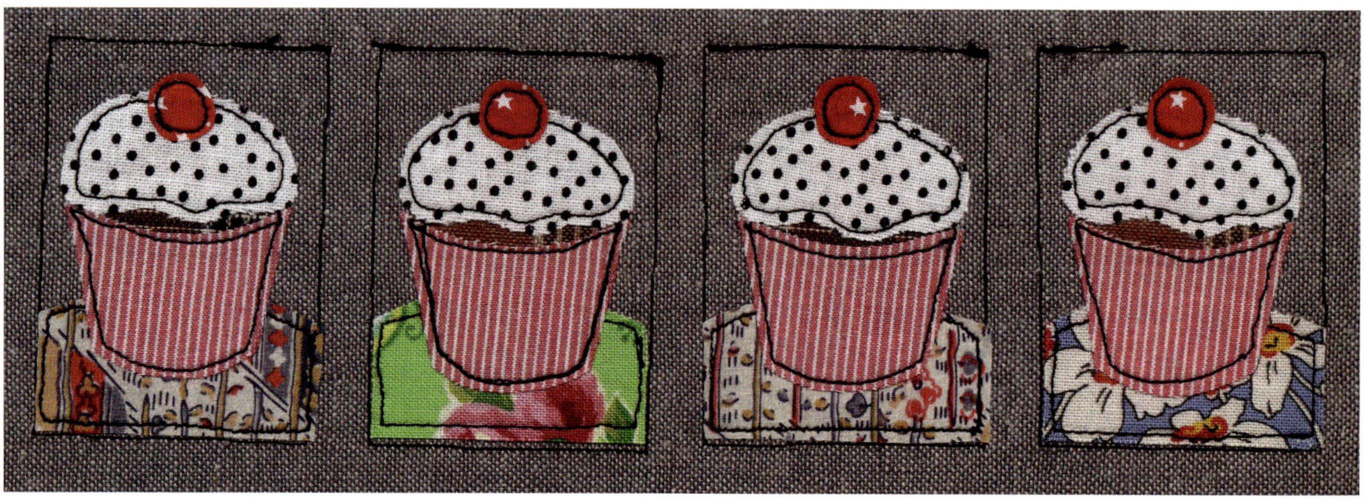

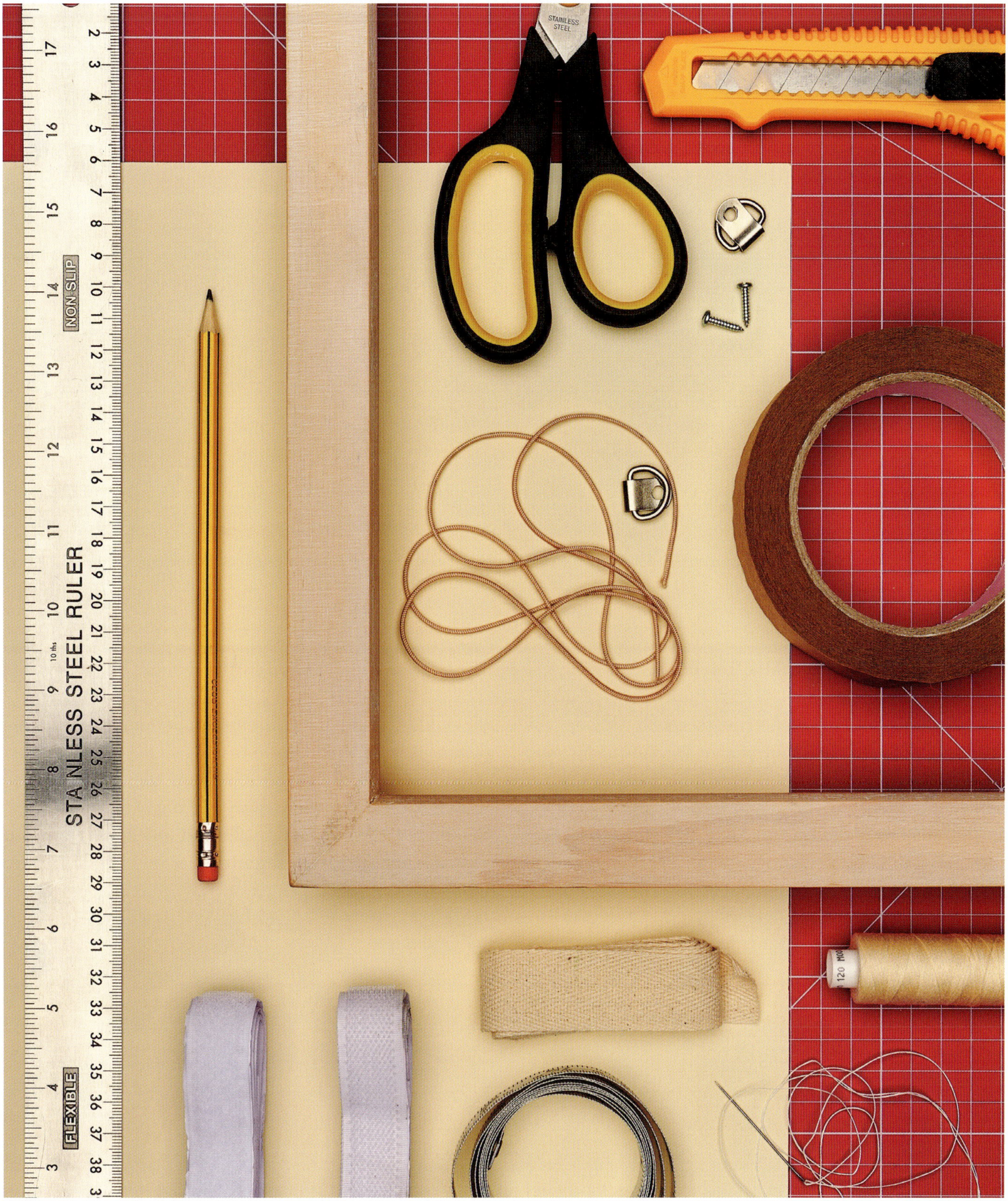

A selection of tools needed for framing *Embellishing a Vintage Cloth.*

3.2 STITCHING THE LOOP TAPE TO THE COTTON TAPE

Set the sewing machine to a zigzag stitch. Using a sewing thread that is similar in colour to the hook and loop tape, thread up the machine, ensuring you have a bobbin of the same colour. Make a double folded hem at each end of the cotton tape, and machine stitch in place.

Pull the hook and loop tape apart. Lay the loop strip of hook and loop tape directly in the centre of the length of cotton tape and stitch to secure.

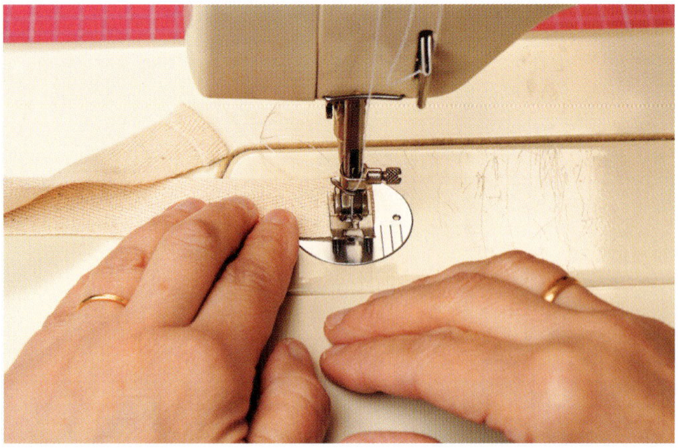

Use a sewing thread similar in colour to the cotton tape and zigzag stitch both ends.

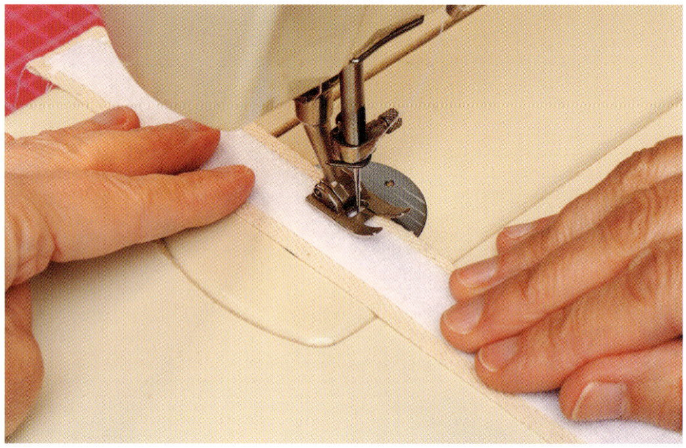

Sew the loop side of the tape onto the cotton tape, again using a zigzag stitch.

3.3 SEWING THE TAPE IN PLACE

Place the assembled piece of cotton tape with the loop tape facing you onto the back of the picture. Position it 1cm ($\frac{3}{8}$in) from each edge and 1cm ($\frac{3}{8}$in) from the top edge and pin it in place.

Thread up a hand sewing needle in the same colour as the tape, run it through a piece of beeswax and make a knot at the end. Using a whip stitch, sew the tape onto the back of the picture using small stitches to ensure that the tape is securely sewn onto the backing fabric. Every so often, check that the whip stitches are not showing on the front of the picture. Sew all the way around the tape, finishing off with a knot where you started. Cut off any waste threads.

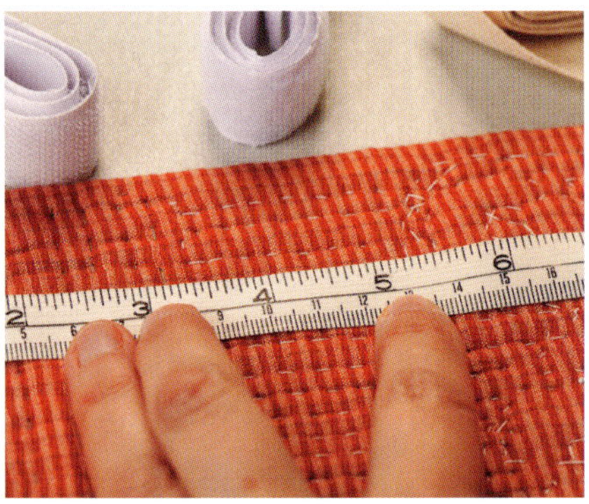

Position the tape 1cm ($\frac{3}{8}$in) from both sides and 1cm ($\frac{3}{8}$in) from the top, and pin in place.

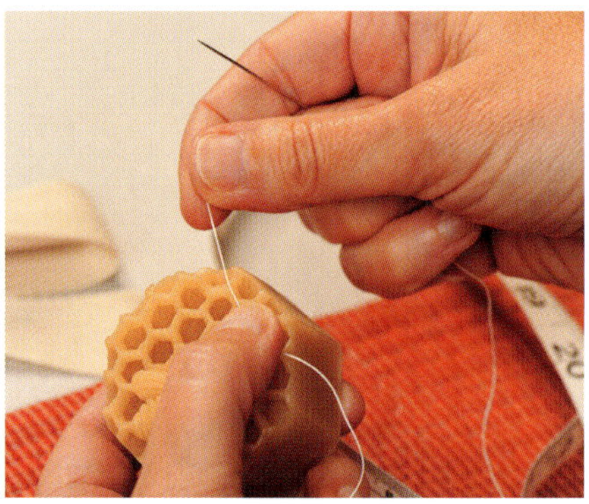

Using beeswax to coat the hand sewing thread will ensure tangle-free sewing.

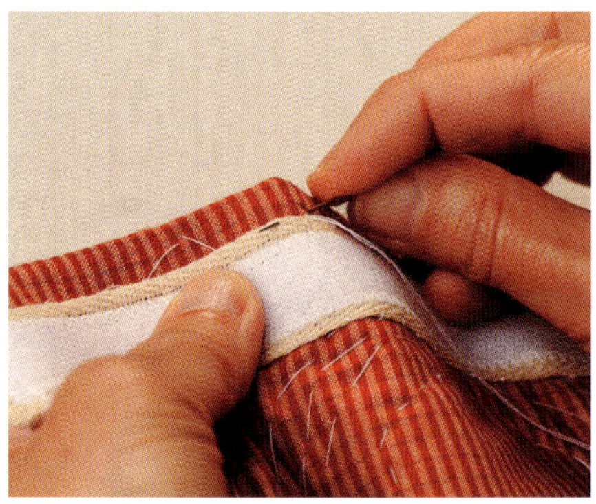

Take your time when sewing the tape onto the back of the picture. This will give a neat finish.

3.4 MEASURING AND MARKING THE MOUNT BOARD

Using the cutting mat, cut the mount board to fit the recess of the frame. Place the picture onto the mount board with the right side facing you, ensuring it is centred between the two sides and with the same distance from the top; it is visually more pleasing for the picture to have a slightly deeper distance from the bottom.

When you are happy with the positioning of the picture, carefully fold back the top of the picture so that you can see the top and sides of the loop tape. Using the pencil, carefully mark the mount board where the end of the loop tape meets the board, and then similarly mark along the top and bottom to show where the hook tape will need to be positioned. Once completed, put the picture to one side.

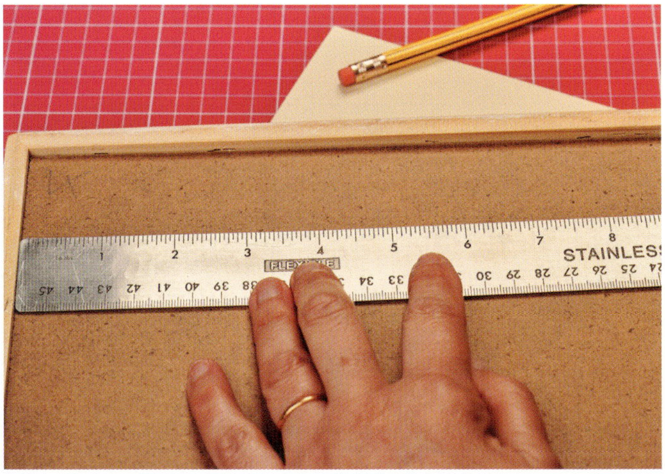

Measure the frame's recess and use a cutting mat to cut the mount board.

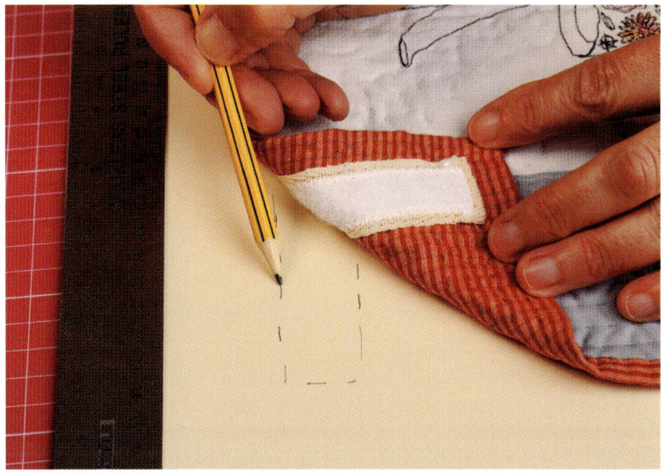

Place the picture on the mount board, measure and position, and mark with a pencil.

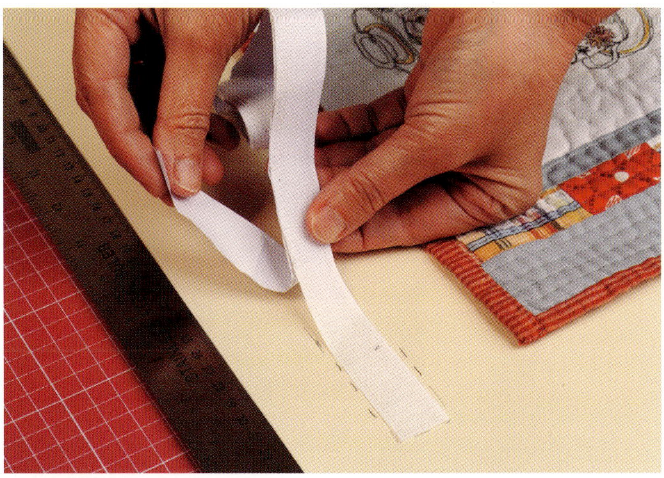

Peel off the protective strip on the hook side of the tape and place within the pencil marks.

3.5 ATTACHING THE HOOK TAPE TO THE MOUNT BOARD

Peel off just the beginning of the protective strip on the hook tape. Align this end of the tape up with one of the edge pencil marks (be aware: the tape is very sticky, so avoid getting anything stuck on it). Continue to peel the protective strip away as you match up the side of the tape to the top pencil marks, and carry on in this way until the hook tape is in place. Using your index finger, gently push along the tape to secure, and leave it for about an hour for the adhesive to dry.

Once dry, place the picture face up onto the mount board, aligning the hook and the loop tape together; you may need to adjust the picture to ensure it is laying flat. Place the assembled picture and mount board into the frame and reassemble the picture frame, reattaching any framing findings. Cut and stick a length of adhesive frame tape over each side where the backing board meets the edge of the frame, ensuring the tape is not visible from the front. Your picture is now ready for hanging.

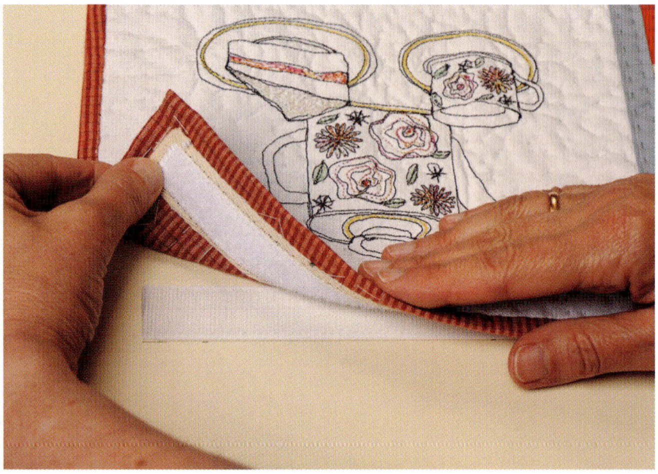

Press the hook and loop tape together. This will attach the picture to the mount board.

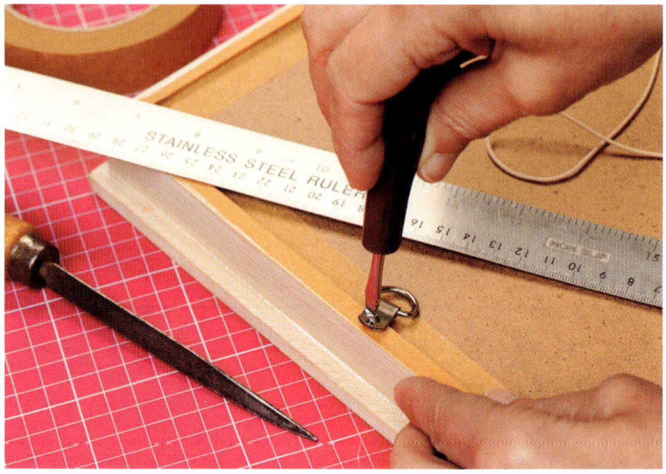

Carefully place the picture in the frame and reassemble using the frame findings.

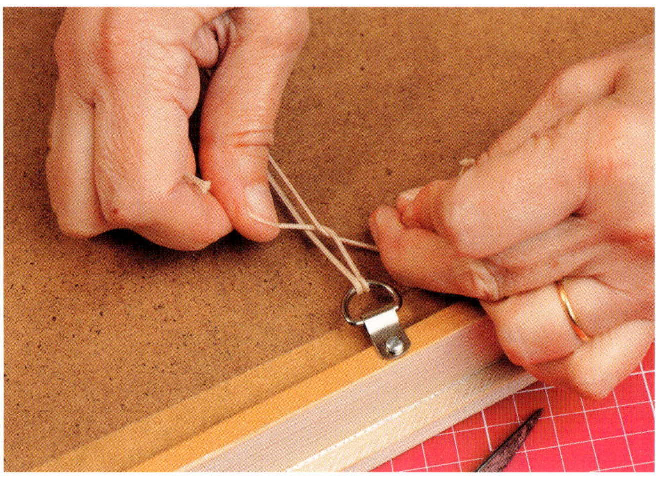

Wrap the frame cord around the picture findings twice. This will make the cord tight.

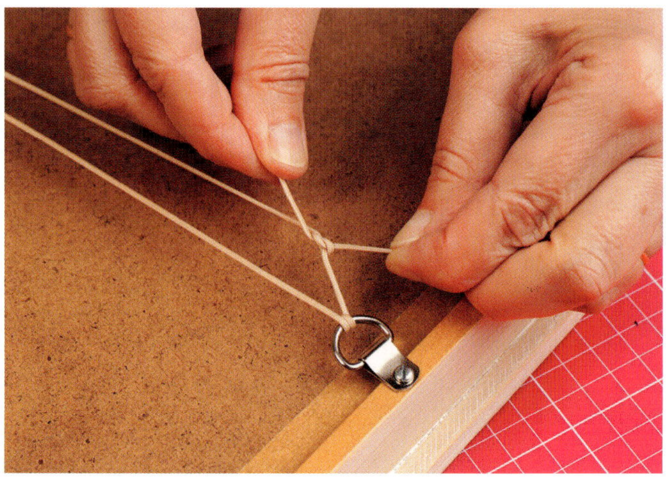

Use a reliable knot, such as a reef knot, to secure the picture cord in place.

LACE MOUNTING A PICTURE ONTO MOUNT BOARD, READY FOR FRAMING IN A BOX FRAME

Lace mounting is a versatile framing technique which is very suitable for presenting any free machine stitched textile pictures that incorporate the background material into the work. This classic but simple technique only requires a needle and thread to secure the textile picture onto a piece of mount board before being housed in its frame. The lacing method will suit any sized picture.

This mounting and framing technique will suit the textiles pictures from: Chapter 6, *Bird of Paradise*; Chapter 7, *Colourful Kites;* and Chapter 8, *Seaside Story*.

YOU WILL NEED

Items from the basic tool kit, as listed in Chapter 1 Tools and Equipment, and the following materials:

- Unglazed wooden box picture frame measuring 25 × 25cm (10 × 10in)
- Adhesive frame tape
- Piece of good-quality mount board in a neutral colour (you will cut to fit your frame)
- Strong hand sewing thread in a similar colour to the mount board (bookbinding thread or a strong thin crochet thread is suitable)
- Sewing thread in a similar colour to the background fabric of your picture
- Eight sprung laundry pegs (wooden or plastic)

4.1 GETTING STARTED: PREPARING THE FRAME AND CUTTING THE MOUNT BOARD

Start by carefully taking your frame apart. Leave any frame findings, such as turnover buttons or point driver staples, in place by gently bending them back. They will be needed when the frame is reassembled.

Measure the frame's recess, then using a pencil, mark the mount board 3mm smaller on each side. Place the piece of mount board on the cutting mat and use a sharp art and craft utility knife to cut the mount board

HANDY HINT ENSURING THE FABRIC-COVERED MOUNT BOARD FITS THE FRAME

When using lace mounting, the mount board is encased by the fabric and is secured by a lacing technique on the back. To ensure that this piece of covered board will fit into your frame, the mount board needs to be cut a little smaller to accommodate the fabric. Before you begin the lacing, double check that both the fabric and mount board will fit snuggly in your frame.

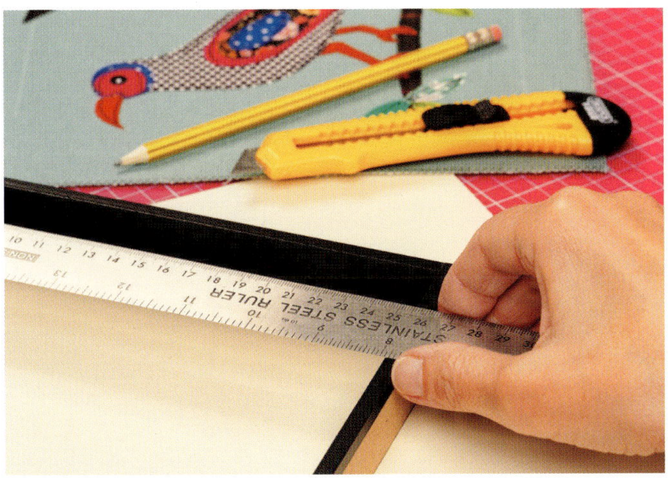

Cut the mount board slightly smaller than the frame to give the picture a snug fit.

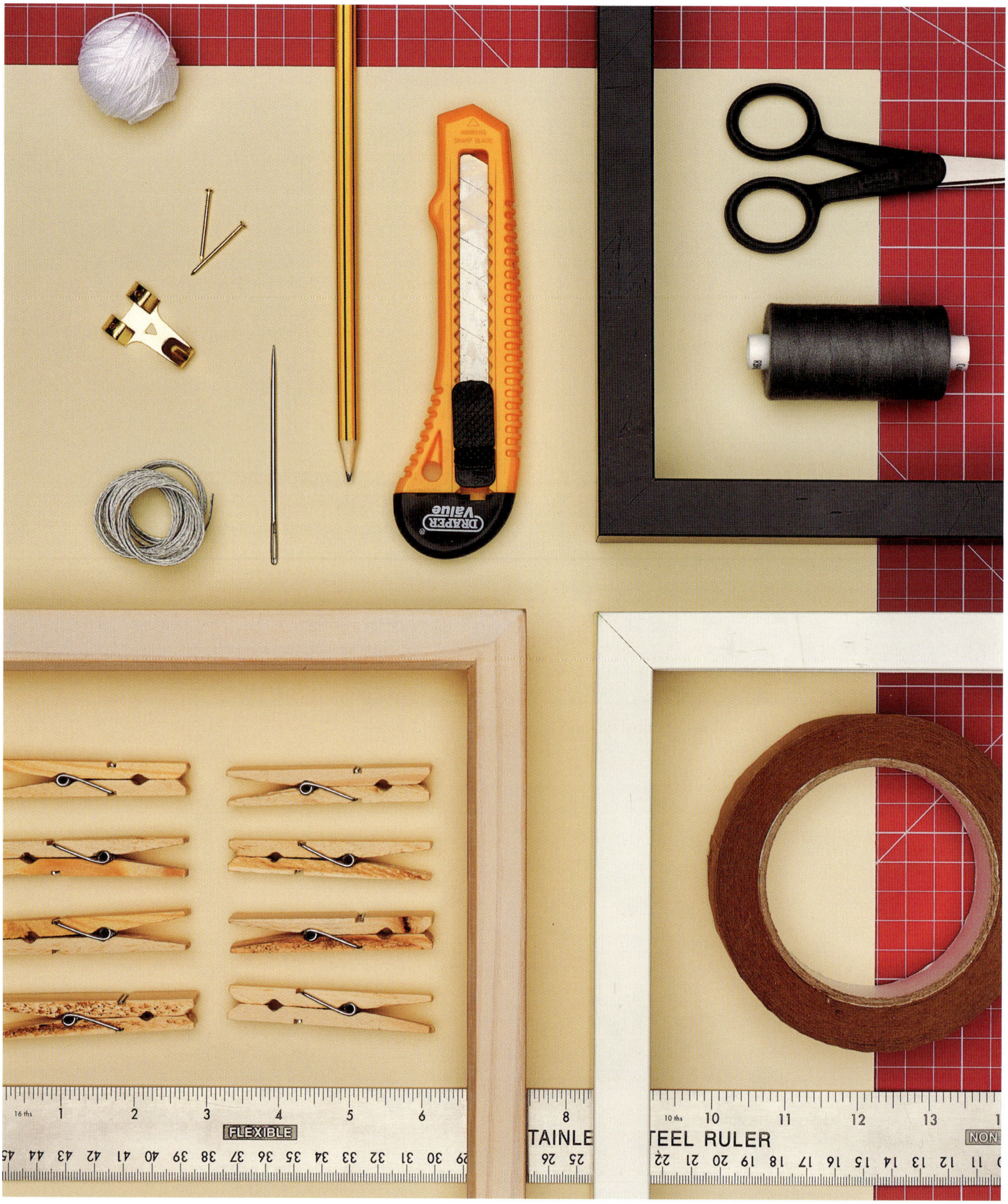

A selection of tools needed for the framing technique of lace mounting. This method will suit *Bird of Paradise*, *Colourful Kites* and *Seaside Story*.

4.2 PLACING THE MOUNT BOARD ON THE PICTURE

Place your picture face down and lay the mount board on top, positioning it centrally. Next, fold over the fabric on the top edge, using two sprung laundry pegs to secure in place; then do the same on the bottom, followed by either side. Turn the picture over and check that you are happy with its position – if you need to adjust it, undo the pegs and reposition.

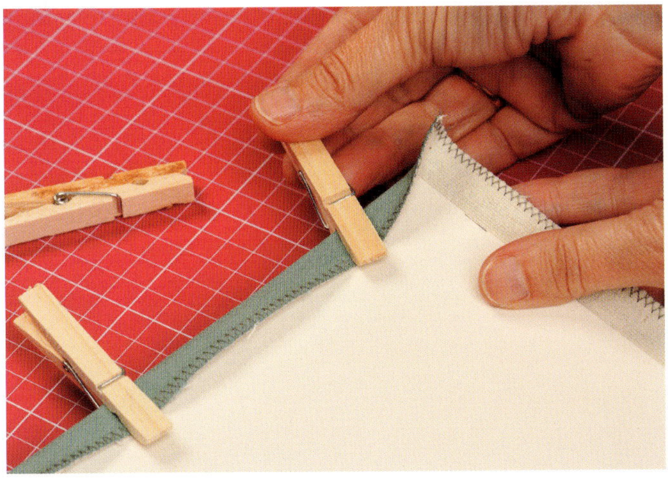

Position the picture on the mount board and secure with sprung laundry pegs.

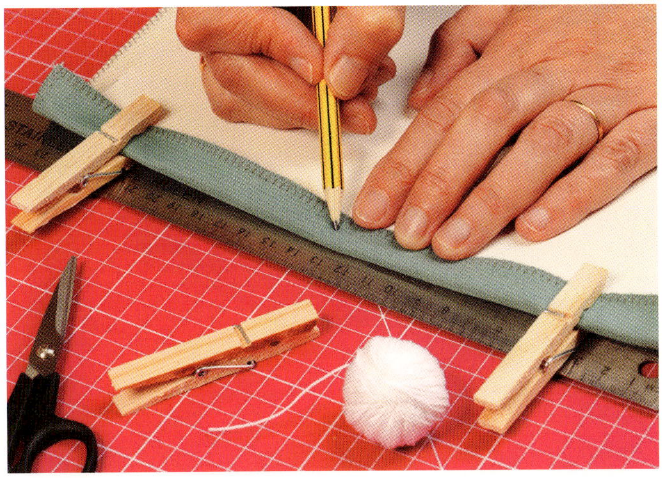

Reposition if necessary, and then mark the middle of the picture along the top edge.

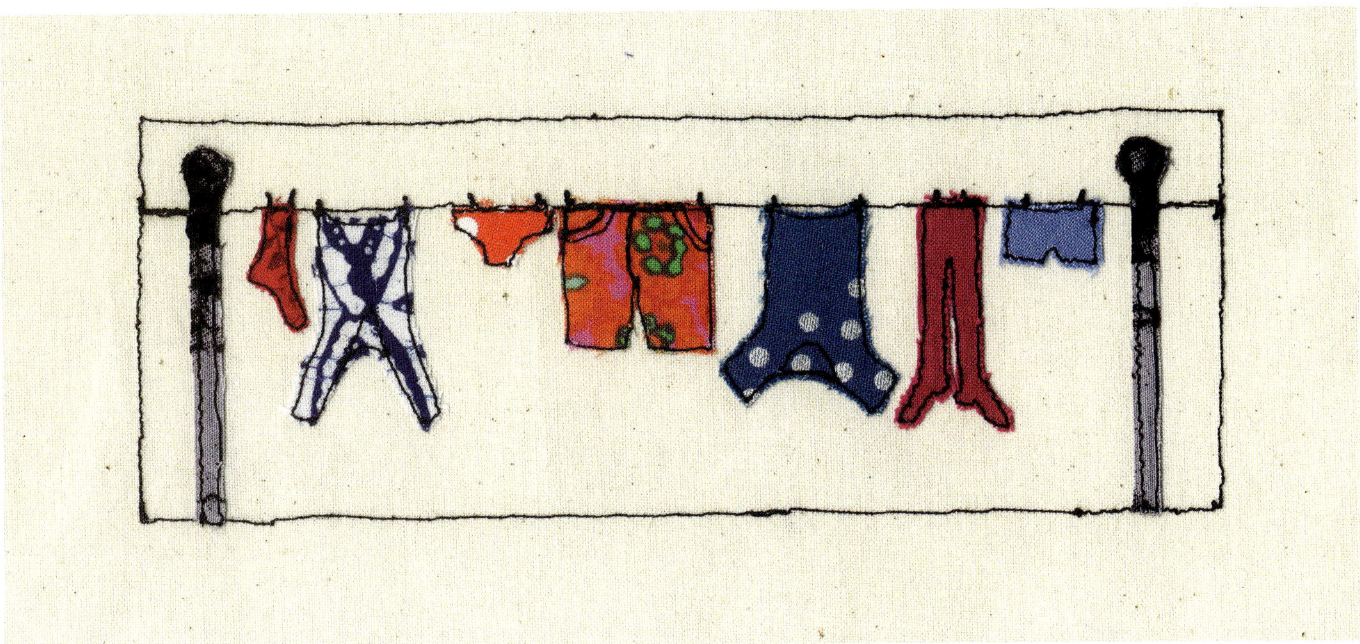

Washing Line by Linda Miller, 7 × 18cm (3 × 7in), fabric appliqué and free machine embroidery. (Photo: Michael Jennings)

4.3 SECURING THE PICTURE IN PLACE, TOP TO BOTTOM

Cut a 1m (40in) length of strong thread, thread up the hand sewing needle and make a knot in the end. With the picture face down, find the middle of the top row.

Push the needle through underneath the fabric lip, 5mm away from the zigzag edge, and pull the thread through so that the knot rests underneath this lip. Push the needle once more through the back of the fabric and pull it tight to create a single whip stitch. Then, take the needle directly opposite to the middle of the bottom edge, push the needle through underneath the bottom lip and pull tight.

Push the needle back through the fabric to repeat the single whip stitch, while pulling the thread tight to secure. Then take the needle back through the first whip stitch at the top and pull the thread tight before knotting off to secure. You should have a double stitch from top to bottom, securing the mount board within the fabric. Cut the thread near the knot to neaten.

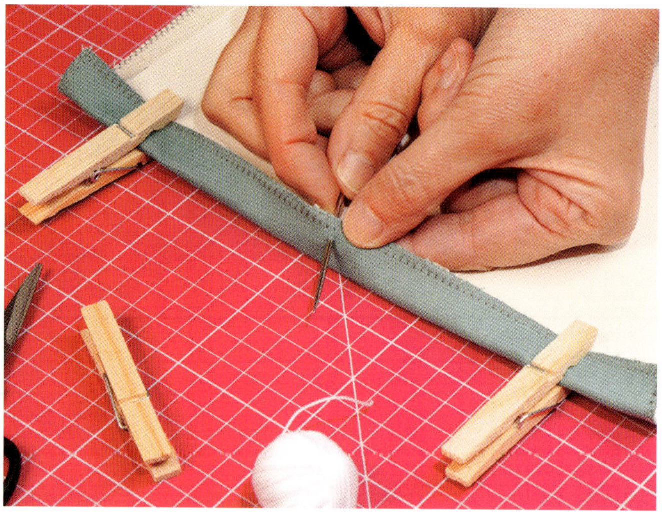

Thread up a sewing needle with 1m (40in) of strong thread and make a knot at the end.

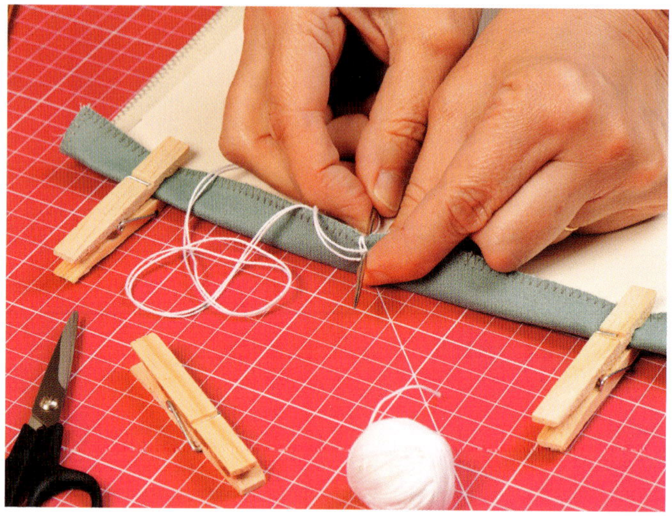

Push the needle underneath the fabric lip and pull it through. Repeat to create a whip stitch.

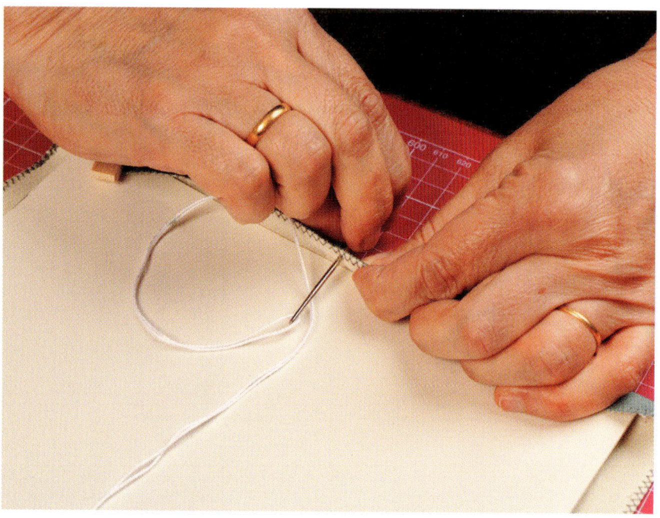

Take the needle to the opposite side and repeat, before knotting and cutting.

4.4 LACING FROM TOP TO BOTTOM: FIRST SIDE

Cut a 2m (2¼yd) length of the strong thread, thread up the hand sewing needle and make a knot in the end. Starting at the top, 2.5cm (1in) away from the first lacing and 5mm in from the zigzag edge, push the needle through the underside of the fabric and make a single whip stitch.

Next, take the needle down to the bottom and push the needle through the underneath of the fabric, 2.5cm (1in) away from the central lacing and 5mm in from the zigzag edge. Then take the needle back up to the top, gently pulling it tight, ready to push the needle back through the underneath of the top, 2.5cm (1in) away from the previous stitch.

Continue in this manner, removing the pegs as you go, until you reach the edge of the mount board. Pull all the lacing tight, however be careful not to pull it too tight to avoid bowing the mount board. Make a single whip stitch and secure with a knot before cutting away the waste thread. You have now laced half of one side of the work.

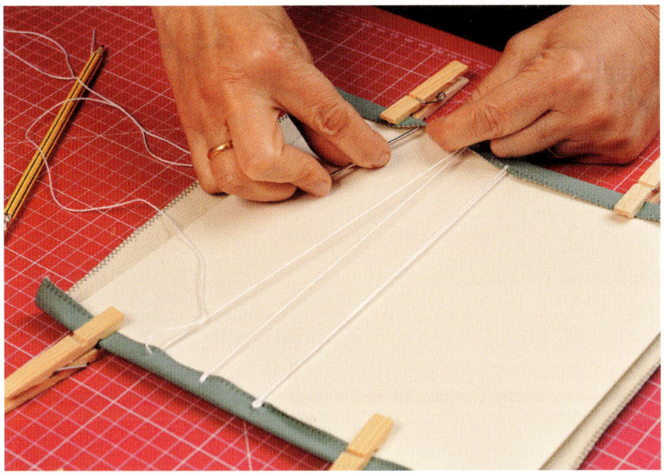

Begin lacing the right-hand side, starting 2.5cm (1in) away from the initial middle lacing.

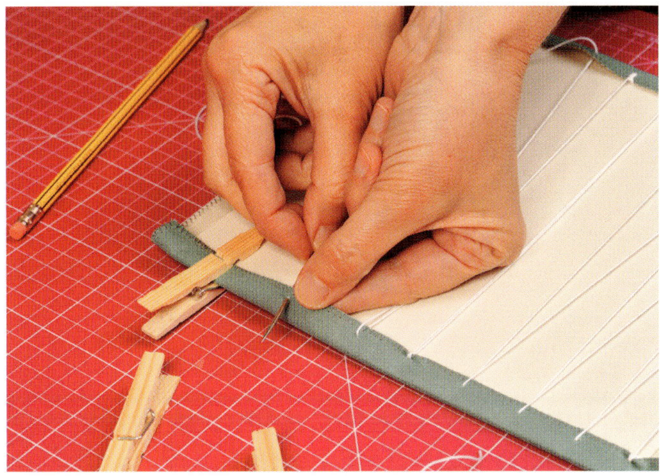

Once the right-hand side has been completed, begin lacing the left-hand side.

4.5 LACING FROM TOP TO BOTTOM: SECOND SIDE

Turn the piece of work through 180 degrees. Rethread the needle with another 2m (2¼yd) length of strong thread and knot. Beginning with a single whip stitch at the top, as before, repeat the previous steps, ensuring that you pull the lacing taut as you go until you reach the other edge of the mount board. Secure with a whip stitch, ensuring the lacing is not too tight and the board is flat.

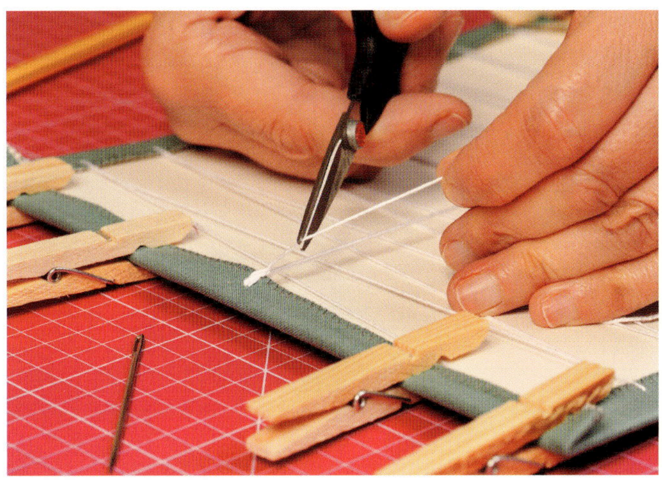

Turn the board 180 degrees, and with another length of thread, repeat the whole process.

4.6 LACING THE SIDES

Turn the work through 90 degrees so that the remaining pegs are top and bottom. Once more, find the middle measurement and using a 1m (40in) length of thread, repeat the initial middle securing stitch. Continue with the lacing of both sides in the same manner as before.

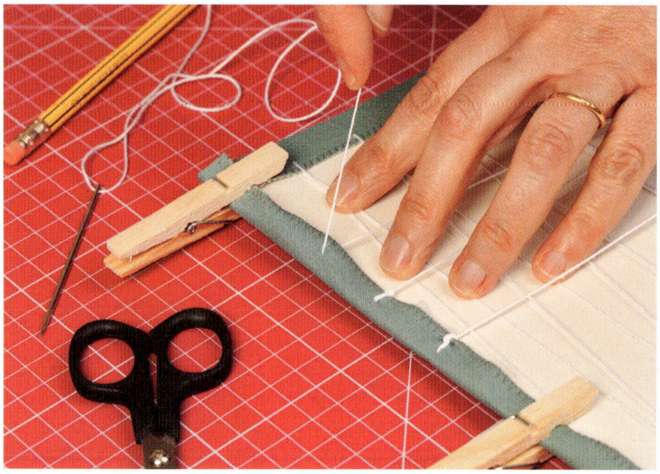

The lacing needs to be taut, but not so tight that the board bows.

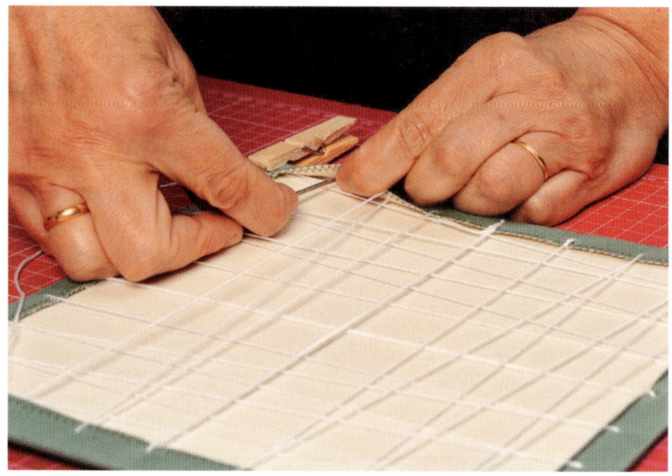

When the end of the thread is reached, knot securely and then rethread.

4.7 WHIP STITCHING THE CORNERS, READY FOR THE FRAME

Thread up a needle using a thread in a similar colour to the picture's background. Whip stitch along the outside edge of each corner to neaten, and fasten it in place before knotting and cutting away the waste thread. Place the picture in the frame, reassemble using the frame findings and neaten with the adhesive tape. The picture is now ready to hang.

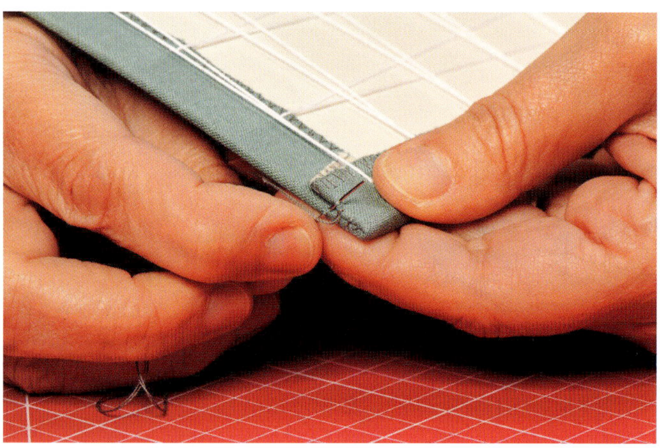

Choose a thread similar in colour to the background and whip stitch each corner.

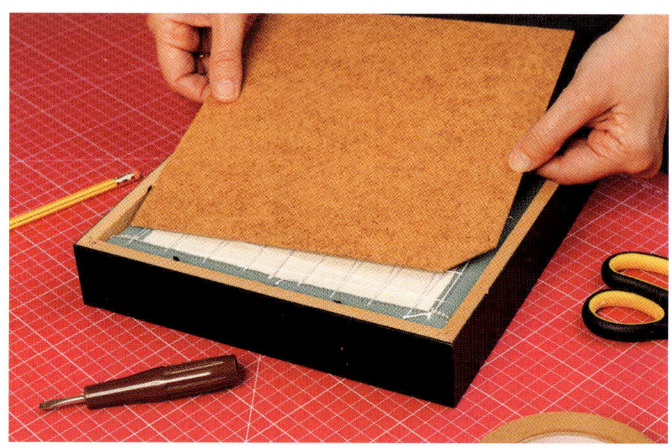

Put the picture into the frame before reassembling with the frame findings and frame tape.

FURTHER THOUGHTS ON FRAMING

Another technique that provides a free-hanging solution is baton mounting, which is similar to the semi free presentation used for *Embellishing a Vintage Cloth*. The textile piece is secured to a baton using hook and loop tape, which is then fixed to the wall. Again, this gives the appearance that the work is gently floating. This economical method is suitable for any sized textile picture that can support its own weight.

A piece of loop tape is first sewn onto a piece of cotton tape and then hand sewn onto the back of the textile picture, ensuring that none of the hand stitches appear on the front. A piece of hook tape is secured to a wooden baton, approximately 6cm (2½in) smaller than the width of the picture, using staples or small upholstery tacks. The baton is then secured to the wall using picture plates and either nails or screws, and the picture is secured using the hook and loop tape.

This elegant solution is useful for pieces that may be considered to be difficult to hang. If the piece in question is very large, uneven in shape or is made from multiple layers, it can simply be repositioned using the hook and loop tape and therefore becomes easy to hang.

Remember, when you are hanging your work, ensure you use the right fixings for your wall and for whatever you are hanging. If the fabric picture is quite light then small nails may suffice; for medium-weight framed pieces, you may wish to use picture hooks; and for very heavy pieces, you may need to use Rawlplugs with compatible screws.

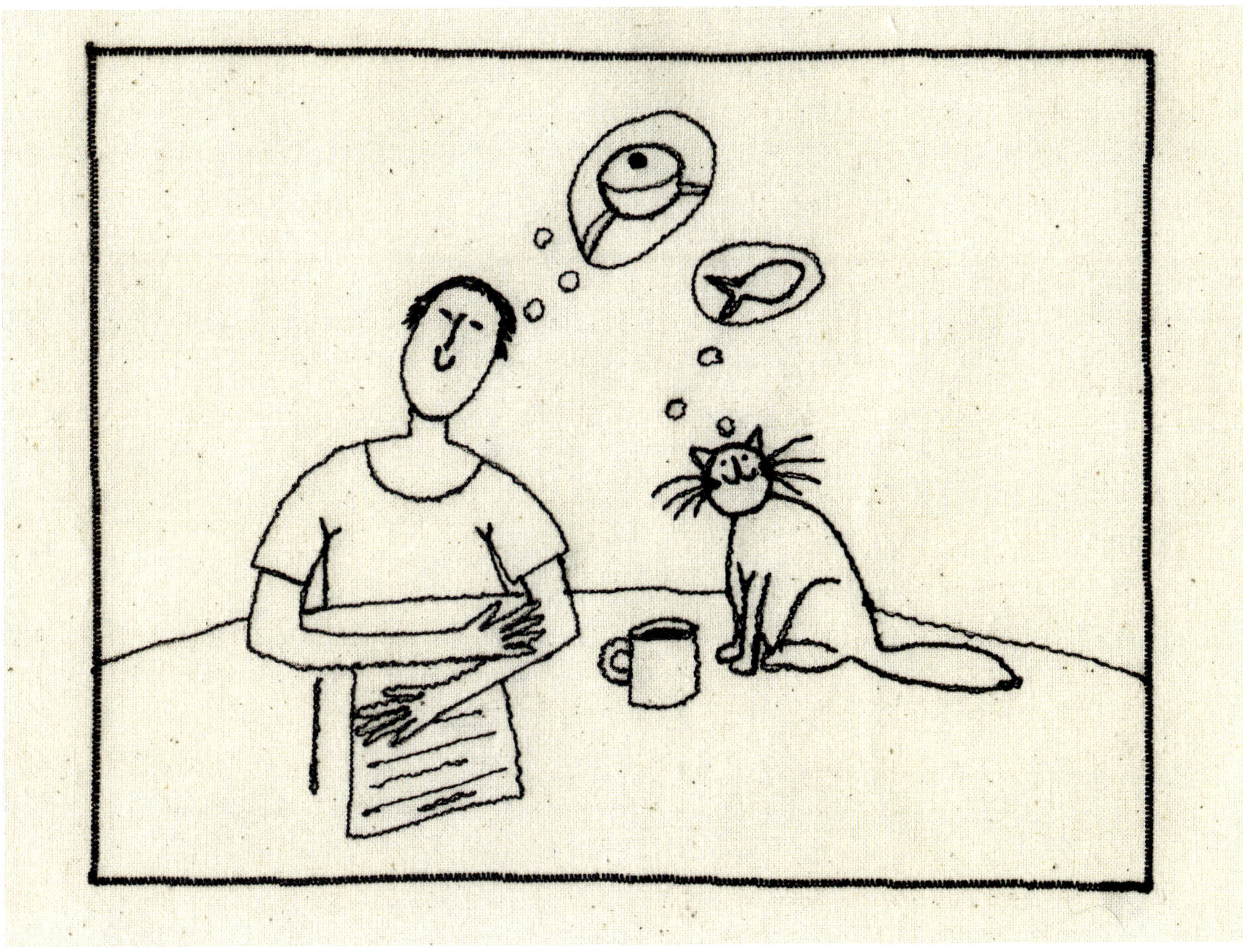

Day Dreaming by Linda Miller, (14 × 18cm (5½ × 7in), free machine embroidery. (Photo: Michael Jennings)

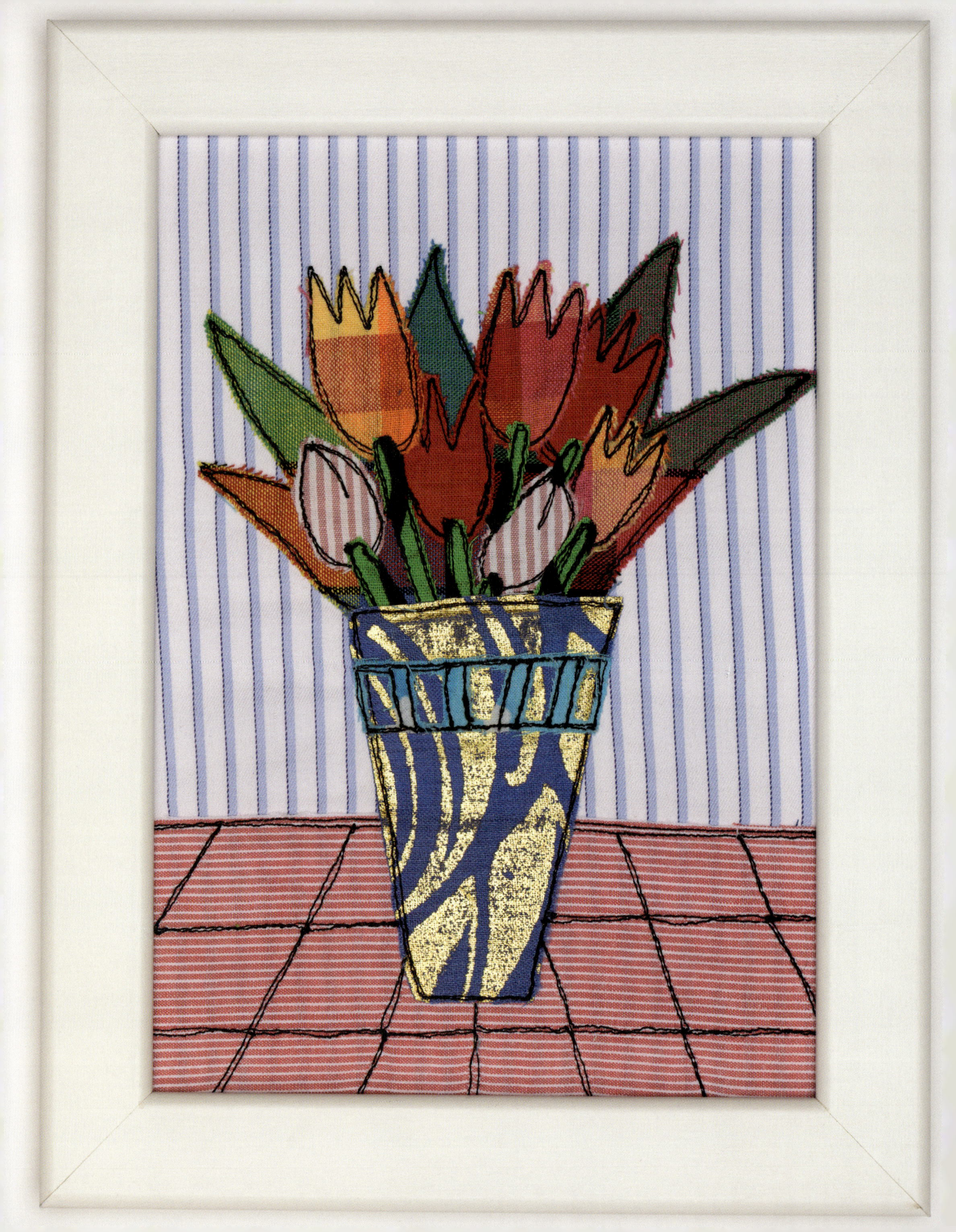

Acknowledgements

This book would not have been possible without the support and encouragement of my friends – you all know who you are, so a huge thank you to each and every one of you!

Thank you to Linda Trueman for introducing me to machine embroidery and setting me on my stitching course with patience and lots of encouragement. My career journey would have been impossible without her.

A massive and special thank you goes to every one of the people listed below. These kind and supportive people all helped in their own unique way, each offering copious amounts of their time and sharing their own and unique skill set with me. Without either one of them, this book would never have got off the ground or got finished.

Fiona Merrikin for all her patience, knowledge and suggestions on how to structure a sentence. Her unlimited time spent on reading, editing, rereading and sharing her command of the English language with me has gone beyond anything I could have asked of her.

Oliver Lane for taking all the step-by-step photographs. His generosity and meticulous attention to detail and lighting are beautifully portrayed in the stunning shots, which are simply perfect. www.lanephoto.co.uk

Sarah Tyssen for her constant energy, kindness and support. Her beautifully understated styling for each photo shoot is just stunning. For always making me laugh as well as baking scones in the name of textiles! www.sarahtyssen.co.uk

Rebecca Ball for her sashiko-inspired needle case and for keeping me supplied with all the gorgeous checks, delicate cottons, bold colours and striped fabrics.

Linda Chew for her hand printed and stitched zip pouch entitled *Georgie's Walk*.

Stephanie Bateman-Sweet for all the retro and vintage fabrics.

Jeff and his Dorset Bees for the best beeswax ever!

Thank you to each one of the artists, makers and designers who generously allowed me to use their work for the mood board created and depicted in the introduction of this book: Hannah Boyd, Caroline Guthrie, Linda Chew, Jill Maguire, Yvonne Miller and Sarah Tyssen.

Yvonne for not minding me using an image of her stitched piece on the supplier's page.

Georgie, my cat and the best critic, who, to show his approval and no matter how well it's hidden, always sits on a newly completed piece of my work.

And lastly and most importantly, a big thanks goes to Michael Jennings for his constant support and encouragement, and for keeping me calm!

Tulips by Linda Miller, 20 × 12cm (8 × 4in), reverse fabric appliqué and free machine embroidery.

Suppliers

Sewing machines
www.berninasewingshop.co.uk

Sewing machine needles
www.schmetz.com/en

Sewing machine supplies and machine embroidery threads
www.sewessential.co.uk

Machine embroidery threads
www.minerva.com

Fabrics and haberdashery items
www.hometownrochester.co.uk
www.cottonpatch.co.uk

Hand sewing needles
www.jjneedles.com

Stream iron and ironing board
www.johnlewis.com

Artists' materials
www.seawhite.co.uk

Art supplies
www.jacksonsart.com

Picture frames and mounts
www.easyframe.co.uk

Embroiderers Guild
embroiderersguild.com

Quilters Guild
www.quiltersguild.org.uk

To dispose of sharps, check with your local recycling centre or pharmacy.

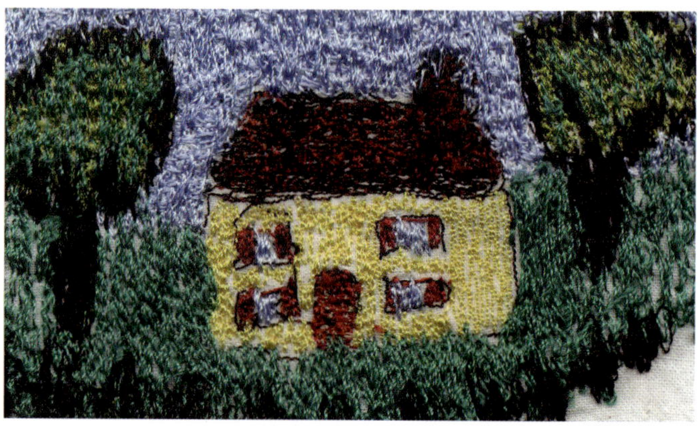

Index

applied fabrics
  fabric appliqué 73–85
  reverse fabric appliqué 87–101

backing 57
basic tool kit 13
bath towel 119
beeswax 17, 114, 122, 130
blanket 119, 121
Bloomsbury Group 103
bobbins
  bringing up the bobbin thread 37
  spools 15, 26
bradawl 119, 122

camera 49, 48, 103
composition 82, 94, 105
corner and edge shaper 20
craft utility knife 19
cutting mat 19
colour
  palette 74–75, 95

domestic textiles 59–61
drawing
  bird 79
  kites 93
  landscape 93
  onto calico 96
  onto fabric with a pen 68
  still life 87–88
  strawberry 36
  with black thread 68
  with stitch 83, 110
  with the sewing machine 90
drawing and recording 87–88

edging 41–44, 57, 70, 85, 101, 115
embroidery hoop
  placing fabric into 35
  wooden 19

fabrics
  base 15
  choosing 47–49
  colourful 95
  decorative 15
  fusible fabric for bonding 15, 80–81, 83, 108
  interfacing, light, iron on 17
  piecing 66–67
  scraps 76, 95
  stabilizing fabric 17, 42–43
flowers
  canna pink sparkler 54–55
  hollyhocks 55–56
  ruby sunflowers 54–56
  yellow heads 109–110
framing
  baton mounting 139
  box frame 119
  lace mounting 133–138
  presentation 117–119
  ready made frames 116–119
  semi free mounting 128–132
  sleeve mounting 124–127
  specialist 118
free machine embroidery
  learning 29–40, 36–37, 51–52
  found objects 9, 105, 106

gallery 9, 117

hand quilting 70
humidity 119
hemming
  double folded hem 124, 130
  single fold hem 126

inspiration
  finding 10, 59, 74, 87, 90, 103, 106
ironing board 21

lightbox 23, 67
lighting
  Anglepoise lamp 23
  daylight bulbs 23, 75
  good lighting 23

masking mape 21
memory cloth 62, 66
mixed media 105–106
mood board 10–11, 105
mount board 21, 119, 121–123, 131, 134, 137
museums 9

narrative cloth 59
needles
  hand sewing needles 15
  machine needles 14, 27
  machine needle sizes 28
notebook 20, 105

paper
  drawing paper 78
  strengthening ready for sewing 113

projects
Bird of Paradise 73
Colourful Kites 87
Embellishing a Vintage Cloth 59
Seaside Story 103
Spring Greens 47
Strawberry Delight 33
pegs
sprung laundry 135, 137, 138
pressing
linen cloth for 21, 41
pencils
HB 20, 68
colouring 20
pens
air-soluble 20, 68
permanent 20
pins 15

quick unpick 20
quilter's hem 71

rotary cutter 19
ruler 21

samplers 59
sewing
by hand 10, 15, 17, 44, 59, 69, 70, 114, 115, 122, 123, 130, 136, 137,
by machine 7, 10, 17, 25, 26, 44, 51, 66
trouble free 21
seam ripper 20
sewing clips 15
sewing machines
choosing 25
drawing with 33, 51
evolution of 7
feed dog teeth 25, 26, 42
feed dogs plate 44
feet, general 14, 26
free machine embroidery foot 14, 23, 26, 35, 37
getting to know 29
health and Safety 30
maintenance 21
tension 23, 29
working with 26–30
sketchbook 20, 87–90
steam iron 21
stitched banners 59
scissors
assorted 19
embroidery 19, 38, 56
paddle 98
stitching
satin stitch 42
stitching by hand 10, 114
stitching by machine 10
stitching in place 112–113
stitching in the ditch 53
zig zag 43–44, 85, 115
sunlight 21, 23, 103, 119,

tape
cotton 128, 130, 139
framing 123, 132, 138
hook and loop 21, 128, 130, 132, 139
tacking fabrics together 69
tailor's chalk 21
tape measure 21
textiles
exploring 9
texture 113
threads
hand sewing threads 17, 28
hand embroidery threads 17, 43
machine threads 17, 28
strong threads
book binding 113, 119, 122, 136, 137
crochet 113, 136, 137
hand 113, 119, 122, 136, 137
tools and equipment 13 – 22

view finder 64
vintage
fabrics 62, 64
feel 106
look 113

whip stitch 57, 71, 124, 127, 130, 136, 137, 138